DATE DUE			
Oct 21 76			

THE AMERICAN WORKING CLASS

Prospects for the 1980s

Edited by

Irving Louis Horowitz

John C. Leggett

Martin Oppenheimer

With the Assistance of
Stanley DeViney

Transaction Books
New Brunswick, New Jersey

Library of Congress Catalog Number: 74-20191
ISBN: 0-87855-081-X (cloth); 0-87855-578-1 (paper)
Printed in the United States of America

Library of Congress Cataloging in Publication Data
Main entry under title:

The American working class.

   Includes bibliographical references and index.
   1. Labor and laboring classes--United States--
Addresses, essays, lectures. 2. Trade-unions--
United States--Addresses, essays, lectures.
I. Horowitz, Irving Louis. II. Leggett, John C.
III. Oppenheimer, Martin.
HD8072.A538 301.44'42'0973 74-20191
ISBN 0-87855-081-X
ISBN 0-87855-578-1 pbk.

Contents

The American Working Class

Part I
The Theory of an American Working Class

1

The American Tradition of Labor Theory and Its Relevance to the Contemporary Working Class

John H. M. Laslett

In a review of academic literature on the American working class published in February 1970, the conservative social critic Irving Kristol claimed that aside from a number of valuable industry-wide studies, the subject of labor theory had become a dull and unfashionable topic on which little that was really new or creative had been written in the United States for a number of years. This was surprising, Kristol added, in view of the perennial importance of labor unions in American society, and the growing signs of tension, both within the official labor movement and in its relations with the outside world. "The membership is restless and increasingly contemptuous of its leadership," he wrote. "The leaders are bewildered, insecure, and increasingly contemptuous of the public. As for the public, it is beginning to wonder whether the institution of trade unionism itself is really 'relevant' to the emerging American society of the 1970's."[1]

Kristol should not have been so surprised. Because of its relatively small size and heavily "economist" tradition, the American labor movement, unlike that in Europe, has never attracted men and women of genius such as Lenin, Gramsci, Rosa Luxemburg, Sorel, or Marx himself into thinking and writing deeply and creatively about the historical role of the working class. As a result, when they have thought about labor at all, the dominant tradition of American social theorists—influenced by a history of pluralist thought stretching back at least to James Madison's treatment of "factions" in *Federalist Paper* No. 10—has tended to treat it as one among a broad range of essentially equal social groupings, each vying for a share in an apparently limitless supply of wealth, status, and power. American Marxists, however, have hardly done better. With some notable exceptions, they have until recently tended to regard American labor within a narrow, deterministic, and vulgar-Marxist form of perspective. Deriving virtually all of their ideas from Europe, they have so far failed to devise an "American" form of Marxism which would serve at once as a viable call to action, and at the same time create a comprehensible model of behavior which can take each of the "exceptionalist" elements in the history of American industrialization into account.

Aside from the Socialist Scholars' conferences, which have produced a number of highly valuable papers on topics associated with labor theory in the past few years,[2] and which have met regularly since 1964, the last major conference to concern itself explicitly with the theory of the labor movement was held by the Industrial Relations Research Association at the University of Wisconsin in December 1950, more than twenty-five years ago. A review of its proceedings[3] indicates that it devoted itself almost wholly to an uncritical reaffirmation of the conservative, job-conscious labor union philosophy of Selig Perlman, the Wisconsin's school's most famous product. His book, *A Theory of the Labor Movement*, which was published in 1928, had by then become by far the most influential attempt to provide a general theoretical explanation of the particular characteristics and behavior of the American working class. Almost no attempt was made at that conference to reexamine the basic tenets of Perlman's *Theory*, despite the tremendous expansion of the labor movement which had taken place in the 1930s and the growth of a more progressive social philosophy under the leadership of the CIO. Since that time, although several scholars have criticized Perlman's work, very little has been done, either by its supporters or by its critics, to evaluate his theory in the light of further historical developments, or to test it against the vast body of empirical research which has since been conducted into various aspects of American working class life.

The purpose of this essay, therefore, is twofold. First, to review briefly and in historical sequence the four or five most important general theories which have been advanced to account for the particular character and outlook of American labor as it has developed over the past one hundred years. Second, to make a preliminary attempt to see what value, if any, these theories may still have in explaining the behavior of American workingmen today.

Two general remarks about the works to be reviewed are in order. First, no proper attempt was made by any of the authors under review to define properly what they meant by labor theory. In most cases, what the various theorists found was a set of rather simple observable patterns in the behavior of small groups of workingmen in their public roles as trade unionists, not an operational model for American working-class behavior as a whole. They made little or no attempt, as social scientists are doing today, to enquire into the private beliefs of workers, or into their views on matters of race, status, religion, or family. Nor did they even examine in detail the attitude of American workers toward politics, beyond certain generalizations concerning old-party loyalty, or expressions of skepticism about undertaking third-party political action. Where no pretense was made at a general theory which went beyond these observable patterns of trade-union behavior no particular harm was done, although this fact in itself sets strict limits to the applicability of their findings to the working class considered as a whole. But where a claim *was* made to a more universal theory which sought to explain working-class behavior generally, but which was in fact based on nothing more than these observed patterns of trade-union activity, unsubstantiated generalizations were made—as I shall suggest in the case of Perlman's theory in particular—which should make us extremely wary of elevating them to the status of a general theory, if we do so at all.

The second remark, which is a corollary of the first, is that until approximately the Second World War, most labor theorists looked at the working class from the point of view of the role played by labor unions viewed as institutional mechanisms for achieving certain social or economic goals. In conducting their research they also examined only the views of a small group of labor leaders, with little regard for the opinions or activities either of the unorganized workers, or of the organized rank and file. Part of the reason for this was that most of them (John R. Commons, Jacob Hollander, George Barnett, and Robert F. Hoxie, to name only a few) were professional academics who—unlike most labor theorists in Europe—rarely played a role within the labor movement itself. It was partly because, in addition to being academics, they were also often social-scientific or Taylor-oriented labor economists. They saw their role as part of an attempt to "solve," or at least to come to grips with, the "labor problem" (as it was called in the nineteenth century) instead of viewing trade-union behavior as part of working-class culture as a whole. In the United States this meant describing and assessing the effectiveness of labor unions as the most characteristic device which working people had developed to cope with the problems created by rapid industrialization and governmental laissez-faire.[4] In view of the fact that up until the 1930s, unlike Germany or England, less than twenty percent of the total American labor force was organized into trade unions, this approach was perhaps understandable. Nevertheless, it limited still further the value of their work for the study of working-class behavior generally, considered either in historical or in sociological terms.

Despite this, however, the remarkable fact is that the small body of theory we are about to examine represents the only coherent set of attempts to examine the behavior of American workingmen within some sort of generalized framework. If it achieves nothing else, this review should enable the contemporary social observer to decide what, from the earlier body of theory, is relevant to the situation of the working class today, and what can safely be assigned to the lumber room of history.

The first major school of American labor theory was the so-called moral uplift or moral conditioning school, which flourished from about 1880 to 1920.[5] This school saw labor unions primarily as manifestations of the worker's desire to improve his intellectual and moral standing vis-à-vis the community as a whole, rather than as protective devices to shelter workers against the effects of industrialization (a view shared by Marxist and job-conscious theorists alike). The moral uplift school was led by two Christian Socialists, Richard T. Ely (1854-1943), of Johns Hopkins University, and Father Richard Ryan (1896-1945), a Catholic cleric and teacher whose thinking was heavily influenced by papal encyclicals on the subject of labor, such as *Rerum Novarum* (1890), as well as by Ely's views. Although they were concerned with such characteristic economic functions of trade unions as arbitration, wage negotiations and strike action, the main contribution of these authors was to emphasize the educational value of labor organizations. In *The Labor Movement in America,* first published in 1886, Ely argued that throughout American history unions had led the fight for free public schooling, political participation, and land reform, and that they were now "perhaps the chief power in this country for temperance." They taught "true politeness and grace in manners." Best of all, the labor movement advocated international peace and social harmony, or as he put it: "The labor movement, as the facts would indicate, is the strongest force outside the Christian Church making for the practical recognition of human brotherhood."[6]

This educational function of trade unions, raising the consciousness level, as we might put it today, was not simply designed for the moral improvement of the individual. Both Ely and Ryan believed in producers' cooperation and public ownership as a more just way of distributing wealth. They evidently thought, moreover, that unions would train their members to believe it also. "Through this process of training," Father Ryan wrote in 1927, "the wage earners will be able in due time to demand a share in the surplus profits and a share in determining all the policies of the industrial concern, and will become fitted to carry on cooperative industries and to sit on the directing boards of publicly owned and democratically managed industrial enterprises."[7]

Although much of this undoubtedly seems quaint and anachronistic to contemporary ears—especially the references to temperance and the cultivation of "true politeness and grace in manners"—the moral uplift school sheds light on the historical antecedents for at least two areas of labor activity which are still of great contemporary concern. One is the traditional role which American labor unions have played in socializing and assimilating a largely immigrant work force to a number of commonly accepted American norms and social goals. Since the decline of massive European immigration caused by the 1924 Immigration Restriction Act, there has been less obvious scope for this particular function of the labor movement. Nevertheless, current attempts to unionize previously neglected domestic or native-born ethnic groups—such as Mexican-Americans into Cesar Chavez's United Farm Workers in California, or former southern blacks into the Detroit UAW[8]—raise once more the issue of what values such groups bring with them to modern industrial society and on what terms they allow themselves to be socialized. Historically speaking, for example, the respectable English-speaking founders of the United Mine Workers of America, although freely admitting blacks and southern-European immigrants into their union, balked at some of the social habits which peasant migrants brought with them from the countryside.[9] If, as I believe, social outlook is as important as institutional tradition in creating proletarian forms of counterculture which can challenge the hegemony of bourgeois rule, then this question is as important in the United States today as it was a hundred years ago. For example, is racial pride to be a positive influence in helping blacks to humanize the degrading and trivializing effects of assembly-line production as socialist ideals once were to poor Jewish garment workers on the Lower East Side? Or is it to continue to be lost and wasted in apathy, submission, or sectarian intraunion quarrels?

Ely's and Ryan's analysis of the progressive social philosophy of the American labor movement also included support for free public schools, land reform, and even some measure of socialization of industry. This serves to remind us that even at the leadership level, American labor unions have by no means always had the narrow job-conscious outlook which they developed under the American Federation of Labor in the early years of the twentieth century, and which in some respects they have reverted to since the decline of the CIO. The dominant interpretation of Selig Perlman and the Wisconsin school of labor economists, which we shall analyze at greater length later on, appeared for some years to convince all but a small group of radicals and social historians that American workers were an exceptionally selfish, narrow-minded lot who had never been interested in anything more than shorter hours and higher wage levels. This outlook also affected the "working class authoritarianism" school of labor sociologists, of which S. M. Lipset still remains the leading expositor. Such an approach has always been unfair, especially during the heyday of the IWW between 1905 and 1917, and in the early years of the history of the CIO. It was especially untrue during the period of the Knights of Labor, which was dominant in the labor movement at the time when Ely wrote *The Labor Movement in America* in 1886, and which, although it was never in any real sense socialist, upheld producer's and consumer's cooperation, equal pay for women, and "a proper share of the wealth that they [the workers] create."[10] Of course, none of this means that we should expect the AFL-CIO to turn suddenly toward socialism. The official labor movement seems just now to be moving even further to the right. It does mean however, that there is nothing inevitable about the way labor ideology has developed in this country, either in the past or by extension in the future. Hence the interesting point for comparative analysis is not why "economism" has played a major role in the American labor movement. It has done so in all labor movements. The question is why it has done so to the exclusion of almost everything else. Part of the answer, I believe, lies in the ongoing influence in this country of a peculiarly tenacious form of labor aristocracy which defeated the Knights of Labor in a struggle for control in the labor movement in the 1880s, and which—because of ethnic, racial, and ideological unpreparedness on the part of unskilled elements in the labor force—has since rarely been effectively challenged.

The second influential school of labor research, the so-called economic-welfare school led by the economist George E. Barnett (1873-1938), who was also of Johns Hopkins, took for granted (without ever defining it) a "general dissatisfaction" with industrialism which caused workingmen to band together and demand greater job security, higher wages, and improved working conditions. The only real question for Barnett—who was heavily influenced by the Webbs in England—was whether economics or politics, that is, trade-union or legislative action, was the more rational, efficient way of securing labor's ends. This raises, indirectly, an issue which has always been important in American labor theory. That is whether, if workers take the legislative route, they will choose to pursue it through one of the two major parties or through a third party of their own making. They have nearly always done the former in the United States, unlike their counterparts in Germany or England, who have established political parties of their own. Barnett, however, did not consider the problem in these terms. Instead, he and his followers conducted a great deal of empirical research into the effects on workingmen of the national-ization of the labor market, and into the characteristics of trade-union members. They also produced the first systematic study of trade-union structure to appear in America, *The Printers,* published in 1909. The main interest of Barnett's work lies in the investigations which he conducted into the internal dynamics and functions of trade unions—a tradition which was to be taken up later by scholars such as Lloyd Ulman, Walter Galenson, or Lipset, Coleman, and Trow in their *Union Democracy* (1956)—not in any fundamental contribution which he made to the theory of the working class.

The third group of American labor theorists, although connected with no single place or university, is somewhat more interesting than the second. Influenced by the instinctual psychology of Thorstein Veblen, and also by the recently translated works of Sigmund Freud, Carleton Parker (1878-1918), Robert F. Hoxie (1868-1916), and Frank Tannebaum (b. 1893) were together responsible for what came to be called the psychologi-cal-environment theory. This school was influential in the years immedi-ately before and after World War I. Like their predecessors, these writers tended to treat workingmen as a single, abstract mass, and to make few differentiations among them on the basis of occupation, race, or social origin. Nevertheless, the psychological-environment school demonstrated more explicit concern than its predecessors for the more general, underly-ing, preinstitutional concerns and aspirations of workingmen, which they conceived of in psychological terms. Their analysis, although it was in some respects simplistic and monocausal, did make it possible to distin-guish between the general characteristics and motives of working-class behavior, on the one hand, and the institutional manifestations of it, on the other. It also made it possible to perceive trade unions as only one among a variety of responses of the working class to general problems of industrial-ization and technological change.

In some ways the most interesting of these three men was Carleton H. Parker, whose *The Casual Laborer and Other Essays,* published posthu-mously in 1920, saw the labor movement arising partly out of economic degradation and the loss of economic independence occasioned by industrial and urban developments, but mainly out of a psychological malad-justment to the life of the factory and the large-scale farm. In the relatively undemanding atmosphere of home and school, Parker argued, the antiso-cial elements among man's instincts (which include anger or pugnacity, revulsion, and revolt at confinement) were either moderated or controlled. But in the sudden transition to the rigid, confining, and degrading work of factory or large-scale ranch, man's antisocial instincts create acute dissatis-faction or frustration with his lot, which is manifested in the creation of unions which serve either as defensive mechanisms or as agents of social revolt. "The problem of industrial labor," he wrote in one essay, "is one with the problem of the discontented businessman, the indifferent student, the unhappy wife, the immoral minister—it is one of maladjustment between a fixed human nature and a carelessly ordered world. The result is suffering, insanity, racial perversion, and danger. The final cure is gaining acceptance for a new standard of normality."[11] Among the programs which Parker advocated to cure the problem were measures for industrial decasualization, and the encouragement of group relationships in industry which would break down the traditional barriers between employer and employee. He also suggested that government and industry should make use of university- and hospital-trained psychologists for advice on ways to overcome worker hostility toward their position.

One difficulty with Parker's theory, aside from its transparently manip-ulative character, is that it was predicated primarily upon his observations among wandering western mineworkers, lumberjacks, or bums, few of whom followed more traditional occupational pursuits, and many of whom joined the IWW. Hence it may be wondered whether Parker's pseudo-anthropological conclusions concerning the "culture of poverty" out of which many of these migrant workers came (and which have been put to interesting use in Melvyn Dubofsky's recent *We Shall Be All: A History of the IWW*) can equally well be applied to the allegedly more settled, factory-oriented labor force in the East. To what degree the eastern, urban labor force is actually more settled in its occupational or geographical mobility patterns than its supposedly more volatile western, or frontier counterpart, has recently become a matter of important historical debate.[12] However, in Frank Tannenbaum's *The Labor Move-ment: Its Conservative Functions and Social Consequences,* published in 1921, as well as in Robert F. Hoxie's *Trade Unionism in the United States,* published in the same year, the leaders of the psychological-environment school went on to apply their theories to the whole American labor force. Their central idea remained that workingmen had become maladjusted by the dehumanizing effects of the machine process, and that the function of trade unions was not simply to improve their economic position, but to reassert some semblance of control by the individual over his own fate.[13]

Robert F. Hoxie, in particular, elaborated a whole pantheon of different types of labor organizations ranging from craft, quasi-industrial, compound craft and industrial unions, to friendly-benefit, revolutionary, and what he called "hold-up" or "guerrilla" unions. He argued that the particular form a labor organization took depended upon the particular constellation of environmental and psychological factors involved.[14]

The great weakness of this body of work, as with most of the theories we are dealing with, is that with the partial exception of Hoxie it was written almost entirely in abstract terms, and made no serious attempt to apply the analytical scheme which it had elaborated to any specific body of workingmen. The central issue with which the psychological-environment school was concerned was, after all, the problem of alienation, although they tended to see it in psychological terms rather than, as a Marxist would, in economic terms. This is, of course, an extremely important issue in discussions of the working class today, as may be seen in a whole series of recent works ranging from Ely Chinoy's *Automobile Workers and the American Dream* (1955), through Robert Blauner's *Alienation and Freedom: The Factory Worker and His Industry* (1964), to Louise Kapp Howe's more recent *The White Majority: Between Poverty and Affluence* (1970). More recently have come still more sensitive, although even less theoretical, compilations of interviews and biographies from the experiences of ordinary workingmen and women both in and out of the work situation, deriving part of their technique from the methods of social survey research, and part from the newly burgeoning field of oral history. Two examples are *Rank and File: Personal Histories by Working Class Organizers,* by Alice and Staughton Lynd (1973), and Studs Terkel's impressive *Working* (1972). The fact that neither Parker's , nor Tannenbaum's, nor Hoxie's work rates even a footnote in any of these volumes indicates what little influence the psychological-environment school now exerts.

The fourth group of American labor theorists is the Marxist school. Numerous writers have, of course, attempted Marxist or neo-Marxist interpretations of the American labor movement, ranging from class conflict interpretations of the workingman's role in the American revolution, to Communist analyses of the New Deal in the 1930s. They have predicated the rise of the labor movement upon technological advances in production which have caused changes in the property relationships between the bourgeois, property-holding class and the working, propertyless class. However muted or transmogrified in the American context, the ultimate cause of unionism is class conflict; the ultimate cause of class conflict is capitalist control of the means of production away from the bourgeoisie, in the interests of production for use instead of profit and the establishment of a more just society. Either explicitly or implicitly, Marxist accounts repudiate what they regard as the utopian or romantic notions of the moral-conditioning theory; the nonrevolutionary (although somewhat more scientific) Fabianism of the economics-welfare school; and the manipulative implications of the psychological-environment school; as well as, of course, the job-conscious theories of the Wisconsin-Perlman school, which limits the worker's response simply to the nature of the opportunity market in which he finds himself, without any deeper analysis of his ultimate destiny or condition.

The recent revival of labor militancy among teamsters, white-collar workers, farm workers, longshoremen and coal miners may well lead the contemporary analyst of the labor movement to this Marxist tradition of labor-union theory with high expectations for its relevance and cogency. If so, he is likely to be disappointed—at least if he reads what may be called the Old Left, or vulgar-Marxist school of labor historiography. There have, of course, been numerous distinguished efforts by individual scholars to apply a general Marxist framework to problems which are either peripherally or centrally concerned with aspects of working class life. One thinks here of the historian Eugene Genovese, or the sociologist C. Wright Mills. But until quite recently those labor theorists who have discussed the America labor movement as such in Marxist terms have nearly always taken each of the Marxist categories of analysis uncritically as givens without any real attempt to examine the theoretical difficulties posed for the model by relatively high wage levels, ethnic or racial fragmentation of the labor force, or a fluid system of social stratification including the very rapid (and un-Marxist) growth in the size of the American middle class.[15] Little effort has been made to rethink Marx's concepts of proletarianization (in terms of Edouard Bernstein's Revisionist argument over upward occupational mobility), or of the dominance in America of bourgeois ideology and values (in terms of arguments by others over embourgeoisement) in relation to the actual circumstances and environment of any significant body of the American working class. Although as works of history they are often competent, the main theoretical interest in reading traditional or Old Left Marxist interpretations of the American labor movement, from William Z. Foster to Philip Foner,[16] is to review the numerous changes in tactics through which revolutionaires active in the labor movement have gone, and to impart blame for their limited success upon leadership sellouts, or "incorrect" tactics on the part of the rank and file.

To give two brief examples, the first Communist *History of the American Working Class,* written in 1928 by Anthony Bimba, begins by giving an interesting chronological account of the development of American working-class movements, only to become progressively more factional as it approaches contemporary times. After generously praising the activities of the American anarchists in the 1880s, for example, Bimba goes on to derogate all opponents of "boring from within" (the Communist tactic at the time his book was written), and to manipulate much of the history of the pre-1914 labor movement in the interests of a proper "line."[17] A more moderate example of this is Nathan Fine's *Farmer and Labor Parties in the United States* which was, as Paul Buhle has pointed out,[18] in many ways the Socialist counterpart of Bimba's work. After cataloging the institutional history of various reform movements in the nineteenth century, Fine turned to a lengthy defense of conservative trade-union Socialists against Left Socialists in the Debs period, and then to a further defense of both against the Communists in the 1920s. Although Fine closes with a clarion call of confidence in the future of the Socialist movement in America, his study is of little more than academic interest to those who would formulate a viable Marxist framework for understanding the present condition of the American working class. As Gabriel Kolko pointed out as long ago as 1966, Old Left Marxism, both in Europe and America, "accepted a paralysing and debilitating optimism which was inherited from the intellectual tradition of the idea of Progress. Defeat as a possibility...was never entertained, and a social theory that cannot consider this notion is not merely intellectually unsatisfactory but misleading as a basis of political analysis and action."[19]

The persistence of this narrow, vulgar-Marxist school of analysis, seen today perhaps most characteristically in the work of Herbert Aptheker and Philip Foner, is all the more disappointing in view of the mass of evidence now being brought to light concerning the repressed early condition, and present dissatisfied status, of much of the American working class. This work is being carried out by a newer generation of sociologists, economists, and historians represented—to take a few random examples—by Herbert Gutman, James Weinstein, Harry Braverman, David Montgomery, Andrew Levinson, and James R. Green.[20] Braverman's and Levinson's work we will refer to again later on. The historians among this group fall into no readily identifiable theoretical category. Certainly not all of them are in any strict sense New Left. What unites them, however, is a common desire to go beyond the narrow, mechanistic perspectives of Old Left, vulgar-Marxist history, and to examine the interplay between community, ideology, family, race, and social class in ways which promise to tell us something in detail for the first time about the difficulties which have inhibited the development of a common working-class culture in the United States.

And yet, to repeat, neither Old nor New Left forms of Marxist social enquiry have so far come near to formulating an "American Marxism" capable at the same time of explaining the "exceptionalist" character of the American industrial experience, and of providing a coherent guide to social action. Some among the Old Left school, indeed, persist in denying that there is anything really "exceptionalist" about American industrialization at all. Part of the reason for this has to do with the inherent difficulty of the subject; part with a "cult of proletarianism" in the radical movement which reinforced native American traditions of antiintellectualism, and discouraged original thought; and part, as we have seen, with the failure of the labor movement itself to make new demands on the body of Marxist theory because of its own inability or unwillingness to present any serious threat to the social system. A further difficulty, I would suggest—and one whose importance has become increasingly noticed as blacks and other minority groups take up an even larger share of jobs among the factory working class—has to do with still unresolved weaknesses in the Marxist schema itself concerning the two areas of enquiry which are likely to be the most critical for the future growth of class consciousness among the American proletariat: Marxist attitudes toward the issue of race and the issue of nationality.

In the 1930s, thousands of black workers joined the American Communist party because it seemed to be the only one which genuinely cared about their fate. But aside from paternalism, white chauvinism, and the great difficulty which the Communist party itself had in overcoming its early use as an arm of Soviet foreign policy, neither it nor its successors have yet been able to resolve the fundamental dilemma created for Marxist theory by conflicts between blacks and other racial minorities' legitimate desires for self-determination, on the one hand, and Marxist analyses of society based upon social class, on the other. In revolutionary Russia, Lenin made use of Ukrainian, Hungarian, and other forms of east-European nationalism as a device to enhance Bolshevism's popular appeal. This tactic was condemmed at the time by Rosa Luxemburg as inconsistent with Marxism's class basis. Nevertheless, it was temporarily adopted by the American Communist party in its 1930s proposal for a territorially independent Southern Black Belt. Not only did the Old Left fail to recognize that the desire for self-determination among American blacks (unlike east Europeans) was rarely linked to the land question, it also found itself, as a consequence of its views in conflict with petty bourgeois pan-African nationalists such as Marcus Garvey, who for all his racial demagoguery succeeded in developing a militant mass black movement where the Communist party failed.[21] Nothing that has happened since, from the Black Panthers to minority movements to end racial discrimination in the labor movement, suggests that this aspect of the problem has been resolved.

We now come to the fifth, and historically speaking, still the most influential theory of the American labor movement; namely the job-conscious theory elaborated by Selig Perlman and the Wisconsin school. In light of the great influence which it has exerted on teaching and research into the fields of labor economics and labor history, somewhat more attention will be paid to its actual content than to that of its predecessors. Strictly speaking, the Wisconsin school was founded not by Perlman but by the eminent progressive and leader of the research team at the University of Wisconsin, of which Selig Perlman was a member, John R. Commons (1862-1945). Commons's numerous empirical investigations led him (most notably in his celebrated article, "American Shoemakers, 1648-1895," first published in 1909) to locate the origins of the labor movement, not as with Marx, in changes in the mode of production. Instead, Commons placed it in the more limited but still vast changes in the nature of the market for labor and for goods which took place as a result of the rapid expansion of the American economy after the Civil War. In this period, the functions of merchant, manufacturer, and worker, which had hitherto been combined in one person, were divided and the individual worker was forced to combine with others to defend the interests of his own separate craft or trade. This laid the intellectual foundations for Perlman's *Theory of the Labor Movement* (1928), much the most celebrated monograph in our literature on the behavior of the American working class.

There are really two parts to Perlman's theory. One takes up the question of why the American labor movement has not adopted socialism, or independent labor politics which Perlman attributes in a rather tautologous fashion to the strength of the institution of private property, to the lack of class-consciousness in America, and to the difficulties of practicing third-party politics in a federal electoral system. The other concerns the issue of what labor's own "organic" or "home-grown" philosophy will be when it is left free from the interference of revolutionary intellectuals. The chief characteristic of the latter, Perlman argued, was to regard labor "merely as an abstract mass in the grip of an abstract force," and to attempt to manipulate it in the direction of revolutionary goals in which, he blithely asserts, it has no intrinsic interest. In America, however (and potentially in Europe also, where Perlman suggested that the influence of intellectuals over the labor movement was in decline), the worker had been able to develop his own organic philosophy. This consisted essentially in dividing control between himself and the employer over the limited opportunities afforded to him by the job in which he was employed. "The safest way to assure this group control over opportunity," Perlman argued, was for the union to "seek, by collective bargaining with the employers, to establish 'rights' on the job,...by incorporating, in the trade agreement, regulations applying to overtime, to the 'equal turn,' to priority and seniority in employment, to apprenticeship, to the introduction and utilization of machinery, and so forth."[22]

Perlman's answer to the question of why workers conceived of their opportunities as limited was twofold. First, a survey of the changes which had taken place in the nature of the market in the nineteenth century— essentially, as far as the United States was concerned, the post-Civil War decades—convinced him that he could no longer operate as a would-be entrepreneur attempting by means of land or currency reform to restore his position as an autonomous economic unit. Instead, he had accepted his position as a wage-earner, seeking by means of collective bargaining, instead of the largely political or legislative means which he had used earlier, to make his position as secure as possible within the particular trade or calling in which he was employed. "The trade unionism of the American Federation of Labor," Perlman wrote, "was a shift from an optimistic psychology, reflecting the abundance of opportunity in a partly settled continent, to the more pessimistic trade union psychology, built upon the premise that the wage-earner is faced by a scarcity of opportunity."

Second, this scarcity consciousness just referred to derived from what Perlman conceived of as a universal psychology among manual workers or workingmen—universal throughout Europe as well as America, once the interfering influence of the intellectual had been withdrawn—according to which the worker accepts inherent limitations in his ability to manipulate the economic world. "The typical manualist is aware of his lack of native capacity for availing himself of economic opportunities as they lie amidst the complex and ever shifting situations of modern business." In contrast, a psychology of unlimited opportunity characterized the entrepreneur, whom Perlman, like Schumpter, thought of as a born risk-taker who could impose his will upon the vagaries of the capitalist system. "Whether he thought the cause of the apparent limitations to be institutional or natural," Perlman concluded, "a scarcity consciousness has always been typical of the manual worker, in direct contrast to the consciousness of abundance of opportunity, which eminates the self-conscious business-man."[23] From a job-conscious psychology created by an age of allegedly shrinking job opportunities, and the development of labor institutions and policies responsive to a wage-earning constituency which was free from the influence of middle-class intellectuals, all else flowed in the shaping of American trade unionism.

It is not difficult to point out the basic weaknesses in Perlman's *Theory,* both in historical and in theoretical terms. Perlman wrote from the perspective of the 1920s, when the conservative craft unionism of the American Federation of Labor was still firmly entrenched. A year after he published his *Theory* in 1928, the Great Depression began, and American capitalism foundered to a degree never before anticipated. The labor movement broke out of its craft-union mold and swiftly encompassed the mass production workers in the years after 1935. Given its commitment to broader social objectives, its willingness to engage in partisan politics, and its encouragement of government involvement in the labor sphere, could the CIO be characterize as pure-and-simple trade unionism? More fundamentally, have not the changes since the 1920s—the incorporation into the labor movement of millions of mass production workers, the development of an economy in which job scarcity no longer seems inevitable, and the immense expansion of the public role of the labor movement—been so far-reaching as to render Perlman's analysis inapplicable? Perlman himself stood by his earlier views. At the 1950 Industrial Relations Research Association symposium, (which took place nine years before his death), he remarked: "In the grasp of the Wisconsin school, the American labor movement, indicative of its basic philosophy, has shown remarkable stead-fastness through times of rapid external change. The objective...is unaltered from Gompers' day; the methods, even outside the immediate vicinity of the job, show no more change than could be accounted for by the changing environment."[24]

The AFL-CIO, particularly after the two halves of the labor movement reunited in 1955, has continued to reveal the powerful grip which the job-conscious philosophy still exerts. Its social idealism has faltered badly, particularly on matters of race and of organizing the marginal and minority workers who lie beyond the mass production industries; its central concern has remained the exercise of control over wage levels, fringe benefits, and other elements in the American worker's general terms of employment. On the other hand, we should ask whether labor's political role, its community involvement, and its abandonment of voluntarism (or aversion to state interference in the affairs of trade unions) do not demand a major reassessment of Perlman's *Theory* on strictly empirical grounds.

Even so, there are fundamental theoretical weaknesses in Perlman's *Theory*. Adolph Sturmthal, for example, taking up an argument earlier disputed at great length between Lenin and the economist school of Russian orthodox Marxists, has pointed out that the radicalization of labor as such by no means always depends upon the external prompting of intellectuals. This is in itself a more orthodox Marxist view which I myself have attempted to elaborate in a recent work on the American labor movement.[25] However, this still leaves open the question of how far a successful socialist party depends upon an alliance being established *between* the two groups, which in many ways it clearly does.

Close study of Perlman's monograph, moreover, reveals that the celebrated scarcity consciousness of the worker—although supposedly deriving from a survey of available economic opportunity and from the worker's inherent awareness of his lack of capacity as an entrepreneur[26]—was in fact deduced solely from a limited number of union contracts and bargaining documents, which in themselves tell us very little either about the worker's psychic predispositions towards capitalism, or about his self-awareness as a putative entrepreneur. In addition, Perlman used both arguments (that based on a supposed survey of available opportunity, and the one based on the worker's inherent limitations as entrepreneur) interchangeably and indiscriminately, without apparently being aware of the enormous implications of the differences between them. It is one thing to assert that the American worker is job-conscious because he has surveyed his range of available opportunities and decided that this is the best tactic for him to pursue. It is even more breathtaking to suggest (with all due respect to Lenin) that all workers everywhere and at all times are *inherently* incapable of anything other than a job-conscious philosophy. Aside from anything else, most historians who have studied the problem would surely agree that such a rigid distinction is implausible, and that at least since the eighteenth century both businessmen *and* manual workers have operated within a framework of limited opportunity, in which the former seeks to impose order on the economic world by means of monopolies and price-fixing, while the latter seeks to do so through trade agreements and work rules.

This is not, of course, to say that the range of opportunities open to the businessman is not always greater than those available to the worker, or that the industrial revolution did not force the worker to defend himself against the depredations of the entrepreneur. The central point to grasp, however, is that whatever name one gives to the predicament, or variety of predicaments, which face the manual worker (whether it be scarcity consciousness, bourgeois exploitation, or psychological maladjustment), those predicaments simply provide a rationale for some form of labor movement. They do not dictate either its philosophy or its form. On the question of form or structure, for example, there is nothing inherent in the predicament of the American manual worker to explain why the American Federation of Labor chose craft unionism as its dominant mode of organization, or resisted mass, industrial unionism for so long. Nor does the predicament of the worker in itself dictate that labor unions should be job-conscious rather than class-conscious in their orientation, or that they should stop short at job-monopoly, instead of reaching for total worker control of industry. One must turn for an explanation to the actual historical influences which have affected the outlook of the American worker, such as ethnic and racial difficulties, high real wage levels, leadership characteristics, or a relatively fluid stratification system, instead of relying on a spurious and deterministic concept of worker psychology, the validity of which has yet to be demonstrated either as a category of actual historical experience or as a viable sociological research tool.

What, then, is the relevance of all this to present studies of the contemporary character and development of the American working class? Before concluding our observations on that question we ought perhaps first to ask whether there has been, since the 1950s, any further contribution to labor theory which represents a major advance over the theories which we have just reviewed. My answer would be that while a number of extremely interesting new areas for research have recently been opened up by social scientists (or, perhaps, taken seriously for the first time), none of them so far have yielded a set of generalizations which can in any sense be called a general theory.

From one direction, we have seen a rapidly growing sensitivity, on the part of sociologists as well as of historians, toward the importance of new or previously neglected minorities or ethnic minorities in the labor force, ranging from C. Wright Mills's and Everett Kassalow's very different studies of the white-collar worker, to the work, respectively, of Joan Moore, Harry Kitano, and Julius Jacobson or Herbert Hill on the increasing importance of Mexican-Americans, Japanese-Americans, and blacks in the labor force.[27] Given their larger numbers and an already strategic position in key industries such as autos, steel, and meatpacking— there are 2.5 million black workers in the AFL-CIO, and they already control most of the UAW local offices in Detroit—it is perhaps natural that the blacks should so far have received the greatest amount of attention. But the developing importance of white-collar and ethnic minority groups of all kinds (even though the latter, of course, have always been part of the traditional working class) have raised issues of status versus class analysis, or of race versus job consciousness, which were almost never considered by the earlier tradition of labor theorists. From the point of view of labor militancy, the Mexican-American farm workers of Texas and California have succeeded in recapturing something of the spirit of the early CIO by integrating national pride with social idealism in their struggle for union recognition. But so far, politically, they show no signs of going beyond the liberal Democratic posture of their earlier New Deal comrades.

From another direction has come a burgeoning and increasingly sophisticated sociological literature on the attitudes, problems, and behavior of contemporary working-class groups at the rank and file level, and sometimes outside of the workplace altogether. Within the union context, we have had Joel Seidman's *The Worker Views His Union* (1958), containing interviews and reflections on the attitudes toward their unions of workers in six different industries; Sidney Peck's *Rank and File Leader* (1963), an analysis of levels of consciousness among shop stewards in a Milwaukee plant in the late 1950s, indicating some degree of anti-Semitism, male chauvinism, and status resentment toward younger workers on the part of the older employees; and John C. Leggett's *Class, Race and Labor* (1968), which correlates regional background, ethnicity, and economic insecurity with the persistence of working-class consciousness in the Detroit work force in the 1960s, to mention only three of the most important works. Outside the union context, there has been Bennett Berger's *Working Class Suburb* (1960), demonstrating the persistence of a sense of working class identity among Ford workers despite the transition from Richmond, California to a San Jose suburb; and Mirra Komarovsky's saddening, but at the same time highly illuminating *Blue Collar Marriage* (1962), showing the loneliness and frustration visited by economic insecurity and traditional assumptions of masculinity upon innumerable working-class wives. Outside formal academic circles, the New Left magazines—*Radical America, Guardian, Socialist Revolution,* Radical Education Project pamphlets—and sometimes even Old Left journals such as *Dissent* or *Science and Society,* have poured forth a veritable flood of reports, opinions, and views.

None of this new literature, with its conflicting and different ideological points of view, has presented any new general theory of the American labor movement, nor has it even attempted to do so. Some of it, however, has provided ammunition for two interrelated sets of debates from which such new theoretical perspectives as we now have can be said to have come. The first of these debates concerns the general political and ideological outlook of the American working class, or what, given present trends in the labor force, its philosophical outlook is likely to become in the future. In itself this is, of course, an old issue. To a great extent in the 1960s, however, it revolved around the hotly debated end-of-ideology thesis—or explanations of American labor moderation in terms of certain recent changes in the American economy and social structure. The second debate, which in part helps to account for and in part itself derives from the first, turns on the equally hotly debated issue of whether, given these same trends in the economy towards a postindustrial society, an industrial working class in the sense that we have hitherto known it will continue to exist at all.

The end-of-ideology argument, although it is usually associated with conservative social theorists such as Seymour Lipset and Daniel Bell—

whose book, *The End of Ideology,* was published in 1960—in fact also derives from positions taken by radicals such as Barrington Moore and Herbert Marcuse. Thus Marcuse in his book *One Dimensional Man* (1964), and in numerous statements since, argues that the American working class has been integrated into the affluent society and "shares in large measure the needs and aspirations of the dominant class."[28] Paul Sweezy and the last Paul Baran, writing in 1966, also came to the conclusion that organized workers in the United States had been "integrated into the system as consumers and ideologically conditioned members of the society."[29] Essentially, however, they assert that the main consequence of the remarkable productivity of American capitalism (and, indeed, of western capitalism generally) since World War II, coupled with the development of sophisticated and successful collective bargaining techniques, has been, to quote Lipset, to "undercut many of the conditions which earlier had led workers to support different forms of class-conscious radical ideology."[30] According to this school, what we should now be concerned with is not the traditional economic grievances of artisans and blue-collar workers (which save for ethnic minorities and other marginal groups are no longer a serious issue) but with the status anxieties, racial attitudes, and—according to Lipset at least—the simplistic, authoritarian attitudes towards politics on the part of the white working class, which survey research techniques allegedly show to be extensive.[31]

One response to this type of argument, put forward in an interesting paper given by Richard Hamilton to the Socialist Scholars' Conference in 1965,[32] has been to challenge the alleged racism and authoritarianism of blue-collar workers suggested by the conservative sociologists on purely empirical grounds. Hamilton argued, for example, correctly in my view, that the working class is no more afflicted by this type of prejudice than are other elements in the American community. Another approach, which has so far been developed more fully in England than in the United States (in John Goldthorpe's *Affluent Worker,* although Bennett Berger's *Working Class Suburb* represents an interesting corollary in the United States) has been to deny that affluence, improved wages and conditions of work, and the benefits of a consumer society have necessarily led to *embourgeoisement* along the lines described.[33] Still a third response, to be seen in the work of Martin Glaberman, Stanley Weir, and numerous other radical commentators, has been to acknowledge that collective bargaining techniques, at least for that portion of the labor force which is organized, may have been able to meet the demands of the contemporary labor aristocracy as regards wages, living standards or working conditions. But this still leaves out many ethnic minorities and other hitherto marginal elements which conservative theorists ignore.[34] The obvious corollary to this argument, which is also in my view well taken, is that collective bargaining is inherently unable to solve problems created by alienation, fragmentation of the work process, bureaucracy, and automation, factors which in the presence of a national crisis—but only then—might still lead to some form of traditional labor revolt. Much the most sensitive treatment of this latter aspect of the problem has been that in Harry Braverman's recent book, *Labor and Monopoly Capital* (1974), which discusses Taylorism, absenteeism, job rationalization, and a whole host of other aspects of the alienation question under the general rubric of "the degradation of work in the twentieth century." The weakness of Braverman's work, although it sets the discussion more firmly than any of its predecessors within Marx's own analytic framework as seen in volume one of *Capital*, is that it offers us no way of judging whether the degradation of the work process in the last generation or so—in what is still, save Japan, technologically the most rapidly changing industrial economy in the world—has been more or less acute than it has been throughout the whole history of industrialization. Thus we are left unable to answer the question posed by Braverman himself in his introduction, whether the recent flurry of rank and file discontent in the labor movement has been "at the usual level, endemic to life under capitalism, or whether it was rising threateningly."[35] The failure of the recent growth of mass unemployment to generate more than a very limited radical response in the United States makes it very difficult, so far at least, to answer Braverman's question with anything other than a negative.

In Italy, in France, in Portugal, and in Great Britain we are, of course, faced with a very different story; perhaps the best refutation of the "end of ideology" argument is simply to point to the rising Communist vote and the ongoing labor unrest among blue-collar workers in these countries, even if it were not easily refuted as nonsensical on other grounds as well. Strictly speaking, however, Bell addressed himself only to advanced industrial societies, which leaves out Portugal, and possibly even Italy, although most assuredly not Great Britain. How far the current British crisis will turn itself from an advanced case of inflation-fueled "economist" discontent into something greater—my own hunch is that it won't—is at this point no more than idle speculation. But to return to the United States, the debate over ideology, although cast in very different terms from that between the earlier job-conscious and Marxist schools, would at least have been recognizable to the pre-1950s tradition of American labor theory. But the second debate, over whether structural changes now occurring in the economy may lead to the creation of a postindustrial (but still capitalist) society in which the very existence of an industrial working class as we have hitherto known it may be called into question, would have been incredible, as well as incomprehensible, to most of the earlier

American theorists. They worked and wrote in a context in which the presence of some kind of industrial proletariat could be taken for granted. Now, however, the conservative school of pluralist sociologists, led again by Daniel Bell, have begun to suggest that changes in technology and in the pattern of consumer demand now taking place will in the long run be so far-reaching as to abolish altogether the traditional concept of a blue-collar proletariat.

The issue has arisen, clearly enough—although so far largely only in America—because of structural change in patterns of employment. As a result of these changes, the proportion of workers employed in goods-producing, mostly blue-collar occupations, while still continuing to rise somewhat in absolute terms (except for those in mining or in agriculture, who continue to decline rapidly in number) is now falling markedly relative to the numbers employed in service, largely white-collar occupations. The effect of this will be, according to one estimate,[36] that by 1980 the proportion of workers employed in the blue-collar field will fall to less than 32 percent of the total work force (it was well over 60 percent in 1935), while the proportion of white-collar workers, especially among government employees (already 7 million in 1968), teachers (already 2 million), scientists and engineers (already about 1.4 million), and engineering and science technicians (already about 900,000 in 1968), will continue to rise sharply. Thus what we may now see emerging is a bifurcated working population, in which the old industrial working class is diminishing in importance and is in any event, according to the end-of-ideology argument, largely satisfied; and a new, better educated, rapidly growing white-collar element which will be largely nonmilitant in its outlook because it already has middle-class status and aspirations.

This latter point has caused perhaps the greatest amount of controversy. Initially, Marxist analysts of this new phenomenon such as C. Wright Mills in his already cited *White Collar* (1951), tended to argue that the new semiprofessional and technical cadres could not be thought of as an autonomous independent class, but would eventually have to move in one direction or another and give their support either to the old industrial working classes or to the business community. But more recently, beginning with French analysts such as Serge Mallet and Andre Gorz, radical American critics of the postindustrial society thesis argued that these new cadres would not simply by virtue of their somewhat higher income become another version of the old and largely conservative aristocracy of labor which had developed in the industrial working class at an earlier period. They argued that these new groups had considerable revolutionary potential—which could be exploited for organizing purposes—because their skills had been broken down and compartmentalized, and they were no longer able to fulfill the creative role for which they had been trained.[37] Thus Herbert Gintis, to take one example, saw the student rebellions of the late 1960s as foreshadowing the revolt of "educated labor" as a whole against capitalism. Even within the New Left, however, there was sharp debate as to what the future loyalties and ideological outlook of these white-collar groups was likely to be. Stanley Aronowitz pointed out, for example, the need to distinguish carefully between the roles of technocrats and technicians, and between those of teachers and governmental employees, before coming to any definitive conclusions. In an essay published in 1971, he questioned the assumption, which had been advanced by a number of other New Left critics, that a rise in educational levels would necessarily lead to mass radicalization among white-collar workers, and concluded rather sharply that at present, "the United States does *not* have a new working class."[38]

But as in the "end of ideology" debate, perhaps the simplest and the most effective response to the postindustrial thesis has come from those who have pointed out that its champions have either anticipated far too much in consigning the traditional proletariat to oblivion, or have simply got their facts wrong. In a remarkable book published in 1974 called *The American Working Class Majority,* Andrew Levinson set out to show, with considerable success, not that Bell's projections concerning the overall future shape were completely out of kilter (that would be impossible) but that his and others' use of figures to show a relative increase in affluence among blue-collar workers, a relative decline in their liberal political outlook, as well as an overall decline in their numbers within the work force, has been much exaggerated. "The majority of Americans are not white-collar, or well off," he writes. "Thirty per cent of blue collar workers are poor and another 30 per cent cannot earn enough to reach the very modest government definition of a middle-class standard of living....American workers are a class apart," Levinson concludes, "with real and legitimate problems and discontents. And unlike the abstract paper coalitions of wildly disparate groups which Liberals have proposed, they are united by common interests and constitute a majority of the American people."[39] If Levinson's analysis is correct, as careful perusal by the reader will, I believe, convince him that it is, it has profound implications for the "embourgoisement," "the end of ideology," "the working class authoritarianism," and "the post-industrial society" schools of analysis. At the very least it has thrown the ball back into their proponents' court.

During the earlier part of this essay we reviewed the previous body of American labor-union theory to see what relevance it had, if any, to the present problems and characteristics of the American working class. Save for Perlman's *Theory*, which is fundamentally shallow, and Marxist theory, which is of course the opposite of shallow but which has so far been incapable of developing an American version of anything like the depth and profundity which Antonio Gramsci, for example, developed for Italy,[40] the value of the remainder for contemporary analysis is extremely limited. Our final purpose is to see that lessons, if any, can be gained for the future by juxtaposing the methodological approach taken to problems of labor theory by the post-1950s generation of analysts, with that taken by scholars of the pre-1950s era, in the light of a brief review of the American tradition of labor theory taken as a whole. On this point, although as I suggested earlier no new theoretical framework has yet emerged which can be said to have entirely displaced those which went before, the greater methodological sophistication of the new group of labor analysts, coupled with their willingness to treat workers as individual human beings with interests and commitments that go beyond their role as members of a labor union, give grounds for hope that a new general theory of the labor movement, if and when it does emerge, will at least be based on both a sounder and a broader range of evidence than the old.

Methodologically speaking, the earlier body of labor theory suffered, in my view, from four main sets of weaknesses which the more recent efforts of labor analysts show signs of being able to overcome. The pre-1950s tradition was guilty, first, of an almost universal tendency (for which both the Perlmanites and their Marxist opponents can equally be blamed) to treat the labor force as a single, abstract entity, or at most as two or three abstract entities, with little attempt to break it down into its component parts, or to examine factors which may have influenced the behavior of workingmen other than those which developed out of the workplace. Robert F. Hoxie of the psychological-environment school was a partial exception here, but he went little further than to recognize the issue. Even a brief review of the mass of empirical work now being done on the racial, ethnic, familial and extra-union roles of working people given in the previous section, however, should convince any future labor theorist that he can no longer afford to ignore the wide variety of contexts, aside from the workplace itself, in which working people operate.

Second, as already suggested, most earlier theorists suffered from an equally debilitating tendency to concentrate upon the trade union as the single most obviously characteristic institution of the working-class movement, and to treat labor theory as though it were confined to a study of the origins, characteristics, and advantages of trade unions. This led, owing largely to the baleful influence of the Wisconsin school of labor economists, to the writing of an extremely narrow, rigid, and dull type of labor history in this country, and to a split between the study of labor-union theory, on the one hand, and the general study of working-class culture, on the other, which has had unfortunate consequences for both. Such tendencies reinforced the predilection of labor theorists either to ignore the pre- or noninstitutional concerns and aspirations of working people (as in the economics-welfare school of George E. Barnett), or (as in the case of Perlman) to base their views upon an explicit or implicit set of assumptions which were set forth in largely abstract terms, and for which they presented very little empirical evidence. Here again, the detailed work now being done on the non- or extra-union activities of working people should enable us to prevent a repeat of this kind of performance.

Third, the pre-1950s tradition of labor-union theory developed generalizations based upon a static model of the labor force which took little, if any, account of changes in its occupational shape or character over time. Elementary statistics concerning changes in patterns of migration, for instance, or changes in the demands of industry for different kinds of labor, such as are now being used as ammunition in the "old"- working-class/"new"-working-class debate should also enable any new labor theorist to avoid that particular pitfall.

Finally, there has been a tendency toward a rigid or deterministic view of labor ideology which I would label ahistorical, not only because it gives us an oversimplified picture of the past, but also because it limits the predictive value of labor theory for the future. Contemporary labor theorists are certainly not wholly free of this tendency, as may be seen in the highly dogmatic assertions concerning working class authoritarianism made by the Lipset school of sociologists, or in the equally elitist and contemptuous attitude toward the working class adopted by such left-wing critics as Marcuse. Generally speaking, however, there has been a much greater degree of sympathy and sophistication in the way in which the various positions adopted by contemporary commentators have been argued. Selig Perlman, for example, dismissed the antimonopoly, producer-orienterd consciousness of the pre-Civil War labor movement as irrelevant and anachronistic to a modern labor movement based upon job-consciousness and a factory economy. It may well be, however, that antimonopolism was indeed appropriate to the labor movement of the early part of the nineteenth century, situated as it was in a relatively small-scale, workshop-oriented economy still largely imbued with rural values. In the same way, a "labor aristocracy" form of explanation may well have been appropriate to the skill-oriented economy of the latter part of the nineteenth century; and an industrial union form of explanation appropriate to the mass-production industries of the first half of this century. Now, as we have seen, the economy is changing again. The predominantly white, blue-collar worker no longer occupies the center of the stage, and in the last years of the twentieth century, assembly-line processes will be largely taken care of by blacks, Chicanos, and other hitherto marginal elements in the labor force, while an increasing number of service, managerial, and technical jobs are filled by white-collar workers with very different backgrounds and skills. Who can say what will happen to the supposedly universal job-conscious theory of labor organization then?

Yet if Perlman put the issue too simply, and if there are many other questions in our study of the working class that we would want to ask besides those concerning job-consciousness, the relevance of his original question still remains. For despite major depressions, active repression by both government and employers, revolutionary changes in the character and types of rewards offered by employment, and appeals from all sides to adopt a different course of action, most American workers have not been willing so far to go beyond the pursuit of rather limited bread-and-butter aims. I have tried to suggest that Perlman's method of establishing the reasons for this was methodologically unsound, and based upon so little empirical evidence as to create doubt in the reader's mind whether he had answered the question at all. But until the unlikely event that the American working class chooses to adopt a different course of action, we must continue to ask why.

NOTES

1. Irving Kristol, "Writing about Trade Unions," *New York Times Book Review,* February 1, 1970, pp. 2, 24. See also Paul Jocobs, *The State of the Unions* (New York, 1963). The most recent general survey, with essays on various aspects of the subject, is *Dissent's* special issue "The World of the Blue Collar Worker" (Winter 1972).
2. The most important of these have been collected in George Fischer, ed., *The Revival of American Socialism: Selected Papers of the Socialist Scholars' Conference* (New York, 1971).
3. Industrial Relations Research Association, *Interpreting the Labor Movement* (Champaign, 1952), pp. 1-69, 83-109.
4. For a further discussion of the role of labor economists in the writing of labor theory and of labor history, see Paul J. McNulty, "Labor Problems and Labor Economics: The Roots of an Academic Discipline," *Labor History* 9(1968): 239-61.
5. This summary of the views of the early American labor theorists is taken from Mark Perlman (Selig's son), *Labor Union Theories in America: Background and Development* (Evanston, 1958), except where otherwise indicated.
6. Richard T. Ely, *The Labor Movement in America* (New York, 1886), p. 138.
7. John A. Ryan, *Declining Liberty and Other Papers* (New York, 1927), p. 218.
8. For insight into these two groups, see Petro Matthiessen, *Sol Si Puedes: Cesar Chavez and the New American Revolution* (New York, 1969); B. J. Widick, "Black City, Black Unions?" *Dissent* (Winter 1972): 138-45; or numerous pamphlets published by the Radical Education Project in Detroit on DRUM

(Dodge Revolutionary Union Movement) and FRUM (the equivalent for Ford), in the late 1960s. One example of the latter is Robert Dudnick, "Black Workers in Revolt" (1969).

9. See, for example, Frank J. Warne, *The Slav Invasion and the Mine Workers: A Study in Immigration* (Philadelphia, 1954), pp. 65-71.

10. *Preamble to the Constitution of...the Knights of Labor.* In John H. M. Laslett, ed., *The Workingman in American Life: Selected Readings* (New York, 1968), p. 41.

11. Carleton H. Parker, *The Casual Laborer and Other Essays* (New York, 1920), p. 59.

12. See, for example, Stephan Thernstrom, "Urbanization, Migration, and Social Mobility in Late Nineteenth Century America," in Barton J. Bernstein, ed., *Towards a New Past: Dissenting Essays in American History* (New York, 1967), pp. 158-75.

13. Tannenbaum went on to argue (although his views on the radical potential of the labor movement were considerably modified in his later book, *A Philosophy of Labor,* 1957), that the worker's desire for security was so great that he would not stop, as Perlman was to argue later, at attempting to share control with the employer over the immediate rewards and character of the job, but would seek to supplant the employer entirely. However, this did not lead Tannenbaum into the Marxist position of arguing for proletarian seizure of the entire means of production, but instead to a more limited form of guild socialism (after G.D.H. Cole, in England) which would be more satisfying to the individual's desire for controlling his own fate.

14. Robert F. Hoxie, *Trade Unionism in the United States* (New York, 1921), pp. 67ff.

15. For an interesting review of Old Left Marxist writing on American labor, see Paul Buhle, "American Marxist Historiography, 1900-1940," *Radical America* 4 (1970): 5-35.

16. For example, William Z. Foster, *American Trade Unionism* (New York, 1950), or his *Misleaders of Labor* (1927). Philip Foner's major work is *The History of the Labor Movement in the United States,* 4 vols. (New York, 1947-65).

17. Anthony Bimba, *History of the American Working Class* (New York, 1937), pp. 10-45, 68-69, 115, 122, 232.

18. Buhle, "American Marxist Historiography," p. 17.

19. Quoted from Gabriel Kolko, "The Decline of American Radicalism in the Twentieth Century," in James Weinstein and David W. Eakins, eds., *For a New America* (New York, 1970), p. 198.

20. For Gutman's work, see various references attached to his "Work, Culture, and Society in Industrializing America, 1815-1919," *American Historical Review* 78 (1973): 531-87. Weinstein has written *The Decline of Socialism in America, 1912-1925* (New York, 1967), and *The Corporate Ideal and the Liberal State, 1900-1918* (New York, 1968); Montgomery, *Beyond Equality* (New York, 1967); and Green, "The Brotherhood of Timber Workers 1910-1913: A Radical Response to Industrial Capitalism in the U.S.A.," in *Past and Present,* 60 (August 1973).

21. Robert L. Allen, *Reluctant Reformers* (New York, 1975), pp. 227-59.

22. Selig Perlman, *A Theory of the Labor Movement* (New York, 1928), pp. 6, 199.

23. Ibid., pp. 214, 239-40.

24. Industrial Relations Research Association, *Interpreting the Labor Movement*, p. 52.

25. In a study of the sources of radicalism in six leading American trade unions at the turn of the century, I found evidence of radicalization resulting from technological displacement, low wages, slum conditions, and other forms of capitalist exploitation. See John H. M. Laslett, *Labor and the Left: A Study of Socialist and Radical Influences in the American Labor Movement, 1881-1924* (New York, 1970), pp. 291-93 ff. For other critiques of Perlman, see Adolph Sturmthal, "Comments on Selig Perlman's 'A Theory of the Labor Movement,'" *Industrial and Labor Relations Review* 4 (1951): 483-96; Charles A. Gulick and Melvin K. Bers, "Insight and Illusion in Perlman's Theory of the Labor Movement," *Industrial and Labor Relations Review* 6 (1953): 510-31.

26. Aside from anything else, both of these concepts assume far too great a degree of rational self-awareness in the decision-making processes of both worker and entrepreneur.

27. C. Wright Mills, *White Collar: The American Middle Class* (New York, 1951); Everett M. Kassalow, "White Collar Unionism in the United States," in Adolph Sturmthal, ed., *White Collar Trade Unions: Contemporary Developments in Advanced Countries* (Urbana, 1966), pp. 305-64; Joan Moore and Afredo Cuellar, *Mexican Americans* (Englewood Cliffs, 1970); Harry Kitano, *Japanese Americans; The Evolution of a Subculture* (Englewood Cliffs, 1969); essays by Julius Jacobson and Herbert Hill in Julius Jacobson, ed., *The Negro and the American Labor Movement* (New York, 1968).

28. Cited in Ernest Mandel and George Novack, "On the Revolutionary Potential of the Working Class," Merit pamphlet (New York, 1969), p. 24.

29. Paul Sweezy and Paul Baran, *Monopoly Capital* (New York, 1966), p. 363.

30. John H. M. Laslett and Seymour Martin Lipset, *Failure of a Dream? Essays in the History of American Socialism* (New York, 1974), p. 27.

31. The initial statement of this position, so far as Lipset is concerned, came in his *Political Man: The Social Bases of Politics* (New York, 1960), ch. 4. His most recent reformulation is to be found in S. M. Lipset and E. Raab, *The Politics of Unreason: Right Wing Extremism in America* (New York, 1970), chs. 1, 9-12.

32. Richard Hamilton, "Class and Race in the United States," in Fischer, *The Revival of American Socialism*, pp. 81-106.

33. John H. Goldthrope et al. *The Affluent Worker in the Class Structure* (Cambridge, 1969).

34. Martin Glaberman, "Marxism, the Working Class and the Trade Unions," in *Studies on the Left* 4 (1964): 65-72; Stanley Weir, "The Labor Revolt," *International Socialist Journal* (April and June 1967).

35. Harry Braverman, *Labor and Monopoly Capital* (New York, 1974), p. 34.

36. Figures here are taken from Daniel Bell, "Labor in the Post-Industrial Society," *Dissent* (Winter 1972): 170-73 ff. For a more extended analysis see various chapters in his *The Coming of Post-Industrial Society* (New York, 1973).

37. Mills, *White Collar*, p. 342; Serge Mallet, *La Nouvelle Classe Ouvrière* (Paris, 1963), pp. 69 ff; André Gorz, *Strategy for Labor* (Boston, 1967), pp. 104-6 ff (first published as *Strategie Ouvrière et Néo-Capitalisme* (1964). See also Alain Touraine, *The Post-Industrial Society* (New York, 1971), first published as *La Société Post-industrialle*, 1969.

38. Herbert Gintis, "The New Working Class and Revolutionary Youth," in *Socialist Revolution* 1 (1970): 13-43; Stanley Aronowitz, "Does the United States have a New Working Class?" in Fischer, *The Revival of American Socialism*, pp. 188-216. For other contributions to the "old"-working-class/"new"-working-class debate, see Donald C. Hodges, "Old and New Working Classes," in *Radical America* 5 (1971): 11-32; and the essays by Bell and Michael Harrington in *Dissent* (Winter 1972): 146-89.

39. Andrew Levinson, *The American Working Class Majority* (New York, 1974), p. 51.

40. See the recently translated works of Gramsci, edited together with an introduction by Quintin Hoare and Geoffrey Nowell Smith in *Selections from the Prison Notebooks of Antonio Gramsci* (New York, 1971), which also, incidentally, includes a highly illuminating chapter on the United States entitled "Americanism and Fordism."

2

Changing Workers in a Changing Economy[1]

S.M. Miller

American workers have been described in clashing ways, depending on the purposes of the commentator and the period. They have been viewed as hardhats and fatcats, complacent in their influence, raging in their racism. Some new and old leftists continue to see them as a class conscious, potentially revolutionary proletariat, the only hope of revolutionary change in capitalist society. Others of the Old and New Left have lost hope in the working class as a revolutionary group: they regard workers as co-opted beneficiaries/victims of the welfare state, or as dwindling remnants of an earlier technological era. Still others, perhaps the bulk of the liberals and ex-Old Left, regard workers and their unions as unworthy of concern and support. They regard workers as antiintellectual, racist, authoritarian. Far from promoting positive change, they are viewed as rear-guardists, hostilely competing for resources that should go to the poor and discriminated. On the other hand, a determined but beleaguered band of liberals retain faith in a resurgence of the New Deal liberal-labor coalition as the basis of progressive social change.

What an extraordinary range of views! It is hard to believe that analysts are talking about the same group of workers. Some notice only particular kinds of conditions; others have special standards for evaluating worker and union behavior, either readily excusing negative practices or expecting higher standards than demanded of corporations and white-collar workers.

HETEROGENEITY

Underlying these difficulties in generalizing about workers is their considerable heterogeneity. We can center on coal miners who display impressive union militancy in a prolonged and turbulent strike. Or we can concentrate on a union like the International Ladies Garment Workers' Union which economically regulates its industry and whose membership has changed ethnically in forty years but whose officials have changed less so. We can talk as though all workers were skilled, highly-paid members of strong construction unions, or as though they all shared the conditions of low-paid, unprotected migrant or "illegal" workers. Many commentators have yielded to the temptation to select a particular slice of contemporary history and generalize from that, or to project a major trend from a minor event.

We never agree on whom to include among workers. Richard Hamilton has argued that foremen should be excluded from studies of blue-collar income and attitudes because their basic situation and outlook differs from those who constitute the manual population. Others believe that the circumstances of many technicians are increasingly similar to those of workers and that they should be included in any discussion of workers. Others argue for the exclusion of low-skilled, low-pay, irregularly employed workers because their conditions and possibilities differ so much from those of skilled and semiskilled workers. Still others identify professionals as a potentially radical "new working class," while some define the "working class" as including most nonmanagerial employees.

For the purpose of this chapter, all manual or blue-collar workers except foremen are included. The term "manual" is broader than blue-collar and includes, in addition to traditional blue-collar workers, others who are not office workers nor factory workers; they are in nonsupervisory positions in service industries. Each statement about workers should be interpreted as saying "some blue-collar workers" or "many blue-collar or manual workers," for a recognition of the heterogeneity among workers is basic to any analysis.

In this chapter, we deal with the current situation of workers in terms of numbers, changing characteristics, income, and racial attitudes. But this brief review of misconceptions about the current situation must be reviewed in terms of the profound shifts in economic structure and policy which are deeply affecting workers. The final section of the paper will deal with these possible shifts and their implications.

NUMBERS

Despite the announcements of the coming of a "service economy" or a "postindustrial society," blue-collar work is not dwindling. True, overall occupational trends show that white-collar work is increasing much more rapidly than blue-collar. This relative decline does not mean that blue-collar employees are decreasing in absolute numbers; the great drop absolutely and relatively has been in agricultural employment. The 1977 total of 29.5 million blue-collar workers was near the all-time high of 29.9 million in 1973, before the deep recession. From 1960 to 1977, the total of blue-collar workers increased by more than 5 million (from 24.1 million to 29.5 million). To this figure should be added most of those in service occupations (12.3 million). The manual total then is 41.8 million, which is only 3.7 million less than that for all white-collar workers.

Male blue-collar workers (24.3 million) in 1977 were 2.6 million more numerous than male white-collar workers (21.7 million). Female workers greatly outnumber males in the white-collar field, predominantly in the lower levels of this broad category. The historical trend also shows the relative importance of male blue-collar work; in 1940, 45.6 percent of the male labor force was in blue-collar work; in 1977, 45.9 percent.[2]

Thus, while blue-collar workers are not a majority of the total labor force, they are not an insubstantial number. Misleading notions about a drop in the number of blue-collar workers partly stem from the assumption that they once predominated in the economy. They never did. Manufacturing employment, a major component of blue-collar work, never much exceeded a third of the total labor force, except in wartime, and was usually considerably lower.

We can understand better the continuing significance of blue-collar workers by comparing them in terms of numbers with the heralded professional worker.

Professionals

Some of those who deprecate the significance and attitudes of workers foresee the emergence of a revolutionary "new working class" of technicians and professionals. While these occupational slots are rapidly growing, this results in part from the low absolute base from which the computations start. The professional and technical category in 1977 constituted only 15.3 percent of the total employed labor force. The absolute increase from 1970 to 1977 in the numbers of professional-technical workers (2.5 million) exceeded the growth of blue-collar employ-ment (1.7 million) by less than a million. If only males are included, the employed blue-collar labor force grew slightly more than the professional and semiprofessional occupations.

Frequently, the figures for the professional-technical classification are confused with data about all white-collar work. Almost half of all white-collar workers are in low-level clerical and sales occupations; more than a fifth are managers and small businessmen, so that less than three of ten white-collar workers (or one-seventh of the labor force) are in professional and technical work.

This "new working class" does not have a high proportion of radicals. The initial responses in the United States to declining demand for professional labor and low or no increases in real income are toward heightened vocationalization rather than toward militancy. But that may change.

Emphasizing the size of the manual categories and minimizing the size of the professional-technical categories should not lead one to conclude that no occupational changes have occurred or that the venerable thesis of a proletarian revolution is tenable. Neither numbers nor outlook make that prediction probable. But, as we shall discuss later, an effective movement for change cannot write off the large group of blue-collar workers.

CHANGING CHARACTERISTICS

Women and Minorities

Within the continuing large category of manual worker, important changes in demographic or ascriptive characteristics are occurring which affect solidarity and militancy. Of blue-collar workers in 1960, 15.1 percent were female; in 1977, 17.7 percent. This rise does not fully reveal the growing importance of women. Restricting the analysis to the "operatives" category, that part of blue-collar work largely done in factories, shows that in 1972 women were already 39.9 percent of the operative labor force; in 1977, this figure had increased to 41.6 percent. By contrast, the 1960 figure was under 30 percent.[3] If we widen our scope and look at blue-collar and service occupations, we find that women held 26.7 percent of these positions in 1960 and 30.6 percent in 1976. Despite the attention to women entering white-collar, particularly managerial and professional, occupations, they are growing in importance in blue-collar ranks.

Minorities, listed in Bureau of Labor Statistics reports as "blacks and others," have grown more slowly than women in blue-collar occupations. In 1960, they furnished 11.5 percent of blue-collar workers; in 1976, 12.3 percent. They were more important in the operatives level, moving from 11.9 percent in 1960 to 14.5 percent in 1976.[4]

Together, women and minorities are 36 percent of the 1977 blue-collar labor force and over one-half of the operative category. The likelihood is for further increases in their share of blue-collar employment with important effects on militancy.

Ascriptive characteristics make it more difficult to organize workers into unions and promote militancy. Schisms may occur on the basis of ascription. Much of what will happen depends on how unions behave toward women and minorities.

Women employees are usually described as difficult to organize into unions and engage in union activities. Some union officials have recognized that when women do participate in union activities, they tend to become heavily involved. Issues which have been heightened by feminist concerns such as wage discrimination and improper treatment are likely to produce greater acceptance by and involvement of women in unions—if unions are receptive.

Black, Puerto Rican, and Mexican-American workers may be militant because of their racial-ethnic bond as well as their class ties. The two influences may fuse together and heighten their militancy and solidarity, making them more vigorous than mainstream workers. Or minority workers may not see their special situations as remedied by trade-union policies. For example, union insistence on strict seniority rules would mean that minorities, the last to be hired, would be first to be fired. The possibilities of antagonism between minority and mainstream workers may be more significant than their common bonds.

A third change is the increasing importance of young workers in blue-collar occupations as older workers retire. Many of the young workers may be less accepting of work and union discipline, although settled economic conditions may temper their unrest.

Over the long run, the fact of an increasingly female and young blue-collar work force may be determining. But in the short run, the issue of race will be more significant. We shall return shortly to this issue.

Another split overlaps these. Differences in the conditions of workers in mainstream and secondary industries may be growing. "Mainstream" industries and factories are characteristically large in size, high in profit, fairly secure, unionized, and oligopolized. The secondary or marginal industries are characterized by small size, low profits, instability, low unionization, and competition. The contention is that a dual or segmented labor market exists in which favored workers (by the standards of employers) are in mainstream industries and factories while less favored workers are in the marginal sectors.

The argument of a dual labor market, which has been contested, is that workers dependent on these industries and factories have different possibilities than mainstream workers. While some may move into mainstream activities, others will long endure the low pay, insecurity, and poor working conditions and fringe benefits of the marginal sectors.

Those in marginal industries are particularly young, minority, and female. To what extent unions will be oriented toward organizing these workers is not clear. The high concentration of employment in large manufacturing concerns (the two hundred largest corporations provide more than 30 percent of manufacturing employment) is paralleled by the density of workers in the sizable number of marginal enterprises. The degree of connection and possibilities of joint action between mainstream and irregular economy workers is central and will be discussed below.

Regional Changes

Two important changes are occurring in the regional distribution of industry and blue-collar workers. The Northeast is experiencing declining firms with the result of high unemployment levels. The South and West are expanding, attracting workers from rural areas and small towns into factories and increasing their share of blue-collar employment. The uprooted in the South are presently resistant to unionization, with some important exceptions. They may become more effectively organized in the future; the resistance, however, from employers like J.P. Stevens can be very great.

Declining economic opportunities in the North may lead to apathy, depression, and withdrawal, or to an enhanced sense of militancy. Thus we have a great deal of uncertainty about the impact of regional changes on the future of the blue-collar labor force. While economic trends seem clear, e.g., continuing decline in the Northeast—the impact of these changes on the outlook of workers is less certain.

INCOME

The "fat cat" view of workers centers on those who earn at least $12,000 a year; the counterview of the downtrodden workers focuses on those who barely reach the minimum wage. Obviously both situations prevail, but the more important issue is not the range (and therefore the heterogeneity) of incomes among workers but the fact that the median annual earnings

($11,688) of male operatives (semiskilled blue-collar workers) in 1976 was almost $4,000 less than the $16,236 that the Bureau of Labor Statistics considered an intermediate standard of living for an urban family of four.

Undeniably, the absolute incomes of workers have advanced markedly since World War II. But three issues must be noted. First, spendable (after tax) average weekly earnings in constant 1967 real dollars (i.e., allowing for price changes) for those who work in manufacturing and have three dependents increased from $90 in 1960 to almost $106 in 1977. In other words, in an eighteen-year period, the average annual increase in after-tax, real income was less than a dollar a week or less than $50 a year! Furthermore, the big advance in real net income occurred between 1960 and 1965: between 1965 and 1977 the total gain amounted to less than $3.50 a week. More stunning is that net real weekly earnings were lower in 1977 than in 1972 and 1973. In sum, net real gains have not been great and some of the improvement has eroded.

Second, expectations regarding what is an adequate level of living have also changed in twenty-five years. Frequently, workers' incomes are judged by the standards of 1945 while the incomes of those better off are evaluated on the basis of contemporary levels and styles. Even those workers with $12,000 plus incomes do not feel that they are doing well or that they have much discretionary income.

Third, hopes for the future cannot be substantial since, after the age of twenty-five, workers' incomes vary little with increasing experience, unlike those of professional and managerial employees. Nor do they have the "fat cat's" comfortable feeling that they don't have to worry about job security—a freedom from fear and risk that is the ultimate luxury. The expansion of the 1950s through the mid-1960s led to a growing confidence in the continuing growth of real income; wages would increase more rapidly than taxes and prices. In the late 1960s, this confidence disappeared as many factory workers discovered little if any gain in their real income. This experience shocked many and continues to be a crucial force in workers' responses.

RACIAL ATTITUDES

Although many workers accept the racist attitudes which are widespread in American society, their attitudes do not constitute a complete rejection of blacks. While they may resist blacks moving next door, they work alongside them in the plant. While they resist (black) people on welfare who they see as indulged in indolence, they support full-employment programs which would guarantee jobs for both blacks and whites. While furious over rioting and looting, they "do not want Negro repression." While they think blacks have gotten away with too much, they don't believe that the past situation of black subjugation is tenable or desirable. They worry about jobs and affirmative action.

Increasing racial tension in many factories is reported. As the numbers of black workers expand, they insist upon obtaining and defending their rights as they define them. Seniority systems and promotional procedures are challenged. In many unions, pressure will be increasingly exerted for black leadership. As black workers become more numerous and more important, the militancy of workers in and out of unions may intensify; racial-ethnic as well as economic class issues may fuse to produce a militancy which has not characterized the unionized working class in this country for some time. But racism is an important divider, and the conflict between black and white workers is not certain to abate even though many white workers have intimate relationships with blacks on the job (but not off the job). As Brendon Sexton has contended, these relationships on the job have greater intimacy than the general relationship of whites and blacks in the upper-middle classes.

What should we make of those complicated statements? My reading is: many workers have strong antiblack feelings, as do many other Americans, but these feelings are not fixed or unchanging. As Samuel Lubell says, workers seek racial peace, not racial change.[5] They are willing to make accomodations if "peace" would follow and if the burden of change were shared by others and not concentrated in their neighborhoods, schools, and jobs. They see many liberal and business establishment figures as saying that they are uninterested in their fate as long as blacks advance and better-off whites are left untouched by improving black opportunities. Their resentment focuses not only on blacks but also on those whites who are seen as disdaining workers and their interests.

Working-class people do not always welcome the advance of minorities; they resist it when it seems to hurt them. But they are not immovable on the race issue. Their racist attitudes have not been the major obstacle to black advancement in this country; the elimination of their racist attitudes will not solve the racist problems in this country. Workers and their unions should and can do better on this issue; so should all of us. I do not see the racial attitudes of workers as an impossible barrier to joint action on issues. On the other hand, white workers are not likely to fashion a just society by themselves. The tragedy for both black and white workers would be a struggle between them.

ECONOMIC CHANGE

An underlying new disturbance is the loss of hope of continuous affluence and economic growth. In the postwar period, the United States and other capitalist countries experienced fairly continuous economic growth and rising real incomes. They now face a long period of halting growth and small improvements, if any, in real incomes. The age of affluence is over.

The future of the American blue-collar labor force depends largely on these changes in national economic conditions. Two important shifts are occurring. First, the fear of inflation is resulting in policies which promote low growth rates and short growth periods. Second, the world economic hegemony of the United States has weakened tremendously. American goods do not compete effectively in the world market, while other nations' goods do compete successfully within the U.S. market; U.S.-based multi-nationals expand their manufacturing output in other countries rather than at home.

A number of measures—which I have termed "the re-capitalization of capitalism"[6] —are proffered to improve America's international position. Many of them will be adopted; how successful they will be is doubtful. The struggle against inflation is assigned high priority in the re-capitalization strategy. That orientation means a deliberate policy of low, slow growth and high levels of chronic unemployment, capped by even higher levels when inflationary dangers heat up. A campaign is underway to accept five percent unemployment or even higher as "normal" or "frictional." For minority groups and youth this normal level is multiplied.

A second plank in the re-capitalization strategy is the promotion of private investment to increase productivity and competitiveness in the world market. This would be pursued by reducing taxes on the well-to-do and corporations. In order to block the inflationary potential of budget deficits arising from lower tax revenues and continuing public expenditures, the demand is for lower governmental outlays, especially on social programs. The impact will be felt particularly by those marginal to the main labor force, although mainstream workers would also be hurt as basic services deteriorate. Wider inequalities will surely result as will the general decay of large cities.

The new wave of investment that may ensue will mean closing down of plants that offer relatively low profit margins and the construction and expansion of more profitable plants. The likely consequence will be further deterioration of the manufacturing base of the Northeast and the displacement of workers whose home localities offer few chances of alternative employment. Regional economic policy will continue to be "job-napping," attempting to entice corporations to locate plants in one place rather than another. Regions will compete in offering low taxes, low wage rates, and a docile labor force.

The new jobs may exceed the number of lost jobs, although that is doubtful since the aim of investment is high productivity. Whatever the number of new jobs, the issue will be where they are located and who gets them—mainstream or marginal workers? Competition for jobs will likely grow.

A third component is a drive for containing wage levels in order to lower the prices of U.S. goods in the international market. Indeed, some corporations have already begun to demand giving up gains previously won by unions. Collective bargaining is likely to become more difficult with the result of much lower increases in real wages than were realized in the postwar period. Indeed, as reported above, the erosion of wage gains has already begun. A chronically high unemployment level would "discipline" many unions into accepting low improvements or giving up some. A particularly sensitive issue for some unions will be the corporation demand to accept reduced employment levels in order to maintain or improve the conditions of remaining workers. This will be a very divisive issue as is the question of sharing work among all employees rather than laying off workers in order to provide full-time employment for high-seniority workers.

If inflation, as many argue, becomes a continuing important issue, then it is likely that there will be increasing reliance on an active incomes policy. Moving from persuasion to mandatory controls on wage increases will mean the further politicalization of wage bargaining in the United States. As in other countries, the focus of argument will become the federal government as the limiter of gains rather than the individual corporations directly involved in negotiations with unions. This politicalization of the wage bargain is likely to lead to greater worker militancy as the situation of individual corporations becomes less significant and the overall functioning of the economy (largely measured by competitiveness in the international market) becomes more central.

Whether or not the federal government actually becomes a more important element in collective bargaining, the likelihood is for a lower or more slowly rising standard of living than before and for considerable strife about wages and working conditions.

A highly successful re-capitalization strategy would increase manufacturing employment in the United States and curtail governmentally-supported white-collar and professional employment.[7]

The advance of office computerization may retard increases in lower white-collar employment. On the other hand, "gray-collar" or technical and white-collar workers, may increase in manufacturing. The number employed in service industries, largely a blue-collar field, may increase. While I hesitate to make projections of the character of the labor force after the sorry predictions which are periodically made, I think that we should not be surprised if the manual labor force in the 1980s does not decline absolutely or relatively.

JOINT ACTION

The variety of changes occuring and their uncertainty of impact mean that political strategies will be very important. There is no inevitable march to greater militancy on the part of workers and unions; there is no inevitable linkage or antagonism with other groups in a society. Whether militancy and joint action develop will depend to a large extent upon the way programs are carried out, particularly the form of the re-capitalization of capitalism, and the degree of willingness of unions, minority groups, liberal organizations, protest groups, and the like to attempt to work together.

No one of these groups is large or effective enough to direct basic macro policy decisions. All of these groups together may not be able to achieve much in these difficult economic and political days of American capitalism. But without some joint action, black and white workers, marginal and mainstream workers, environmentalists and the growth-oriented will all suffer.

The most likely scenario is an increasing effort to split mainstream workers from marginal (black) workers. An active policy of trying to push down wages of mainstream workers may lead to a heavy price in disturbance. The accomodation to this turbulence would be some strengthening of the conditions of mainstream workers, while those of marginal workers might deteriorate even more. A likely way is through reduced taxation on workers and sharp curtailment of those public services which are primarily beneficial to marginal workers. Over time, there is also likely to be a deterioration in the social security programs benefiting retired workers.

High-level unemployment and small wage improvements are likely to result in unrest even if some tax and social measures seek to offset them. How this unrest will be directed is an open issue. It may lead to personalistic and religious solutions; it may move in a more political way. If the response is political, then the issue is to what extent can the joint interests of a variety of groups be fostered? Or will the interests of narrow groupings of mainstream workers be central?

An economic platform is needed that pulls together the interests of both mainstream and marginal workers, and at the same time, deals with the broad issues of the economy. Full employment bills such as Humphrey-Hawkins, even in a strong rather than weak version, are inadequate. They do not propose alternatives to the re-capitalization strategy which are economically and politically attractive. The absence of a vital and viable liberal-left-union strategy leaves the political macro economic stage to conservative approaches of unlikely effectiveness and likely damage to many.

The molding of a program that is compelling to large numbers of heterogeneous workers and other groups in society is essential. Blue-collar workers should be viewed as part of a potential, although loose, coalition which can produce important changes, or more accurately, bar negative, regressive policies. Instant success is not likely. It will take some time to develop new policy platforms to challenge the delegitimation of governmental actions which help the vulnerable, and to learn how disparate groups can overcome their differences and focus on their common needs. The linkages will not be easy to obtain or maintain. How unions—which are experiencing turnovers of leadership, voting down of agreements, and other signs of member unrest—respond will be a vital element in the development and maintenance of linkages. On some issues, such as social security, unions are in the vanguard of progressive actions. But there is great uncertainty about other issues.

Avoiding racial splits, increasing members' allegiances, and developing programs of broad, rather than only sectoral, appeal are significant challenges to trade unions. They may not succeed in doing these things, but if they do not, it will be a sorry time for the majority of Americans. Joint action will be ineffective without workers and their unions playing a key role. There is a large number of workers; unions are organized influences with a broad national agenda, unlike many of the specialized or localized interest organizations which have emerged in the sundering of Kennedy-Johnson liberalism.

To promote joint action, more realistic views of the changing characteristics, conditions, and outlook of blue-collar workers are necessary.

NOTES

1. Some sections of this paper are adapted from S.M. Miller and Martha Bush, "Can Workers Transform Society" in Sar. A. Levitan, ed., *Blue-Collar Workers*, (New York: McGraw-Hill, 1971), pp.230-52.
2. Data are from *Statistical Abstract, 1977*, Table 660, p. 406. The 1940 datum is from *Historical Statistics of the United States: Colonial Times to 1970*, part 1, Table Series D, 182-232, p. 139.
3. Data from *Statistical Abstract 1977*, Table 660, p. 406. Also see *Historical Statistics of the United States*, vol. 5, pp. 139-40.
4. *Statistical Abstract 1977*, Table 661, p. 407.
5. Samuel Lubell, *The Hidden Crisis in American Politics* (New York: Norton, 1970), p. 77.
6. See articles by S.M. Miller, "The Re-Capitalization of Capitalism," in *The International Journal of Urban and Regional Research* (June 1978), and in *Social Policy* (forthcoming).
7. It is doubtful whether defense industries, an important locus of professional employment, will contract. While many multinationals do not benefit from governmental expenditures on these industries, they observe the rule of not criticizing corporate practices and well-being.

3

Race, Class, and the New Ethnicity: The Holy Ghost of Social Stratification

Irving Louis Horowitz

Recent attitudes and behavior of working-class Americans, sometimes called the "new ethnics," have deeply shocked and bewildered many acute commentators. The supposed return to militant self-identification has led one radical to claim that "the working-class white man is actually in revolt against taxes, joyless work, the double standards and short memories of professional politicians, hypocrisy and what he considers the debasement of the American dream."[1] The same display of muscular working-class behavior has led an equally radical critic to assert that "the hard-hat labor unionists, and they are by no means limited to the building trades, have joined with the military elite and their political spokesmen. This suggests the great danger of the rise of a proto-fascist workers movement in the United States. Whatever social and cultural forces may be invoked to explain this development, it is already manifesting itself in a variety of ways. The racist hard-hats from many unions are the potential street fighters of American fascism."[2] From the foregoing statements it is difficult to surmise who is in greater need of depolarization—the working class or its intellectual saviors.

WHO IS AN ETHNIC?

Whatever actual evidence we have is considerably more ubiquitous and nondescript than either projections for an ethnic-based fascism or for an ethnic-based new socialism. At the level of attitudes, several generalizations can be made: first, working-class ethnics for the most part are neither more nor less prejudiced against the black community than the wealthier classes.[3] Second, classical aspirations of upward mobility and geographical relocation along class rather than ethnic lines still permeate working-class ambitions.[4] Third, traditional class allegiances to the party system remain essentially as fluid or as fixed as they have been for other classes.[5] Fourth, it has been questioned whether feelings of alienation and anomie have affected the working class any more than other social sectors. The working class in general continues to favor government welfare and income maintenance programs, at least those affecting them in particular.[6]

Even at this late date, there remains no clear definition of the phrase: working class; no statement, even at a statistical level, of any special economic squeeze against the working class; and finally, there remains the highest doubt that a problem specific to blue-collar workers or to white ethnics as such exists. Social problems seem universal, affecting blue-collar and white-collar people alike, affecting ethnics and blacks alike, and affecting different nationalities and religious groups alike. In short, economic problems are endemic to the United States of America, and the ethnic aspects of these problems are simply expressions of such universal class dilemmas.[7]

Whether or not the general wisdom is accurate, the rise of a new literature on blue-collar ethnics does herald something novel in the social sciences. At the least, earlier analyses based on the end of class interests, class ideologies, and class politics have receded to the point of either a memory or a whisper, only to be replaced by a verbal celebration of ethnic interests, ethnic ideologies, and ethnic politics. The only certainty is that such exaggerations too will pass.

Any attempt to define ethnicity raises at least three sociological problems: (1) who is an ethnic; (2) how can ethnicity be distinguished from other social variables and character traits; and (3) what can ethnicity predict—what are its behavioral consequences? Before coming to terms with the current ideological and political uses of ethnicity, it may be worthwhile to describe the ideological sources of the current celebration of ethnicity. The general characterization of ethnicity in the social science literature can be summarized under seven headings.

1. It is frequently claimed that ethnics are neither very rich nor very poor, nor part of either the ruling class or the underclass. Rather, they are often identified with either the blue-collar working class or the lower-middle class.

2. The current literature presents highly selective idiosyncratic definitions of ethnicity. Jews and Japanese are often excluded by intellectual fiat from the ethnic category on the basis of their middle or upper-middle class position, and on the basis of their upward mobility through education; other times, they are included as a political category of an "anti-WASP" sort.

3. Ethnicity *within* lower-class groups or racial groups such as blacks seems to be excluded from discussion. Thus, for example, distinctions and differences between East African blacks and Jamaican blacks are very rarely spoken of by those defining or employing the term "ethnicity."

4. There is a strong tendency to describe ethnics in terms of whites living in the urban complex or in the inner city, in contrast to whites living in suburban or nonurban regions.

5. A distinction is often made between nativists and ethnics, that is, between people who have Protestant and English-speaking backgrounds and those with Catholic and non-English speaking backgrounds, although in some cases (for instance, the Irish), ethnics may be identified solely on the basis of religion.

6. Ethnics are said to have in common a vocational orientation toward education, in contrast to a liberal arts or humanities orientation. They tend to be nonacademic, antiintellectual, and highly pragmatic. Interestingly, although blacks are perhaps the best illustration of a vocationally-oriented subculture, they are not generally categorized as ethnics.

7. Ethnics are usually said to possess characteristics and attitudes identified with those on the political Right: strong patriotic fervor, religious fundamentalism, authoritarian family patterns, and so forth. Indeed, characterizations of ethnicity and conservatism show such a profound overlap that the only difference would appear to be the currently positive attitude toward such behavior on the part of the learned observers.[8]

Determining who is an ethnic has more to do with sentiment than with science. The concept defines a new, positive attitude toward those who fit the model. One now hears "them" spoken of as middle class, lower-middle class or working class in contrast to lower class. "They" are said to be part of a great new wave of populism: the struggle against opulence on one hand and welfare on the other. As such, the concept of ethnicity claims a political middle ground. It does not celebrate a national consensus nor does it accept the concept of a class struggle. Its ideologists perceive of ethnics as a series of interest groups rather than a social class. There is an unstated kinship between classical liberalism and the ideology of ethnicity. It promotes the theme of cultural pluralism and cultural difference more distinctly than it does social change or social action.[9] This helps to explain why dedicated civil libertarians have moved their attentions and affections from the black underclass to the white ethnic class.[10]

One of the more customary ploys in refocusing attention away from blacks and towards ethnics is to point to quantitative parity. The new ethnics take note of the fact that there are nearly as many Americans of Italian and Irish extraction as there are of African extraction. The supreme difficulty in this sort of quantitative exercise is the absence of qualitative common sense: the blacks have a unique and special history in America that provides them with a solidarity and a definition quite apart from other Americans; whereas the Italians and Irish, and other ethnic groupings as well, have a far weaker sense of delineation and definition. The blacks (and this they share uniquely with the Jews) represent a group apart; the new ethnics represent groups which would like the future payoffs, but not the historic penalties, of becoming a group apart.[11] Now it might well be the case that even blacks will be rendered by sharpening class divisions to the point where racial commonalities dwindle. If this should be the case, then it is more likely that class factors rather than ethnic factors would become the beneficiary of such economic cleavages.[12]

ROOTS OF ETHNICITY

The rise of ethnicity as a separate factor reflects the existence in America of what has been called a cross-cutting culture that reduces any sense of common identity among those who comprise the 90,000,000 members of the total working class, of whom fewer than one-fourth are organized into unions. Observers have discussed the persistence of ethnic identity from this vantage point. Michael Parenti has observed that in a single weekend in New York, separate dances for persons of Hungarian, Irish, Italian, German and Polish extractions are advertised in the neighborhood newspapers and the foreign language press. Herbert Gans and Gerald Shuttles have discussed the persistence of a tightly knit network of relationships among Italians living in Boston and in Chicago. Occupationally, the $5,000 to $10,000 category embraces secretaries and assembly-line workers, senior clerks and cab drivers. Geographically, workers spread out over the south with its racially dominated politics, midwest where fear of communism is a serious sentiment, and the northeast where problems of traffic congestion and state financial support for parochial schools excite political passions.[13]

Ethnicity refers then to a cluster of cultural factors that define the sociogram of the person beyond or apart from the racial or class connections of that person. It defines the binding impact of linguistic origins, geographic backgrounds, cultural and culinary tastes, and religious homogeneity. In this sense, the concept of ethnicity is not only distinguished from class but in a certain respect must be considered its operational counterpart. It provides the cultural and theological linkages that cut through class lines and form new sources of tension and definition of inclusionary-exclusionary relationships in an American society grown weary of class perspectives on social reality.

In part, the renewed emphasis upon ethnicity signifies the decline of the achievement orientation and the return to an ascriptive vision. Generational success can no longer be measured in terms of job performance or career satisfaction. Therefore, new definitions of group membership are sought in order to generate pride. These often take the form of a celebration of ethnic origins, and a feeling that such origins somehow are more significant to group cohesion than is class or race.

The notion of ethnicity, like other barometers of disaffection from the nation-state, is indicative of problems in self-definition. Americans have long been known to have weak class identification. Most studies have shown that class identification is weak because class conflict is thought foreign to American society; nearly everyone claims to be a middle-class member.[14] Few see themselves at either end of the class spectrum. In fact, one analyst suggested that "it is not implausible to suggest that the 1980 census data will show that greater numbers of Americans will be living in $25,000 plus households than in poverty."[15] As a result, class as a source of status distinction is strong, but as a source of economic mobilization it is weak.[16] In a sense, the concept of ethnicity closely emulates the concept of race, for race, unlike class, is based upon ascription rather than achievement. But ethnicity defines a community of peoples having language, religion, and race in common. For some, it further entails a commonality of tastes, what Novak has termed "gut issues."[17] For example, Poles and Italians share religious similarities, but they are not likely to share language identities. The church has long recognized ethnicity on the basis of linguistic and national origin, and not simply the universal ministerial claims of Catholicism.[18]

Determining the behavioral consequences of ethnicity entails the difficulty of establishing whether there are common political demands or even common economic conditions that all national and linguistic minorities share. Aside from the fact that a bare majority of ethnics participate in Democratic party politics, there is little evidence that ethnics do in fact share common political goals. There seem to be greater gaps between first- and second-generation Irish and Poles than between Irish and Poles of the same generation. Hence the actual power of ethnicity as an explanatory variable must be carefully evaluated and screened.

In large measure, the new ethnicity reflects rather than shapes the new politics. The present era represents a new kind of emphasis. The collapse of federalism, the strain on the American national system, and the consequent termination of the melting-pot ideology has led to a situation where ethnicity in a sense fulfills the thirst for community—a modest-sized community in which the values of rural America as well as rural Europe could be simulated in the context of a post-industrial world, yet without the critique implied by the radical and youth movements.

Disillusionment with the American system and its inability to preserve a universal series of goals has led to a reemergence of community-centered parochial and particularistic doctrines. Indeed, the positive response of the American nation to the historical injustices heaped upon the black people has made it seem that ethnicity could achieve the same results by using a similar model of social protest.

There has been a notable shift of attitudes at the ideological level. What once appeared to be a minority problem with its attendant drives toward integration into the American mainstream has now become an ethnic problem with its attendant drives toward self-determination apart from the American mainstream. To be more precise, there has been an erosion of that mainstream. With the existence of 20 to 30 million first- and second-generation Italian-Americans, 9 to 10 million Spanish-speaking Ameri cans, some 13 million Irish Americans (these often overlapping with 48 million Catholics), who in turn share a country with 6 million Jews and 23 million blacks, the notion of majority status for white Protestant America has been seriously eroded. The notion of the WASP serves to identify a dominant economic group, but no longer a uniquely gifted or uniquely destined-to-rule political or cultural group. Thus, ethnicity has served to express a genuine plurality of interests, without necessarily effecting a revolution in life-styles or attitudes. Equality increasingly becomes the right to be different and to express such differences in language, customs, and habits, rather than a shared genuine plurality of interests, without necessarily effecting a revolution in life-styles or attitudes. Equality increasingly becomes the right to be different and to express such differences in language, customs, and habits, rather than a shared position in the white Angle-Saxon Protestant ethos which cominated the United States up and through the end of World War II and the Cold War period.

Ethnicity is also an expression of the coming into being of new nations throughout the Third World—African nations, Asian nations, Latin American socialist states, Israel as a Jewish homeland, the reemergence of Irish nationalism. The international trend toward diversified power bases has had domestic repercussions on minority standing in the United States. The external reinforcement of internal minorities has changed the self-image of these internal minorities. The new ethnics are (in part at least) the old minorities in an era of postcolonialism, in an era of capitalism on the defensive, at least as a cultural ideal if not as an economic reality. Thus, whether ethnicity takes revolutionary or reactionary forms internally, its rise to conceptual and ideological preeminence is clearly a function of the breakup of the old order in which Anglo-American dominance went uncontested.

RACE, RELIGION, AND ETHNICITY

The concept of ethnicity is not only an attempt to simulate the strategy of the blacks for gaining equality through struggle; it is also patterned after the main tactic of the Jews for gaining equality through education. Whether such simulation or imitation will be successful depends on whether ethnicity is an overriding concept or simply a word disguising differences of a profound sort between linguistic groups and religious groups. The fact of being Irish may be of binding value, but the fact of being Protestant Irish or Catholic Irish certainly would take precedence over the ethnic unity. Similarly, being a Ukraine may be a binding value as long as Ukraines are defined exclusively in nonreligious terms. For the Ukrainian Jews certainly do not participate in the same ethnic goals, despite a shared geographic and linguistic background. Hence, the concept of ethnicity may explain little in the way of behavior unless it can be demonstrated that it forms the basis of social solidarity and political action, and is not simply a residual category.

The new emphasis on ethnicity is distinguishable from the old emphasis on minority groups in the United States primarily because it represents repudiation of the "melting-pot" ideology, but more significantly, a breakdown in what used to be known as the majority. It is terribly difficult to have minority studies in a world where the major impulse is weak, nonexistent, or defined as another minority. Hence, the rise of ethnicity as a rallying point seems to be in inverse proportion to the decline of white Anglo-Saxon Protestantism as a consensus framework. The latter, too, has turned ethnic. Ethnicity has become a relative concept instead of a subordinate concept.

The call for "Ethnic Power," modeled as it is upon the past decade of civil rights struggles, provides a perfect illustration of the limits of model construction. It involves a blurring of the special circumstances of blacks in the United States. It would not be entirely amiss to recall that the black presence in the United States was largely involuntary, whereas the ethnic minority presence was largely voluntary. Moreover, the black experience in America was linked to the plantation as a total institution and connected to their degradation as a people; white immigration (ethnic immigration) involved participation in the building of America and particularly in the building of its industrial life. Thus, while modes for ethnic separatism are premised on the black movement, at the same time they display little awareness of the different circumstances of black participation in American affairs throughout the last one hundred years.

A latent function of current appeals to a new ethnicity are directly related to the Great White Hope, to the theme of ethnics preventing blacks from becoming the major power bloc in urban America. As such, ethnicity becomes not just a response to present superordinate traits of the dominant American sectors. Ethnicity becomes a euphemism for the fight against crime in the streets and for the fight to maintain a white foothold in the major urban centers. Support for the claims of ethnicity must also be viewed as a reaction to the flight of hugh sectors of the middle class to suburban America, thus leaving the white working-class ethnics to absorb the full impact of black militants and black organizations in the American cities.

The celebration of ethnicity is not so much a recognition of the special contribution of Europeans to America as it is the manufacturing of a new conservatism. Ethnicity gives expression to an organized group of white working-class Americans dedicated to the maintenance of their comparative class positions. As such, ethnicity becomes yet another hurdle for black Americans to jump in order to gain equity in this society. An overt struggle between whites and blacks is intellectually unpalatable; hence, ethnicity emerges to defuse racial tension by shifting the struggle to the loftier plane of downtrodden blacks and denigrated ethnics.

At an entirely different level, the celebration of ethnicity has brought about strange new alliances or the potential for new coalitions. After years of struggle in support of black egalitarianism and in particular black institutions of higher learning, Jews are now being criticized as never before by their black colleagues. Whatever the roots of black nationalism, its first contact is with the Jew as landlord, shopkeeper, and realtor. Whether the turn of the Jewish community to ethnics will resolve their problems with blacks is difficult to ascertain. In fact, what is being jeopardized is the special philanthropic relationship which has existed throughout the twentieth century between the black and Jewish communities, and which perhaps is epitomized by such established black leaders as the late Martin Luther King and such Jewish leaders as the deceased Rabbi Stepher Wise. But this was bound to end—as blacks established their own sources of political power and Jews discovered others, especially Israelis, in dire need.

The middle class character of the alliance between blacks and Jews has long been understood. Its focus on education as the main source of upward mobility rules out the possibility of revolutionary coalition. And as young blacks move more conscientiously toward success through education, and as an older generation of Jews move with equal rapidity toward reformist goals, the historic alliance between these two peoples becomes seriously jeopardized as they come to compete for the same goals and essentially with the same skills. The educational model proved efficacious for the postwar blacks, more so than has been anticipated. As a result, blacks turned toward a political participatory model, operationally defined by a direct challenge to, and search for, a share in government power. Be that as it may, declaration of support by the Jewish community, or its self-declared representatives, on behalf of the ethnic urban white working class, has little more than symbolic significance. Class barriers between peoples continue to be clearly more durable than the commonality of race.

Various organization efforts to sensitize and depolarize, although well-intentioned and intellectually sincere, start from a fundamentally erroneous premise; namely, that the key polarity is presently between black America and ethnic America. Such a formulation does permit various organizations, especially Jewish middle-class organizations, to perform their historic role of honest broker and friend at both courts. However, the likelihood is that, despite the differences between Poles and blacks in cities such as Detroit or Gary, their problems arise from common sources—a lack of steady jobs, poor upgrading procedures, lack of meaningful retraining programs, and a breakdown of urban development—all of which should (if the proper conclusions are drawn) create the basis for class solidarity rather than simple ethnic separation along racial or religious lines.

It can be understood why some organizational leaders of the Jewish community would seek rapprochement with ethnic groups. However, since the ethnics themselves often define the Jews as outside ethnicity, and since the class formations that separate ethnic America from Jewish America continue unabated, the possibility of alliance seems remote and, when executed, tenuous. It may represent a tactical side bet in a specific community where Jewish-ethnic interaction is high, but little else. Again, the cross-cutting characteristics of race, class, and ethnicity tend to make nonpolitical coalitions exceptionally difficult to maintain over any period of time.

The special tactical relationships between blacks, Jews, and ethnics is really the crux of any future working-class consensus in the United States. In terms of stratification, the United States has become a three-track nation. The blacks are identified as being either on the government payroll or on the government dole. The Jews are identified as being entrepreneurial kingpins in America. The ethnics are seen, or perceive themselves, as the true heirs of the working-class spirit.[19] In this sense, the growing tendency of Communist parties throughout the world to accept, if not adopt outright, anti-Semitic postures is a very real response to its working-class and black constituencies—which see Jews very much as the exploiters rather than exploited, and likewise see them as elements unwilling to participate in the American way of life by virtue of their alleged dual allegiance to Israel. In this sense, Soviet anti-Semitism is a convenient ideological pose for prearranged policies.

Even the executive director of The National Association for the Advancement of Colored People has recognized that blacks subconsciously apply a higher standard in the expectations of Jewish attitudes than of any other group, and hence become deeply disturbed when Jewish response to manifestations of black anti-Semitism are often in terms of the European holocaust rather than the American ghetto experience.

> There is a positive factor at work in Negro-Jewish relations—above and beyond the close and analytical scrutiny which both are accustomed to render to the issue of their relationship. This is the working partnership which has developed among professionals in the respective organizations and among officials and academicians, whose daily pursuits bring them into close and continual contact. The antennae of representatives in those categories are highly sensitive; they respond to warning signals with consultations; efforts to mediate tension spots; and attempts to achieve formulations, which will accomodate at either end.[20]

This kind of "adaptive prophylaxis" offsets respective levels of apprehension, or irritation, in the different constituencies. Leading black and Jewish organizations have worked to reach agreement on equal employment opportunity: the troublesome issue is whether federally imposed guidelines and timetables would, or should, assume the aspect of preferential quotas. The type of racial and religious compromise that will be reached will clearly not only defuse the issue of employment for minorities, but largely determine the ethnic posture.[21]

Black-Jewish competition has been defused, but more among religious leaders than ordinary citizens. Black Christians and more liberal Jewish organizations have assumed leadership in overcoming the intense racial-religious dichotomies of the past decade. To this very extent the tactic of accommodating the new ethnicity will lose its impulse. The more traditional alignments of blacks and Jews on a liberal axis will confront the white ethnic one on a conservative axis. It might be argued that such competition is merely illustrative of false consciousness, that the "real" issue remains economic. Such a point of view automatically and mechanically assumes a primacy of the economic. This very unwillingness to take seriously the competition of race, ethnicity, and religious clusters is in part responsible for the renaissance of ethnicity to begin with.

STRATEGIC USES OF ETHNICITY

Ethnicity is at least as much a tactic as a definition. The new ethnicity is a statement of relatively deprived sectors seeking economic relief through political appeals. Traditionally, such relief was found through the trade-union movement. However, the growing bureaucratization of trade unions has signified a parallel decline of faith in class warfare. To seek relief from factory-owners or managers has come to seem less efficient than appeals or, if necessary, threats leveled directly at the federal government. For example, during the 1973 energy-fuel crisis, the mass representatives of the Teamster Workers, over and above either trucking managers or union officials, demanded wage benefits directly from the government corresponding to the new price hikes. The political apparatus provided such fiscal compensation due to rises incurred from higher operating costs. Collective bargaining became transformed into state decision making. And this process has only accelerated during the entire 1970s.

Direct bargaining processes between an outside group and the federal administration are not new. The essential tactic of black organizational life, certainly since the New Deal and intensified after World War II, was precisely a direct negotiation with the political system, in this manner circumventing the economic subsystem. The efficacy of this newer political model is attested to by health and welfare legislation, civil rights rulings, Supreme Court decisions on educational opportunity, and presidential commissions on minority rights. Negotiations between mass outsider groups and state officialdom achieved more results than the previous search for economic equality through class struggle. This shift from economic to political realms has come to be shared by ethnic representatives, by those who seek to obtain from the government for Americans of Polish, Italian, or Irish extraction similar rights to those achieved by the blacks' leadership.

The dilemma of this approach arises not so much in the model; indeed, to extract promises and seek restitution from federal agencies does seem more promising that to achieve wage benefits from industry. Rather, the dilemma resides one step further back in time: in the differential histories of the black people vis-à-vis the ethnic groups who seek to emulate this racial style within American politics. Even the most ardent defenders of the new ethnicity admit to substantial differences between race and ethnicity on this score.

> The new ethnicity does *not* entail: (a) speaking a foreign language; (b) living in a subculture; (c) living in a "tight knit" ethnic neighborhood; (d) belonging to fraternal organizations; (e) responding to "ethnic" appeals; (f) exalting one's own nationality of culture, narrowly construed. Neither does it entail a university education or the reading of writers on the new ethnicity. Rather, the new ethnicity entails: first, a growing sense of discomfort with the sense of identity one is supposed to have—universalist, "melted," "like everyone else;" then a growing appreciation for the potential wisdom of one's own gut reactions (especially on moral matters) and their historical roots; a growing self-confidence and social power; a sense of being discriminated against, condescended to, or carelessly misapprehended; a growing disaffection regarding those to whom one had always been taught to defer; and a sense of injustice regarding the response of liberal spokesmen to conflicts between various ethnic groups, especially between "legitimate" minorities and "illegitimate" ones. There is, in a word, an inner conflict between one's felt personal power and one's ascribed public power; a sense of outraged truth, justice, and equity.[22]

The new ethnicity is thus a strategic matter of discomfort, dissatisfaction, and disaffection. It is not a question of oppression or subjugation. As a result, it is hard to avoid the conclusion arrived at by Myrdal, that the new ethnicity is not a populist movement, but an elitist demand by a rootless third-generation intelligentsia.

In addition to a missing urge to reach the masses for whom they pretend to speak, the writers on historical identity rather systematically avoid the problem of poverty and all that is related to it. To this also belong the limited horizons, the lack of a rational perception of themselves and the nation, and a reluctance to organize with other groups having the same interests to press their demands through the means freely provided by a democratic America. It is poverty and all this, not the lack of historical identity, that holds American ethnics down. At the same time, it permits the formation of policies that run counter to the American dream of a free and democratic society that creates happiness for all its people, from wherever they come.

The "enemy" the ethnic intellectuals commonly put up as a target— i.e., those people in America who believe in the perfection of the melting pot—is a straw man. For several decades I have been closely following events in this country, and I have seldom met any fairly well-educated American who subscribed to the melting-pot with the naivete customarily attributed to those who supposedly held that idea.

That America is a pluralistic society where people with different cultural backgrounds have to live together and mold a nation is an obvious fact. And that this creates problems and difficulties is also obvious. But America in general has shown great capacity to absorb cultural patterns from diverse sources.[23]

This set of demands made by "voluntary ethnics" may very well not be representative of the wishes or desires of Americans of Polish, Italian, Irish, or other European extractions. His summary of the distinction between problems of identity and those of poverty indicates the excessive psychologism underlying at least one part of the new ethnicity.

In its most sophisticated form, the strategy of ethnicity is made in terms of the migration, absorption, and identification of new groups. In its celebrationist form it is said that America has been uniquely able to incorporate all new groups into its social life and political experience.[24] The current charge is that such integration and incorporation is largely chimeric in nature. The evidence for this is that the culture costs of immigration, no less than the class exploitation of ethnic groups, has been vastly understated.

Lost in the ethnic interstices of the American social structure, the larger question of class is never engaged, nor is even at issue. This kind of ethnic reductionism forces us to accept as predetermined what society defines as truth. Only through ethnicity can identity be securely achieved. The result is that ethnic questions which could, in fact, further our understanding of the relationship of individuals to social structures are always raised in a way that serves to reconcile us to a common heritage of miserable inequities. Instead of realizing that the lack of a well-defined stratification structure, linked to a legitimated aristocratic tradition, led Americans to employ the language of ethnic pluralism in exchange for direct divisions by social class, we continue to ignore the real factors of class in our society.[25]

The same cross-cutting problem exists in the current sophisticated expressions of ethnicity no less than earlier forms. While blacks are included among the ethnics in the sophisticated version, the politics of ethnicity tends to counterpose its own needs over and above the racial requirements of blacks. Beyond that, the extent of the failure or success of culture pluralism to modify the culture modism of American industrialization is an empirical issue not easily decided in terms of the moral superiority of pluralism over monism.

Weighting the ethnic factor with respect to race, religion, and class remains an issue not only in terms of the identification that people have with ethnicity, but also its galvanizing impact. We have first the empirical question of the ability of ethnicity to generate political action. Implicit in a great deal of literature on ethnicity is an automatic assumption that ethnicity and working-class membership are axiomatic, while the blacks are identified as lower class, or outside the system of the working class. Sociologists have often exaggerated the idea of a lower-class culture.[26] More to the point, there has been a profound misreading of the actual distribution of the blacks in American society—for if they have a distinctive culture, they nonetheless form an essential human core in the U.S. labor force, particularly in service industries, government work, and heavy-duty labor.[27] They represent between 15 to 16 percent of the labor force, in contrast to 11 percent of the population as a whole. They are becoming unionized at a more rapid rate than their white ethnic colleagues.[28] They are also a crucial factor in assembly-line activities such as steel and autos. What sets them apart is not that they are low class while the white ethnics are working class, but that the bulk of black labor (because of its historical marginality and nontechnical characteristics) remains nonunionized, while a larger percentage of white ethnic labor (also deriving from historical sources such as immigrant syndicalist backgrounds and specialized craft forms of labor) is and has been for some time largely unionized. Accentuating the gap between lower-class black culture and working-class white ethnicity is a profoundly conservative reading of actualities—one that disguises the acute responsibilities of an American labor force sharply divided between the one-fourth which is highly organized, in contrast to the three-fourths which are poorly organized, if organized at all.

This concept of ethnic organization as a precondition for class solidarity is a theme struck by any number of commentators. Richard Krickus has summed up this sentiment with particular force:

> With rising self-awareness, the appearance of vigorous leadership, and the evolution of organizational structures, many black communities can meet the minimum requirement necessary for coalitions. Because similar structures do not exist in most white ethnic communites, a coalition with blacks is not yet feasible. Until the white ethnics, through heightened group identity, generate new leaders and develop new organizational props, the precondition for coalition activities will not materialize in their communities. [29]

But the author of these sentiments makes it clear that the purpose of such organizational pluralism is more ambitious.

> If the white ethnics are to cooperate with and work toward common goals with their nonwhite neighbors, they must acquire the means to articulate their demands in a more effective fashion. Through this process of articulation a clear view of their own self-interest will surface. This in turn is a precondition to their working together with other groups that share many problems in common with them.[30]

The assumption is often made that there is a lock-step arrangement between ethnic identification, followed by confrontation, which in turn will presumably create the basis for ethnic and racial harmony. The notion of collective self-interest or group self-interest, so important in the development of the black civil rights movement, thus becomes the strategic model for ethnic self-improvement. The dilemma exists nonetheless since it might well be that distinctions and differences between Catholics and Protestants, or for that matter, between ethnic enclaves within Catholicism, will exert far more influence that the simple consensus required to make ethnicity a successful strategy and response to racial identity.

Ultimate class identities can readily become blurred by the immediate ethnic pluralities. The rhetoric of racial and ethnic antagonism may be heightened rather than lessened by the assumption that separate organizational forms are now required for both black and ethnic groupings. To define tensions between ethnics and blacks without clearly demarcating the similarity of their class interests, which might also involve an identity of class hostilities, serves to exacerbate rather than eliminate tensions. It is to assume that specialized groups and momentary tactical considerations must always prevail over long-run tendencies and trends in the class composition of American society. It is also to assume that Jews as ethnic types have a sameness that also makes them part of this solution based on ethnicity. It might just as easily be the case that Jews too reveal profound antagonism within their numbers based on considerations of class and religion. For example, there remains a considerable spread in the class and occupational ladder among Jews, and perhaps an even wider disparity between orthodox, reformed, conservative, reconstructionist, and other varieties of Jewish religious practice. Further, on the grounds of national and ethnic backgrounds, Jews of East European and Asian or Middle Eastern origins show wide disparities. And of course, beyond that are the gulfs of a more political sort, between Zionists, non-Zionists, and even anti-Zionists. To perceive Jews as one unified phalanx is thus to credit them with far greater unity than they in fact possess. It is also to assume that the world of Jews is necessarily forged exclusively by threat mechanisms from outside groups. It is to deprive them of the very organic integrity said to be an identifying hallmark of other ethnics.

The world of ethnicity is filled with strategies based upon models largely derived from other groups. The selective and subjective method of defining membership in an ethnic group permits the concept to be employed in any number of political contexts. It might well be that however flawed the concept of ethnicity may be at the theoretical level, it can nonetheless serve as a rallying cry for those groups who are dismayed and disturbed by the breakup of ethnic communites in American society. The Jews, in particular, are castigated for being the first to abandon the urban ship in favor of suburbia. But why ethnicity must, perforce, take an urban rather than a suburban form is rarely examined, much less critically dealt with.

Within the political framework of American mass society, it might be that ethnicity functions as a conservative manifestation against the breakup of community. In substance, although clearly not in form, this is similar to left-wing radical and racial nationalist groups who likewise exhibit tendencies toward communal apartness, and racial and religious efforts at firm exclusionary-inclusionary relationships. The difference is that the new ethnicity seems to be more concerned with order than community.

Patterns of disaffiliation have found expression throughout all sectors of American society. Those who identify with the past, like those who trust only in the future, have similar problems with the present system of affluence; but quite clearly, they have posed different solutions. It is plain that forms of social change will be scarcely less painful in the United States than they have been elsewhere. Such forms involve coalitions and consolidations of a type that may, in the long run, lead to racial harmony and class unity. However, the more likely immediate outcome will be a forging of ethnic sensitivity that will tend to minimize and mitigate against such efforts at unification and national integration.

There are those who look forward to a great age of unification between lower-class blacks and working-class whites. But unification, even on the basis of expediency and political coalition still seems remote. Not only is the social system unable to provide much hope for such a coalition, but the structure of unionism on one hand and racial separatism on the other conspire to frustrate race-class fusion.[31] That the concept of ethnicity has created one more large-scale strain in the two-hundred year history of the American society is a reflection of the growing intensity of separatist politics and industrialist economics. The ultimate fruits of a policy of racial supremacy has been the intensification of interest group politics. Race and ethnicity have both threatened the survival of the social system, and yet neither seems prepared to offer an option for all other peoples living within the United States. In addition to class and race, ethnicity must now be seen as a measure of disintegration in the American sociopolitical system. Indeed, however weak this variable might be, the fact that it has left the sociology texts for the neighborhoods is indicative of the tragic ruptures in a nation unable to overcome the collapse of federalism at home and the shrinkage of imperialism abroad.

Ethnicity is in substance a surrogate concept, an expression of disintegration and deterioration of the national economic system and national social priorities. Like other notions of a particularistic nature, its importance derives more from those who are excluded than those who are included. It is a response to a collective anomie, an era in which the halcyon days of confident national priorities and arrogant international goals have become remote. Representative government has turned unrepresentative. Regulatory mechanisms have turned oppressive and bureaucratic. Large factory management and factory unionism have joined forces to present the ordinary laborer with an unresponsive structure. The drive for economic rationalization has led to the multinational corporation and international cartelization at an accelerated rate. This conglomerate push has underscored the economic impotence of the ordinary person; the tendency toward subsystemic approaches is reflected in the turn toward ethnicity.

The revival of ethnicity as a working-class value is paralleled by the middle-class return to race, sex, property, and other definitions for surmounting the vacuity and vapidity of post-industrial capitalist life. The weakness of the success ethic and the achievement orientation is revealed in middle-class youths' emphasis on rurality, fundamentalism, psychologism, and other forms of the *Gemeinschaft* community of fate that presumably was left behind with the old world and its feudal relationships. Those groups identified with the blueing of America[32] are no more content with the progress of this nation than are those who are part of the greening of America.[33] That expressions of discontent should take different forms in different classes is certainly not without precedent, but what is surprising is the uniformity of the demand to get beyond the present malaise, the widespread resentment that makes clear that the old sociological consensus and the old political checks and balances are no longer effective mechanisms against disaffection of large portions of American society.[34]

If ethnicity is a surrogate concept, it remains necessary to make plain on behalf of what it is a surrogate. Politically, it represents a demand for larger participation in the federal bureaucracy; economically, it is a demand for higher rewards for physical "hand" labor, at the expense of mental "head" labor; and culturally, it is a statement of the rights of groups to their distinctive life-styles. Beyond that, however, are the historical dimensions: the return to ethnicity, insofar as it is more than an intellectual pipedream, is also a return to community: a pristine era in American life, before the melting-pot ideology boiled out the impurities of the immigrant generation with a weird mixture of external pressure and internalized guilt.

The return to ethnicity is more than a restatement of ascribed values; it hearkens back to a period in which family allegiances, patriarchal authority, foreign languages, and the meaning of work itself had a certain priority over career and monetary achievement. On this point there can be little question that the prime targets are the blacks, who have employed the welfare model in order to gain a measure of influence and even self-respect, and the Jews, especially those of the second and third generation, who have employed the educational model to create the basis for rapid upward mobility. The problem is that the new ethnics have a hard time thoroughly identifying with the former model, and an equally hard time gaining access through the latter model. Tragically enough, they lack a model of their own.

By extension, it might be claimed with justification that Jews have largely employed the concept of social class both to explain the American system and to live within its parameters. The blacks have generally employed a concept of racial nationalism to explain why, despite the appearance of wealth, they have been kept out of the advantages of the class network. It is predictable, under the circumstances, that the rise of an ethnic consciousness would lead to a search for large-scale explanations as to why many people of Catholic faith, Polish-Italian-Irish-Ukrainian ancestry, and working-class membership seemed to be so inexorably locked into the American system at its lower, but not lowest, points. Ethnicity provides a sense of homogeneity without attempting to impose either a class or racial analysis to a conservative set of ethnic workers.

Tendencies toward individualization and privatization are evolving into a durable counterculture: on one side are students, blacks, and chicanos. On the other are ethnics: Poles, Catholics, day laborers, and all the whites who have failed to milk or melt into the "system." Whether the response has been Left or Right is less important than the impulse to resist encroachments on "little people"—the public turned ethnic with a missionary vengeance. The making of the new minorities points up the huge shift in the United States from a nation of factory workers to a nation of marginals, i.e., service-oriented personnel. The response, in some measure, whether put in terms of racial politics or ethnic politics, is a demand for a politics of scale, in which the possibility for the control of decision making and policy making would be restored to communities of responsibility. This impulse toward community is a possible source of new coalitional efforts, whether under the label of populism or welfarism, that might provide some hope for a reinvigorated politics. But for the present, ethnicity as a basic concern and a root concept should neither be dismissed nor celebrated.

Since a critical part of my argument is that ethnicity is an important, but nonetheless supplemental, variable in the analysis of American social structure and social stratification, it is entirely fitting to conclude this paper with a brief examination of ethnicity and its impact on American foreign policy. Too often, a phenomenon such as class, race, or ethnicity is dealt with exclusively as a domestic matter, hence reducing the frame of analysis to the most obvious and conventional. In point of fact, by examining how ethnicity functions in a foreign policy context, the researcher is better able to assess the relative, no less than absolute, worth of any given stratification variable. And I do believe that such an examination will bear out my contention that ethnicity is a strategic as much as a structural phenomenon, one whose measurable importance is subject to policy initiatives at least as often as to political reflexes.

POLITICS OF ETHNICITY

The amount of research and theorizing that has gone forth concerning ethnicity in this recent period is of such a magnitude that one must wonder why so little has been done thus far on the impact of ethnic and national minority groups in the formation of U.S. foreign policy.[35] Sometimes, the most obvious aspects of an issue elude us precisely because of their prima facie character. In this instance, the overseas origins of most ethnics, and presumably their continuing concern with events taking place in the mother or father country of origin, in large measure explain the importance of the subject at hand: the impact of ethnic groups on U.S. foreign policy.

Interestingly enough, the consensus among researchers seems to be that the actual amount of impact has been minimal; far less than one would predict given the large number of immigrant peoples involved in gross aggregate terms. A number of papers come perilously close to suggesting that the independent and dependent variables should be reversed: that U.S. foreign policy serves to galvanize ethnic sentiments as much, if not more, than the other way around. If for no other reason than to articulate these data in a systematic manner for the first time, one would have to say that discussions about ethnicity have been raised to a new level of coherence and intelligence.

Rather than burden these remarks by nitpicking, or suggesting specific methodological strategies or theoretical remedies that might strengthen (or for that matter weaken) ongoing research efforts, I would like to address myself to eleven points—six of which can be considered in the realm of political enquiries and five in the realm of sociological concerns—which might help to explain the rather weak and even confused impact that ethnic groups have had in the forging of U.S. foreign policy, or at least on conceptualizing foreign policy. For if the impact of ethnics has been somewhat ambiguous in congressional quarters, there can be no ambiguity about the relative absence of ethnic impact at the judicial and executive levels.

First, an extremely important point is what might be called the area of interethnic-group rivalries. Such rivalries tend to minimize any interest-group impact by creating a cancellation or veto effect; that is, one ethnic group becoming hostile or remaining indifferent to the needs of another. For example, the specific demands for national independence and autonomy by Lithuanians, Latvians, and Poles are rarely, if ever, coordinated with demands for Jewish circles seeking to emigrate from the Soviet Union. Although they may have a shared animosity toward the Soviet system, and although some leaders within these emigré groups have sought collaboration, at the same time they retain their own deep inherited animosities toward each other. Similarly, differences between religious subvariables within ethnic groups may mediate or vitiate the impact of ethnic politics. In considering the extent to which the structure of Catholic churches in certain industrial parts of the United States are divided along national lines—that is, Italian Catholics, Polish Catholics, Irish Catholics, and so on—one can see what a formidable obstacle it is to generate ethnic politics that would have sufficient impact to moderate, much less cancel, established U.S. foreign policy. In short, when the aggregate numbers are further refined, we have a problem of a critical mass, an absence of a hegemonic standpoint that would make ethnics speak with a united voice toward common ends.

Second, another aspect that vitiates ethnic group politics is the complex nature of struggles being waged overseas. The conflicts between Biafra and Nigeria had the earmarks of a fundamental schism: Biafra asserting the right of each nation to self-determination, confronting Nigeria with its claims of the necessity of national cohesion over and against separatist demands. There are no absolute rights or wrongs at this racially hegemonic level, just decisions and choices that American blacks had to confront and clearly did by choosing different sides of that struggle. Similarly, and more recently, the Angolan struggle pitted Soviet-backed Cuban armed forces versus military groups supported by the United States and even South Africa. One might say that the blacks in America were caught between the devil and the deep blue sea—a choice between superpowers at one level and white satellites sending in guerrilla forces at quite another level. But such is the world of overseas struggles. To make ethnic solidarity, even black solidarity on Third World matters obvious or prima facie, is to miss the point of the complexity of real events. While we are on the subject of American blacks, there is Haiti where one finds a black republic, but also a dictatorial regime that is clearly anathema to most American black citizens. This would indicate that the ethnic variable, even at its more compelling levels, probably remains less compelling and less pronounced to its adherents than other variables such as class, religion, or nation.

Third, while on the subject of dissent, we must not forget that one contributing element in the survival of ethnic politics, whatever the strength and weakness of specific ethnic formations, is the breakdown, or at least the absence, of national American goals. We are clearly at the end of an era based upon national celebration and perennially rising expectations. The reappearing ghost of Malthus haunts Marx and Keynes alike. Shortages, boycotts, resource shortfalls, all raise the specter of falling expectations. Whatever measure social researchers use, it is clear that a sense of cohesion has given way to a sense of separation. But such separation often is limited to survivalist goals of the ethnic groups within their adopted nation, without much possibility of expanding such goals to overseas policy-making contexts.

Fourth, it might be argued that a breakdown of national American goals has led to a return of pluralism—a pluralism emerging as a secular nationalism rather than a clerical theology. In the nineteenth century, pluralism really meant the proliferation of a plethora of Protestant church groups. The pluralism of the early twentieth century had meant the opening up of the economic valves to new groups, including new levels of mass participation in social movements aimed to stimulate the voluntary improvement of American life. One might say that the emergence of ethnicity represents a third-stage rocket in the takeoff of pluralism: one that is based on the importance of secular national concerns in decision making at personal levels—that is marriage partners, work establishments, and so on. But again, such a pluralism, while strengthening the U.S. capacity to insure its survival, even in the face of its current collective anomie, hardly adds up to a unified ethnic power bloc capable of influencing U.S. foreign policy.

Fifth, there is a problem of strategy that is hidden behind the phrase "hyphenated peoples." How long in spatial and temporal terms is the hyphen between the terms Greek-Americans, Afro-Americans, and Jewish-Americans? Or, to be more specific, what weight does the ethnic factor prior to the hyphen assume in relation to the American after the hyphen? For such strategic decisions determine in large measure not only attitudes toward U.S. foreign policy, but ultimately issues of allegiance to America in a time of absolute conflict. We need only remind ourselves how rapidly support for German-American Nazi Bonds evaporated in 1940-41 once the United States entered World War II. Thus, even when ethnic groups in America receive strong overseas reinforcements and endorsements, when ethnicity is a clear obstacle to U. S. foreign policy, it collapses under the weight of the national interest.

Sixth, we should also be aware that political decisions involve not just a strident defense of overseas interests of ethnic groups, but also some careful calculations of what America means to these groups. For to run the risk of complete isolation from a U.S. foreign policy context is to insure ethnic defeats and frustrations. This is just as true for Afro-American groups who have to decide on the importance of African language, culture, and customs vis-à-vis participation in American affairs, as it is for Jewish groups who, while seemingly having struck a balance between allegiance to the United States and commitment to the national goals and destinies of Israel, nonetheless are constantly faced with pressures that at the very least weaken, if not entirely cancel, the impact of ethnic groups forging U.S. foreign policy. Even when there is relative solidarity in the goal orientation of such ethnic groups, only a concomitant drive by the national polity can effectuate changes in a desired way. Thus we are faced with converting a problem of punctuation—the hyphen—into a problem of social science: how do groups organize their politics in order to maximize both American and ethnic ends? For without showing what is in it for America, ethnic pressure groups are foredoomed to failure.

Let us now turn to five sociological phases of the ethnic factor in U.S. foreign policy: I would submit that they are equal in importance, if fewer in number, to problems posed by ethnic politics. They should at least be operationalized and categorized so that no misinterpretations of the limits of ethnicity are permitted to filter through the analytic grids being offered.

Seventh, the initial sociological factor is that ethnic politics often involved generational solidarity. Common language, a shared culture, and a struggle to maintain and transmit that inheritance to subsequent generations born and reared within a strictly American context provided the basis for ethnic solidarity. The problem here is nearly insurmountable. It involves the maintenance of dual cultures within a political and economic system that largely rewards high participation in the American culture, and maximum utilization of the English language. There are so many crosscurrents among the young that a considerable amount of ethnic politics is drained off in maintaining ethnic loyalties rather than extending such ethnicity to the policy-making arena. In this sense, the ethnic factor can be sharply contrasted to membership in the trade-union movement. There is no ethnic personage comparable to George Meany: nothing in ethnic politics that witnesses one leader coughing and 15 to 18 million members sneezing. That, in a sense, is exactly what the ethnic factor lacks in sociological terms, because the purpose of ethnicity is to distinguish not just the ethnic subculture from the larger culture, but the ethnic group from other ethnic groups. The search for distinction and distinctiveness serves to weaken, on sociological grounds, any overall political impact on international grounds.

Eighth, the crossover points between religion and ethnicity also serve to dramatically weaken any direct ethnic impact on political affairs. The needs of a religious grouping are by no means isomorphic with those of an ethnic grouping. The Catholic church, which often reveals clear lines of ethnic demarcation between Irish, Polish, Italian, and other ethnic forces still registers a general orientation that overrides, to some extent at least, specific nationalities that the church represents. This is true to an even greater extent in the Greek community, where the power and potency of the Greek Orthodox church served to dampen, and in many instances still, opposition to the Greek military junta, despite the obvious sentiments of the Greek-American community for democratic government in the old country. Similarly, in the Jewish world the pluralization process has gone on unabated. Orthodox, Conservative, Reform, and Reconstructionist temples and synagogues compete with each other for membership loyalties and affections. They provide a particularistic flavor to Jewish-American life that limits singular Jewish impact on U.S. foreign policy, even with respect to Israel. Thus, the crosscutting impact of religiosity and ethnicity must be viewed as a major deterrent to an organized expression of ethnic politics in America.

Ninth, there is a clear problem of organization involved in ethnic politics. In former decades earlier in the century, and even in the mid-nineteenth century, ethnic groups were social rather than political in character. Their concerns were insurance policies, bank loans to the landsman, services to specialized charities that did not trust the larger culture, burial plots to insure cultural continuity as well as eternal salvation. All of these activities were so worthwhile, but so readily absorbed by the general culture in more recent years. Jewish fraternal organizations, for example, can no longer compete with New York Life or Metropolitan Life in terms of insurance policy benefits. Hence, they are faced with either going out of business or finding new causes. Given Roberto Michel's iron-law of oligarchy, we know that organizations do not voluntarily remove themselves from the world simply because they have no social function. What they do is find new functions. Chief among these are the causes of brethren less favored by fortune and fate living in Europe, Asia, or Third World contexts. This clear differential permits the ethnic and fraternal societies and clubs to mobilize moral sentiments as well as muster economic support for these less fortunate ethnic groups. In other words what we have, in part at least, is a change in function in order to guarantee organizational continuity, and not simply a response to daily tragedy and travail taking place in an overseas context.

Tenth, what we are witnessing in American society is a unique event. The end of the achievement society and the emergence of the ascription society is clearly upon us. As traditional forms of mobility begin to shut down, new forms of social distinctions emerge. Social mobility comes upon the hard fact that the third- or fourth-generation daughter or son of a medical doctor, accountant, or engineer cannot aspire to anything more than their parental generation in economic terms. One might argue that the entire generational revolt of the 1960s was a backhanded recognition that going up on the occupational ladder of mobility no longer made sufficient sense to merit the effort. As a result, there has been a huge return to ascribed features of social life: to matters of race, sex, and religion, as well as to national origin. Ethnicity became a telling differentiation between people who in a previous generation were marked only by competing on the way up the occupational ladder of success. Now that the ladder has been opened wide, the bases of differentiation must clearly shift. It becomes pointless to discuss America in terms of the theory of the melting pot, given the absence of achievement as the common denominator. The pot has already melted. The question becomes, in effect, what form of solidification remains to be tapped? This is an extremely important sociological aspect of the current ethnic revival, especially the search for ethnicity as a factor in the formation of interest-group politics at home rather than abroad.

Eleventh, a serious factor inhibiting the expansion of ethnic politics is the potency of the United States as a centrifugal force—even in the absence of older *Gemeinshaft* forms of authority. We must never ignore the push factors that led people out of their native lands as well as the pull factors that brought them to America. Ultimately, the passions for exercising a decisive influence in U.S. policy toward other nations is dampened by a foreknowledge that the country of origin was not so perfect when these people emigrated and is of dubious improvement years later. Often, the literature recites animosity for ethnics who have "forgotten" their ancestral hunting grounds. Regrettably, these same critics have more precisely forgotten the reasons for the century of immigration between 1850 and 1950. If America did not always turn out to be a promised land, there was little doubt in the minds of the emigrés that they were moving from lands often without the promise of equity, justice, or freedom. Thus, the limited capacity for impacting foreign policy is not necessarily a sign of confusion or weakness, nor the absence of will or interest on the part of the ethnic peoples to shape relevant policy.

In the very act of forging pluralistic doctrines of political behavior, ethnic groups have carried over the ideology of pluralism to the inner workings of their own organizational life. And in the very process of such democratization they have become linked with general American interests, norms, and values. As a result, ethnicity has probably contributed more to the forging of an American consensus than it has to the erosion of that consensus which seemingly characterizes other critical pivots such as class, race, and sex in the hierachy of social stratification.

NOTES

1. Pete Hamill, "The Revolt of the White Lower Middle Class," *New York Times,* April 14, l969.
2. Herbert Hill, "Racism and Organized Labor," *New School Bulletin, 28* (February 8, 1971).
3. Richard F. Hamilton, "Black Demands, White Reactions, and Liberal Alarms," *Blue Collar Workers,* Sar Levitan, ed. (New York: McGraw-Hill, 1971), p. 135.
4. Angus Campbell, *White Attitudes Toward Black People* (Ann Arbor: Institute for Social Research, University of Michigan, 1971), pp. 43-44.
5. Barbara Mikulski "Who Speaks for Ethnic America," *Divided Society: The Ethnic Experience In America,* Colin Greer, ed. (New York: Basic Books, 1974), pp. 355-59.

6. Andrew M. Greeley, *Why Can't They Be Like Us? Facts and Fallacies about Ethnic Differences and Group Conflicts in America* (New York: Institute of Human Relations Press, 1969), pp. 45-55.
7. Sar Levitan, *Blue-Collar Workers: A Symposium on Middle America* (New York: McGraw-Hill, 1971), pp. 13-20.
8. Robert Coles, *The Middle Americans: Proud and Uncertain* (Boston: Little, Brown, 1971).
9. Cf. Michael Novak, "The New Ethnicity," *The Center Magazine* 7 (July/August 1974).
10. Thomas J. Cottle, "The Non-Elite Student: Billy Kowalski Goes to College," *Change,* 3 (March/April 1971): 36-42; and *Time's Children, Impressions of Youth* (Boston: Little, Brown, 1971).
11. Milton Friedman, "Kensington, U.S.A.," *La Salle College Magazine,* 11 (Fall 1967); reprinted and distributed by the American Jewish Committee.
12. William J. Wilson, *The Declining Significance of Race* (Chicago: University of Chicago Press, 1978); and Charles V. Willie and William J. Wilson, "The Inclining vs. the Declining Significance of Race" (a debate), *Society* 15 (July/August 1978): 10-21.
13. John Howard, "Public Policy and the White Working Class," *The Use and Abuse of Social Science,* ed. by I. L. Horowitz (New Brunswick, New Jersey: Transaction Books/E. P. Dutton, 1971), pp. 65-66.
14. Richard Centers, *The Psychology of Social Classes* (Princeton, New Jersey: Princeton University Press, 1949).
15. Ben J. Wattenberg, *The Real America: A Surprising Examination of the State of the Union* (Garden City, New York: Doubleday, 1974). pp.64-65.
16. Harold M. Hodges, *Social Stratification: Class in America* (Cambridge, Mass.: Schenkman, 1964), pp. 101-6.
17. Novak, "The New Ethnicity," pp.18-25.
18. Greeley, *Why Can't They Be Like Us?,* pp.46-48.
19. Novak, "The New Ethnicity," pp.18-25.
20. Michael Novak, "White Ethnic," *Harper's Magazine* 243 (September 1971), pp. 44-50.
21. John A. Morsell, "Ethnic Relations of the Future," *The Annals of the American Academy of Political and Social Science* 408 (July 1973): 83-93.
22. Novak, "The New Ethnicity," p. 19.
23. Gunnar Myrdal, "The Case Against Romantic Ethnicity," *The Center Magazine* 7 (July/August 1974): 26-30.
24. Oscar Handlin, *Race and Nationality in American Life* (Boston: Little, Brown, 1957).
25. Colin Greer, *Divided Society: The Ethnic Experience in America* (New York: Basic Books, 1974), pp. 34-35.
26. Lee Rainwater, "Crucible of Identity: The Negro Lower Class Family," *Daedalus,* whole no. 95 (1966): 172-216; and *Behind Ghetto Walls: Black Family Life in a Federal Slum* (Chicago: Aldine-Atherton, 1970), pp. 361-97.
27. Thomas R. Books, "Black Upsurge in the Unions," *Dissent,* 17 (March/April 1970): 125-38.
28. Bayard Rustin, "The Blacks and the Unions," *Harper's Magazine* 242 (May 1971), pp. 73-81.
29. Richard J. Krickus, "Forty Million Ethnics Rate More Than Bromides," *The Washington Post,* (August 31, 1969).

30. Richard J. Krickus, "The White Ethnics: Who Are They and Where Are They Going?" *City* 5 (May/June 1971): 23-31.

31. John C. Leggett, *Class, Race, and Labor: Working Class Consciousness in Detroit* (New York: Oxford University Press, 1968), pp. 144-54.

32. Peter Berger, "The Blueing of America," *The New Republic* 164 (April 1971), pp. 20-23.

33. Charles A. Reich, *The Greening of America: How the Youth Revolution Is Trying to Make America Livable* (New York: Random House, 1970).

34. Naomi M. Levine and Judith M. Herman, "The Ethnic Factor in Blue Collar Life," National Project on Ethnic America, American Jewish Committee (mimeograph, 1971).

35. An exception to the role of ethnicity in an international framework is the work done by Abdul A. Said and his associates. Cf. *Ethnicity in an International Context: The Politics of Disassociation* (New Brunswick, N.J.: Transaction Books, 1976); and *Ethnicity and U.S. Foreign Policy* (New York: Praeger Publishers, Praeger Special Studies, 1977).

Part II
Cleavages and Changes within the Working Class

4

A Theory of Ethnic Antagonism: The Split Labor Market*

Edna Bonacich

Societies vary considerably in their degree of ethnic and racial antagonism. Such territories as Brazil, Mexico, and Hawaii are generally acknowledged to be relatively low on this dimension; while South Africa, Australia, and the United States are considered especially high. Literally hundreds of variables have been adduced to account for these differences, ranging from religions of dominant groups, to whether the groups who migrate are dominant or subordinate, to degrees of difference in skin color, to an irreducible "tradition" of ethnocentrism. While some writers have attempted to synthesize or systematize some subset of these,[1] one is generally struck by the absence of a developed theory accounting for variations in ethnic antagonism.

One approach to this problem is to consider an apparent anomaly, namely that ethnic antagonism has taken two major, seemingly antithetical forms: exclusion movements, and so-called caste systems.[2] An example of the former is the "white Australia" policy; while South Africa's color bar illustrates the latter. The United States has shown both forms, with a racial caste system in the South and exclusion of Asian and "new" immigrants[3] from the Pacific and eastern seaboards respectively. Apart from manifesting antagonism between ethnic elements, exclusion and caste seem to have little in common. In the one, an effort is made to prevent an ethnically different group from being part of the society. In the other, an ethnically different group is essential to the society: it is an exploited class supporting the entire edifice. The deep south felt it could not survive without its black people; the Pacific coast could not survive with its Japanese. This puzzle may be used as a touchstone for solving the general problem of ethnic antagonism, for to be adequate a theory must be able to explain it.

The theory presented here is, in part, a synthesis of some of the ideas used by Oliver Cox to explain the Japanese-white conflict on the U.S. Pacific coast and by Marvin Harris to analyze the difference between Brazil and the deep south in rigidity of the "color line."[4] It stresses the role of a certain kind of economic competition in the development of ethnic antagonism. Economic factors have, of course, not gone unnoticed, though until recently sociological literature has tended to point them out briefly, then move on to more "irrational" factors (even such works as *The Economics of Discrimination* by Becker).[5] A resurgence of Marxian analysis has thrust economic considerations to the fore,[6] but I shall argue that even this approach cannot adequately deal with the problem posed by exclusion movements and caste systems. In addition, both Marxist and non-Marxist writers assume that racial and cultural differences in themselves prompt the development of ethnic antagonism. This theory challenges that assumption, suggesting that economic processes are more fundamental.

No effort is made to prove the accuracy of the following model. Such proof depends on a lengthier exposition. Historical illustrations are presented to support it.

ETHNIC ANTAGONISM

"Ethnic" rather than "racial" antagonism was selected as the dependent variable because the former is seen to subsume the latter. Both terms refer to groups defined socially as sharing a common ancestry in which membership is therefore inherited or ascribed, whether or not members are currently physically or culturally distinctive.[7] The difference between race and ethnicity lies in the size of the locale from which a group stems, races generally coming from continents, and ethnicities from national subsections of continents. In the past the term "race" has been used to refer to both levels, but general usage today has reversed this practice.[8] Ethnicity has become the generic term.

Another reason for choosing this term is that exclusion attempts and caste-like arrangements are found among national groupings within a racial category. For example, in 1924 whites (Europeans) attempted to exclude whites of different national backgrounds from the United States by setting up stringent immigration quotas.

The term "antagonism" is intended to encompass all levels of intergroup conflict, including ideologies and beliefs (such as racism and prejudice), behaviors (such as discrimination, lynchings, riots), and institutions (such as laws perpetuating segregation). Exclusion movements and caste systems may be seen as the culmination of many pronouncements, actions, and enactments, and are continuously supported by more of the same. "Antagonism" was chosen over terms like prejudice and discrimination because it carries fewer moralistic and theoretical assumptions.[9] For example, both of these terms see conflict as emanating primarily from one side: the dominant group. Antagonism allows for the possibility that conflict is mutual; i.e. a product of interaction.

THE SPLIT LABOR MARKET

The central hypothesis is that ethnic antagonism first germinates in a labor market split along ethnic lines. To be split, a labor market must contain at least two groups of workers whose price of labor differs for the same work, or would differ if they did the same work. The concept "price of labor" refers to labor's total cost to the employer, including not only wages, but the cost of recruitment, transportation, room and board, education, health care (if the employer must bear these), and the costs of labor unrest. The degree of worker "freedom" does not interfere with this calculus; the cost of a slave can be estimated in the same monetary units as that of a wage earner, from his purchase price, living expenses, policing requirements, and so on.

The price of a group of workers can be roughly calculated in advance and comparisons made even though two groups are not engaged in the same activity at the same time. Thus in 1841 in the colony of New South Wales, the Legislative Council's Committee on Immigration estimated the relative costs of recruiting three groups of laborers to become shepherds. Table 1 shows their findings. The estimate of free white labor, for example, was based on what it would take to attract these men from competing activities.

FACTORS AFFECTING THE INITIAL PRICE OF LABOR

Labor markets that are split by the entrance of a new group develop a dynamic which may in turn affect the price of labor. One must therefore

distinguish initial from later price determinants. The initial factors can be
divided into two broad categories: resources and motives.

TABLE 1
Estimated Cost of Three Types of Labor to be Shepherds in New South Wales, 1841*

	Free Man (White)			Prisoner (White)			Coolie (Indian)		
	£	s.	d.	£	s.	d.	£	s.	d.
Rations	16	18	0	13	14	4	9	6	4
Clothing	-	-	-	3	3	0	1	1	8
Wages	25	0	0	-	-	-	6	0	0
Passage from India	-	-	-	-	-	-	2	0	0
Total per Annum	41	18	0	16	17	4	18	8	0

*From Yarwood.

Resources

Three types of resources are important price determinants. These are:

1. Level of Living, or Economic Resources—The ethnic groups forming
the labor market in a contact situation derive from different economic
systems, either abroad or within a conquered territory. For members of an
ethnic group to be drawn into moving, they must at least raise their wage
level. In general, the poorer the economy of the recruits, the less the
inducement needed for them to enter the new labor market. Crushing
poverty may drive them to sell their labor relatively cheaply. For example
Lind describes the effect of the living level on the wage scale received by
immigrant workers to Hawaii:

> In every case [of labor importations] the superior opportunities for
> gaining a livelihood have been broadcast in regions of surplus
> manpower, transportation facilities have been provided, and finally a
> monetary return larger than that already received has been offered to
> the prospective laborer. The monetary inducement has varied con-
> siderably, chiefly according to the plane of living of the population
> being recruited, and the cheapest available labor markets have, of
> course, been most extensively drawn upon.[10]

Workers need not accept the original wage agreement for long after they have immigrated, since other opportunities may exist; for instance, there may be ample, cheap land available for individual farming. One capitalist device for keeping wages low at least for a time is to bind immigrants to contracts before they leave the old economy. The Indian indenture system, for example, rested on such an arrangement.[11]

2. Information—Immigrants may be pushed into signing contracts out of ignorance. They may agree to a specific wage in their homeland not knowing the prevailing wage in the new country, or having been beguiled by a false account of life and opportunity there. Williams, for example, describes some of the false promises made to draw British and Germans as workers to West Indian sugar plantations before the advent of African slavery.[12] Chinese labor to Australia was similarly "obtained under 'false and specious pretences.' "[13]

The possibilities for defrauding a population lacking access to the truth are obvious. In general, the more people know about conditions obtaining in the labor market to which they are moving, the better can they protect themselves against disadvantageous wage agreements.

3. Political Resources—By political resources I mean the benefits to a group of organizing. Organization can exist at the level of labor, or it can occur at higher levels, for example, in a government that protects them. These levels are generally related in that a strong government can help organize its emigrants. There are exceptions, however: strong emigrant governments tend not to extend protection to their deported convicts or political exiles; and some highly organized groups, like the Jews in the United States, have not received protection from the old country.

Governments vary in the degree to which they protect their emigrants. Japan kept close watch over the fate of her nationals who migrated to Hawaii and the Pacific coast; and the British colonial government in India tried to guard against abuses of the indenture system (for example, by refusing to permit Natal to import Indian workers for their sugar plantations until satisfactory terms had been agreed to).[14] In contrast Mexican migrant workers to the United States have received little protection from their government, and African states were unable to intervene on behalf of slaves brought to America. Often the indigenous populations of colonized territories have been politically weak following conquest. Thus African nations in South Africa have been unable to protect their migrant workers in the cities.

In general, the weaker a group politically, the more vulnerable it is to the use of force, hence to an unfavorable wage bargain (or to no wage bargain at all, as with slavery). The price of a labor group varies inversely with the amount of force that can be used against it, which in turn depends on its political resources.

Motives

Two motives affect the price of labor, both related to the worker's intention of not remaining permanently in the labor force. Temporary workers tend to cost less than permanent workers for two reasons. First, they are more willing to put up with undesirable work conditions since these need not be endured forever. If they are migrants, this tolerance may extend to the general standard of living. Often migrant temporary workers are males who have left the comforts of home behind and whose employers need not bear the cost of housing and educating their families. Even when families accompany them, such workers tend to be willing to accept a lower standard of living since it is only short term.

Second, temporary workers avoid involvement in lengthy disputes. Since they will be in the labor market a short while, their main concern is immediate employment. They may be willing to undercut wage standards if need be to get a job, and are therefore ripe candidates for strike-breaking. Permanent workers also stand to lose from lengthy conflict, but they hope for benefits to their progeny. If temporary workers are from elsewhere, they have no such interest in future business-labor relations. Altogether, temporary workers have little reason to join the organizations and unions of a permanent work force, and tend not to do so.

1. Fixed or Supplementary Income Goal—Some temporary workers enter the market either to supplement family income, or to work toward a specific purchase. The worker's standard of living does not, therefore, depend on his earnings on the job in question, since his central source of employment or income lies elsewhere. Examples of this phenomenon are to be found throughout Africa:

> . . . the characteristic feature of the labor market in most of Africa has always been the massive circulation of Africans between their villages and paid employment outside. In some places villagers engage in wage-earning seasonally. More commonly today they work for continuous though short-term periods of roughly one to three years, after which they return to the villages....the African villager, the potential migrant into paid employment, has a relatively low, clearly-defined and rigid income goal; he wants money to pay head and hut taxes, to make marriage payments required of prospective bridegrooms, or to purchase some specific consumer durable (a

bicycle, a rifle, a sewing machine, a given quanity of clothing or textiles, etc.).[15]

Such a motive produces the "backward-sloping labor supply function" characteristic of many native peoples in colonized territories. In addition to the general depressing effects on wages of being temporary, this motive leads to a fairly rapid turnover in personnel, making organization more difficult and hindering the development of valuable skills which could be used for bargaining. If wages were to rise, workers would reach their desired income and withdraw more quickly from the market, thereby lessening their chances of developing the political resources necessary to raise their wages further.

2. Fortune Seeking—Many groups, commonly called sojourners, migrate long distances to seek their fortune, with the ultimate intention of improving their position in their homeland.[16] Such was the case with Japanese immigrants on the west coast and Italian immigrants in the east. Such workers stay longer in the labor market, and can develop political resources. However, since they are temporary they have little incentive to join the organizations of the settled population. Instead they tend to create competing organizations composed of people who will play a part in their future in the homeland, i.e. members of the same ethnic group.

Sojourner laborers have at least three features which affect the price of labor: lower wages, longer hours, and convenience to the employer. The Japanese show all three. Millis cites the U.S. Immigration Commission on the question of relative wages:

> The Japanese have usually worked for a lower wage than the members of any other race save the Chinese and the Mexican. In the salmon canneries the Chinese have been paid higher wages than the Japanese engaged in the same occupations. In the lumber industry, all races, including the East Indian, have been paid higher wages than the Japanese doing the same kind of work. As section hands and laborers in railway shops they have been paid as much or more than the Mexicans, but as a rule less than the white men of many races.[17]

And so on. The lower wage level of Japanese workers reflects both a lower standard of living, and a desire to get a foothold in the labor market. As Iwata puts it: "Their willingness to accept even lower wages than laborers of other races enabled the Japanese to secure employment readily."[18]

Millis describes a basket factory in Florin, California, where Japanese workers had displaced white female workers because the latter were unwilling to work more than ten hours a day or on weekends.[19] The Japanese, anxious to return to Japan as quickly as possible, were willing to work twelve to fourteen hours per day and on weekends, thereby saving their employers the costs of a special overtime work force.

The Japanese immigrants developed political resources through a high degree of community organization. This could be used for the convenience of the employer by solving his recruitment problems, seeing that work got done, and providing workers with board and lodging. In the case of seasonal labor, the Japanese community could provide for members during the off-season by various boarding arrangements and clubs, and by transporting labor to areas of demand.[20] These conveniences saved the employer money.[21]

As the reader may have noted, I have omitted a factor usually considered vital in determining the price of labor, i.e. differences in skills. I would contend, however, that this does not in itself lead to that difference in price for the same work which distinguishes a split labor market. While a skilled worker may be able to get a higher paying job, an unskilled laborer of another ethnicity may be trained to fill that job for the same wage. Skills are only indirectly important in that they can be used to develop political resources, which in turn may lead to a difference in wage level for the same work.

PRICE OF LABOR AND ETHNICITY

Ethnic differences need not always produce a price differential. Thus, if several ethnic groups who are approximately equal in resources and/or goals enter the same economic system, a split labor market will not develop. Alternatively, in a two-group contact situation, if one ethnic group occupies the position of a business elite and has no members in the labor force (or in a class that could easily be pushed into the labor force, e.g. low-capital farmers) then regardless of the other group's price, the labor market will not be split. This statement is a generalization of the point made by Harris that the critical difference in race relations between the deep south and Brazil was that the former had a white yeomanry in direct competition with exslaves, while the Portuguese only occupied the role of a business elite (plantation owners).[22]

Conversely, a split labor force does not only stem from ethnic differences. For example, prison and female labor have often been cheaper than free male labor in western societies. Prison labor has been cheap because prisoners lack political resources, while women often labor for supplementary incomes.[23]

That initial price discrepancies in labor should ever fall along ethnic lines is a function of two forces. First, the original wage agreement arrived at between business and new labor often takes place in the labor group's point of origin. This is more obviously a feature of immigrant labor, but also occurs within a territory when conquered peoples enter their conquerors' economy. In other words, the wage agreement is often concluded within a national context, these nationalities coming to comprise the ethnic elements of the new labor market. One would thus expect the initial wages of co-nationals to be similar.

Second, nations or peoples that have lived relatively separately from one another are likely to have developed different employment motives and levels of resources (wealth, organization, communication channels). In other words, the factors that affect the price of labor are likely to differ grossly between nations, even though there may be considerable variation within each nation, and overlap between nations. Color differences in the initial price of labor only seem to be a factor because resources have historically been roughly correlated with color around the world.[24] When color and resources are not correlated in the "expected" way, then I would predict that price follows resources and motives rather than color.

In sum, the prejudices of business do not determine the price of labor, darker skinned or culturally different persons being paid less because of them. Rather, business tries to pay as little as possible for labor, regardless of ethnicity, and is held in check by the resources and motives of labor groups. Since these often vary by ethnicity, it is common to find ethnically split labor markets.

THE DYNAMICS OF SPLIT LABOR MARKETS

In split labor markets, conflict develops between three key classes: business, higher paid labor, and cheaper labor. The chief interests of these classes are as follows:

1. Business or Employers—This class aims at having as cheap and docile a labor force as possible to compete effectively with other businesses. If labor costs are too high (owing to such price determinants as unions), employers may turn to cheaper sources, importing overseas groups or using indigenous conquered populations. In the colony of Queensland in Australia, for example, it was believed that cotton farming would be the most suitable economic enterprise:

> However, such plantations (being too large) could not be worked, much less cleared, by their owners; neither could the work be done by European laborers because sufficient numbers of these were not

available—while even had there been an adequate supply, the high rates of wages would have been prohibitive. This was a consideration which assumed vast importance when it was realized that cotton would have to be cultivated in Queensland at a considerably lower cost than in the United States in order to compensate for the heavier freights from Queensland—the more distant country from England. It seemed then that there was no possibility of successful competition with America unless the importation of some form of cheap labor was permitted.[25]

Cheaper labor may be used to create a new industry having substantially lower labor costs than the rest of the labor market, as in Queensland. Or they may be used as strikebreakers or replacements to undercut a labor force trying to improve its bargaining position with business. If cheap labor is unavailable, business may turn to mechanization, or try to relocate firms in areas of the world where the price of labor is lower.

2. Higher Paid Labor—This class is threatened by the introduction of cheaper labor into the market, fearing that it will either force them to leave the territory or reduce them to its level. If the labor market is split ethnically, the class antagonism takes the form of ethnic antagonism. It is my contention (following Cox)[26] that, while much rhetoric of ethnic antagonism concentrates on ethnicity and race, it really in large measure (though probably not entirely) expresses this class conflict.

The group comprising higher paid labor may have two components. First, it may include current employees demanding a greater share of the profits or trying to maintain their position in the face of possible cuts. A second element is the small, independent entrepreneur, like the subsistence farmer or individual miner. The introduction of cheaper labor into these peoples' line can undermine their position, since the employer of cheaper labor can produce at lower cost. The independent operator is then driven into the labor market. The following sequence occurs in many colonies: settlement by farmers who work their own land, the introduction of intensive farming using cheaper labor, a rise in land value and a consequent displacement of independent farmers. The displaced class may move on (as occurred in many of the West Indies when African slave labor was introduced to raise sugar), but if it remains, it comes to play the role of higher paid labor.

The presence of cheaper labor in areas of the economy where higher paid labor is not currently employed is also threatening to the latter, since the former attracts older industries. The importance of potential competition cannot be overstressed. Oftentimes writers assert the irrationality of ethnic antagonism when direct economic competition is not yet in evidence owing to few competitors having entered the labor market, or to competitors having concentrated in a few industries. Thus Daniels belittles the role of trade unions in the Asiatic Exclusion League by describing one of the major contributors as "an organization whose members, like most trade unionists in California, were never faced with job competition from Japanese."[27] It does not take direct competition for members of a higher priced labor group to see the possible threat to their well-being, and to try to prevent its materializing. If they have reason to believe many more low-priced workers are likely to follow an initial "insignificant trickle" (as Daniels describes the Japanese immigration, failing to mention that it was insignificant precisely because a larger anticipated flow had been thwarted, and diverted to Brazil)[28] or if they see a large concentration of cheaper labor in a few industries which could easily be used to undercut them in their own, they will attempt to forestall undercutting.

Lest you think this fear misguided, take note that, when business could override the interests of more expensive labor, the latter have indeed been displaced or undercut. In British Guiana the local labor force, composed mainly of African exslaves, called a series of strikes in 1842 and 1847 against planters' attempts to reduce their wages. Plantation owners responded by using public funds to import over 50,000 cheaper East Indian indentured workers.[29] A similar situation obtained in Mississippi, where Chinese were brought in to undercut freed blacks. Loewen describes the thinking of white landowners: "the 'Chinaman' would not only himself supply a cheaper and less troublesome work force but in addition his presence as a threatening alternative would intimidate the Negro into resuming his former docile behavior."[30] Such displacement has occurred not only to nonwhite more expensive labor, but, as the effects of slavery in the West Indies show, to whites by white capitalists.

3. Cheaper Labor—The employer uses this class partly to undermine the position of more expensive labor, through strikebreaking and undercutting. The forces that make the cheaper group cost less permit this to occur. In other words, either they lack the resources to resist an offer or use of force by business, or they seek a quick return to another economic and social base.

With the possible exception of sojourners, cheaper labor does not intentionally undermine more expensive labor; it is paradoxically its weakness that makes it so threatening, for business can more thoroughly control it. Cox makes this point in analyzing why Pacific coast white and Asian workers could not unite in a coalition against business:

> . . . the first generation of Asiatic workers is ordinarily very much under the control of labor contractors and employers, hence it is easier for the employer to frustrate any plans for their organization.

Clearly this cultural bar helped antagonize white workers against the Asiatics. The latter were conceived of as being in alliance with the employer. It would probably have taken two or three generations before, say, the East Indian low-caste worker on the Coast became sufficiently Americanized to adjust easily to the policies and aims of organized labor.[31]

Ethnic antagonism is specifically produced by the competition that arises from a price differential. An oversupply of equal-priced labor does not produce such antagonism, though it too threatens people with the loss of their job. However, hiring practices will not necessarily fall along ethnic lines, there being no advantage to the employer in hiring workers of one or another ethnicity. All workingmen are on the same footing, competing for scarce jobs.[32] When one ethnic group is decidedly cheaper than another (i.e. when the labor market is split) the higher paid worker faces more than the loss of his job; he faces the possibility that the wage standard in all jobs will be undermined by cheaper labor.

VICTORY FOR MORE EXPENSIVE LABOR

If an expensive labor group is strong enough (strength generally depending on the same factors that influence price), they may be able to resist being displaced. Both exclusion and caste systems represent such victories for higher paid labor.

1. Exclusion—Exclusion movements generally occur when the majority of a cheaper labor group resides outside a given territory but desires to enter it (often at the request of business groups). The exclusion movement tries to prevent the physical presence of cheaper labor in the employment area, thereby preserving a nonsplit higher priced labor market.

There are many examples of exclusion attempts around the world. In Australia, for instance, a group of white workers was able to prevent capitalists from importing cheaper labor from India, China, Japan, and the Pacific Islands. Attempts at importation were met with strikes, boycotts, petitions, and deputations.[33] Ultimately, organized white labor pressed for strong exclusion measures, and vigilantly ensured their enforcement. As Yarwood puts it: "A comparison of the records of various governments during our period [1896-1923] leaves no doubt as to the special role of the Labour Party as the guardian of the ports."[34] In other words, a white Australia policy (i.e. the exclusion of Asian and Polynesian immigrants) appears to have sprung from a conflict of interests between employers who wanted to import cheap labor, and a labor force sufficiently organized to ward off such a move.

California's treatment of Chinese and Japanese labor is another example of exclusion. A socialist, Cameron H. King, Jr., articulates the threatened labor group's position:

> Unskilled labor has felt this competion [from the Japanese] for some time being compelled to relinquish job after job to the low standard of living it could not endure. The unskilled laborers are largely unorganized and voiceless. But as the tide rises it is reaching the skilled laborers and the small merchants. These are neither unorganized nor voiceless, and viewing the menace to their livelihood they loudly demand protection of their material interests. We of the Pacific Coast certainly know that exclusion is an effective solution. In the seventh decade of the nineteenth century the problem arose of the immigration of Chinese laborers. The Republican and Democratic parties failed to give heed to the necessities of the situation and the Workingman's party arose and swept the state with the campaign cry of "The Chinese must go." Then the two old parties woke up and have since realized that to hold the labor vote they must stand for Asiatic exclusion.[35]

King wrote this around the time of the Gentlemen's Agreement, an arrangement of the U.S. and Japanese governments to prevent further immigration of Japanese labor to the Pacific Coast.[36] The agreement was aimed specifically at labor and not other Japanese immigrants, suggesting that economic and not racial factors were at issue.

Exclusion movements clearly serve the interests of higher paid labor. Its standards are protected, while the capitalist class is deprived of cheaper labor.

2. Caste—If cheaper labor is present in the market, and cannot be excluded, then higher paid labor will resort to a caste arrangement, which depends on exclusiveness rather than exclusion. Caste is essentially an aristocracy of labor (a term borrowed from Lenin),[37] in which higher paid labor deals with the undercutting potential of cheaper labor by excluding them from certain types of work. The higher paid group controls certain jobs exclusively and gets paid at one scale of wages, while the cheaper group is restricted to another set of jobs and is paid at a lower scale. The labor market split is submerged because the differentially priced workers ideally never occupy the same position.

Ethnically distinct cheaper groups (as opposed to women, for example, who face a caste arrangement in many Western societies) may reside in a territory for two reasons: either they were indigenous or they were imported early in capitalist-labor relations, when the higher paid group could not prevent the move. Two outstanding examples of labor aristocracies based on ethnicity are South Africa, where cheaper labor was primarily indigenous, and the U.S. South, where they were imported as slaves.

Unlike exclusion movements, caste systems retain the underlying reality of a price differential, for if a member of the subordinate group were to occupy the same position as a member of the stronger labor group he would be paid less. Hence, caste systems tend to become rigid and vigilant, developing an elaborate battery of laws, customs, and beliefs aimed to prevent undercutting. The victory has three facets. First, the higher paid group tries to ensure its power in relation to business by monopolizing the acquisition of certain essential skills, thereby ensuring the effectiveness of strike action, or by controlling such important resources as purchasing power. Second, it tries to prevent the immediate use of cheaper labor as undercutters and strikebreakers by denying them access to general education thereby making their training as quick replacements more difficult, or by ensuring through such devices as "influx control" that the cheaper group will retain a base in their traditional economies. The latter move ensures a backward-sloping labor supply function[38] undesirable to business. Third, it tries to weaken the cheaper group politically to prevent their pushing for those resources that would make them useful as undercutters. In other words, the solution to the devastating potential of weak, cheap labor is, paradoxically, to weaken them further, until it is no longer in business' immediate interest to use them as replacements.

South Africa is perhaps the most extreme modern example of an ethnic caste system. A split labor market first appeared there in the mining industry. With the discovery of diamonds in 1869, a white working class emerged.[39] At first individual whites did the searching, but, as with the displacement of small farms by plantations, they were displaced by consolidated, high-capital operations, and became employees of the latter.[40] It was this class together with imported skilled miners from Cornwall (lured to Africa by high wages) which fought the capitalists over the use of African labor. Africans were cheaper because they came to the mines with a fixed income goal (e.g. the price of a rifle) and did not view the mines as their main source of livelihood. By contrast, European workers remained in the mines and developed organizations to further their interests.

Clearly, it would have been to the advantage of businessmen, once they knew the skills involved, to train Africans to replace the white miners at a fraction of the cost; but this did not happen. The mining companies accepted a labor aristocracy, not out of ethnic solidarity with the white workers but:

(as was to be the case throughout the later history of mining) they had little or no choice because of the collective strength of the white miners....The pattern which was to emerge was that of the Europeans showing every sign of preparedness to use their collective strength to ensure their exclusive supremacy in the labour market. Gradually the concept of trade unionism, and, for that matter, of socialism, became accepted in the minds of the European artisans as the means of maintaining their own position against non-white inroads.[41]

The final showdown between mine owners and white workers occurred in the 1920s when the owners tried to substitute cheaper nonwhite labor for white labor in certain semiskilled occupations. This move precipitated the "Rand Revolt," a general strike of white workers on the Witwatersrand, countered by the calling in of troops and the declaration of martial law. The result was a coalition between Afrikaner nationalists (predominantly workers and small-scale farmers being pushed off the land by larger, British-owned farms) and the English-speaking Labor Party.[42] The revolt "showed the lengths to which white labour was prepared to go to defend its privileged position. From that time on, mine managements have never directly challenged the colour-bar in the mining industry."[43]

The legislative history of much of South Africa (and of the post-bellum deep south) consists in attempts by higher priced white labor to ward off undercutting by cheaper groups, and to entrench its exclusive control of certain jobs.[44]

This interpretation of caste contrasts with the Marxist argument that the capitalist class purposefully plays off one segment of the working class against the other.[45] Business, I would contend, rather than desiring to protect a segment of the working class supports a liberal or laissez-faire ideology that would permit all workers to compete freely in an open market. Such open competition would displace higher paid labor. Only under duress does business yield to labor aristocracy, a point made in *Deep South*, a book written when the depression had caused the displacement of white tenant farmers and industrial workers by blacks:

> The economic interests of these groups (employers) would also demand that cheaper colored labor should be employed in the "white collar" jobs in business offices, governmental offices, stores, and banks. In this field, however, the interests of the employer group conflicts not only with those of the lower economic group of whites but also with those of the more literate and aggressive middle group of whites. A white store which employed colored clerks, for example, would be boycotted by both these groups. The taboo upon the

employment of colored workers in such fields is the result of the political and purchasing power of the white middle and lower groups.[46]

In sum, exclusion and caste are similar reactions to a split labor market. They represent victories for higher paid labor. The victory of exclusion is more complete in that cheaper labor is less available to business. For this reason I would hypothesize that a higher paid group prefers exclusion to caste, even though exclusion means they have to do the dirty work. Evidence for this comes from Australia where, in early attempts to import Asian labor, business tried to buy off white labor's opposition by offering to form them into a class of "mechanics" and foremen over the "coolies."[47] The offer was heartily rejected in favor of exclusion. Apartheid in South Africa can be seen as an attempt to move from caste to the exclusion of the African work force.

Most of our examples have contained a white capitalist class, a higher paid white labor group, and a cheaper, nonwhite labor group. Conditions in Europe and around the world, and not skin color, yield such models. White capitalists would gladly dispense with and undercut their white working-class brethren if they could, and have done so whenever they had the opportunity. In the words of one agitator for excluding Chinese from the U.S. Pacific coast: "I have seen men...American born, who certainly would, if I may use a strong expression, employ devils from Hell if the devils would work for 25 cents less than a white man."[48]

In addition, cases have occurred of white workers playing the role of cheap labor, and facing the same kind of ethnic antagonism as nonwhite workers. Consider the riots against Italian strikebreakers in the coal fields of Pennsylvania in 1874.[49] In the words of one writer: "Unions resented the apparently inexhaustible cheap and relatively docile labor supply which was streaming from Europe obviously for the benefit of their employers."[50]

Even when no ethnic differences exist, split labor markets may produce ethnic-like antagonism. Carey McWilliams describes an instance:

> During the depression years, "Old Stock"—that is, white, Protestant, anglo-Saxon Americans, from Oklahoma, Arkansas, and Texas—were roundly denounced in California as "interlopers." The same charges were made against them that were made against the Japanese: they were "dirty," they had "enormous families"; they engaged in unfair competition; they threatened to "invade" the state and to "undermine" its institutions. During these turgid years (1930-1938) California attempted to exclude, by various extra-legal devices, those yeoman farmers just as it had excluded the Chinese and

Japanese. "Okies" were "inferior" and "immoral." There was much family discord when Okie girl met California boy, and vice versa....The prejudice against the Okies was obviously not "race" prejudice; yet it functioned in much the same manner.[50]

CONCLUSION

Obviously, this type of three-way conflict is not the only important factor in ethnic relations. But it does help explain some puzzles, including, of course, the exclusion-cast anomaly. For example, Philip Mason develops a typology of race relations and finds that it relates to numerical proportions without being able to explain the dynamic behind this correlation.[52] Table 2 presents a modified version of his chart. My theory can explain these relationships. Paternalism arises in situations where the cleavage between business and labor corresponds to an ethnic difference. A small business elite rules a large group of workers who entered the labor market at approximately the same price or strength. No split labor market existed, hence no ethnic caste system arises. The higher proportion of the dominant ethnicity under "Domination" means that part of the dominant group must be working class. A labor element that shares ethnicity with people who have sufficient resources to become the business elite is generally likely to come from a fairly wealthy country and have resources of its own. Such systems are likely to develop split labor markets. Finally, competition has under it societies whose cheaper labor groups have not been a major threat because the indigenous population available as cheap labor has been small, and/or exclusion has effectively kept business groups from importing cheap labor in large numbers.

This theory helps elucidate other observations. One is the underlying similarity in the situation of blacks and women. Another is the history of political sympathy between California and the South. And, a third is the conservatism of the American white working class, or what Daniels and Kitano consider to be an "essential paradox of American life: [that] movements for economic democracy have usually been violently opposed to a thorough-going ethnic democracy."[53] Without having to resort to psychological constructs like "authoritarianism," this theory is able to explain the apparent paradox.

In sum, in comparing those countries with the most ethnic antagonism with those having the least, it is evident that the difference does not lie in the fact that the former are Protestant and the latter Catholic: Protestants are found in all three of Mason's types, and Hawaii is a Protestant-dominated territory. It does not lie in whether the dominant or subordinate group moves: South Africa and the deep south show opposite patterns of movement. It is evident that some of the most antagonistic territories have been British colonies, but not all British colonies have had this attribute. The characteristic that those British colonies and other societies high on ethnic antagonism share is that they all have a powerful white, or more generally higher paid working class.

TABLE 2
Numerical Proportion of Dominant to Subordinate Ethnic Groups*

	Category	
Domination	Paternalism	Competition
	Situations	
South Africa (1960) 1-4	Nigeria (1952) 1-2000	Britain (1968) 50-1
U.S. South (1960) 4-1	Nyasaland (1966) 1-570	U.S. North (1960) 15-1
Rhodesia (1960) 1-16	Tanganyika 1-450	New Zealand 13-1
	Uganda 1-650	

*Adapted from Mason.

NOTES

*   Reprinted with permission from *American Sociological Review* 37 (October 1972): 547-59.

1.   For example, Stanley Lieberson, "A Societal Theory of Race and Ethnic Relations," *American Sociological Review* 26 (December 1961): 902-10; Philip Mason, *Patterns of Dominance* (London: Oxford University Press, 1970); Donald L. Noel, "A Theory of the Origin of Ethnic Stratification," *Social Problems* 16 (Fall 1963): 157-72; R.A. Schermerhorn, *Comparative Ethnic Relations* (New York: Random House, 1970); and Pierre L. van den Berghe, "Paternalistic versus Competitive Race Relations: An Ideal-Type Approach," in *Racial and Ethnic Relations,* ed. Bernard E. Segal (New York: Crowell, 1966) pp. 53-69.

2.   I do not wish to enter the debate over the applicability of the term "caste" to race relations [cf. Oliver C. Cox, *Caste, Class and Race* (New York: Modern Reader, 1948) and Allison Davis, B.B. Gardner, and M.R. Gardner, *Deep South* (Chicago: University of Chicago Press, 1941]. It is used here only for convenience and implies no particular theoretical bent.

3. The term "exclusion" has not usually been applied to immigrant quotas imposed on eastern and southern European immigrants; but such restrictions were, in effect, indistinguishable from the restrictions placed on Japanese immigration.

4. Cox, pp. 408-22; Marvin Harris, *Patterns of Race in the Americas* (New York: Walker, 1964). pp. 79-94.

5. Gary Becker, *The Economics of Discrimination* (Chicago: University of Chicago Press, 1957).

6. For example, Robert Blauner, "Internal Colonialism and Ghetto Revolt," *Social Problems* 16 (Spring 1969): 393-408 and Michael Reich, "The Economics of Racism," in *Problems in Political Economy,* ed. David M. Gordon (Lexington, Mass.: Heath, 1971), pp. 107-13.

7. This usage contrasts with that of van den Berghe, *Race and Racism* (New York: Wiley, 1967), pp. 9-10, who reserves the term "ethnic" for groups socially defined by cultural differences. In his definition, ethnicity is not necessarily inherited. I would contend that, while persons of mixed ancestry may be problematic and are often assigned arbitrarily by the societies in which they reside, inheritance is implied in the common application of the word.

8. For example, Schermerhorn; and Tamotsu Shibutani and Kian M. Kwan, *Ethnic Stratification* (New York: Macmillan, 1965).

9. See Schermerhorn.

10. Andrew W. Lind, *An Island Community* (New York: Greenwood, 1968), p. 199.

11. K. L. Gillion, *Fiji's Indian Migrants* (Melbourne: Oxford University Press, 1962), pp. 19-38.

12. Eric Williams, *Capitalism and Slavery* (Chapel Hill: University of North Carolina Press, 1944), p. 11.

13. Myra Willard, *History of the White Australia Policy to 1920* (London: Melbourne University Press, 1967), p. 11.

14. Cf. C.J. Ferguson-Davie, *The Early History of Indians in Natal* (Johannesburg: South African Institute of Race Relations, 1952), p. 9.

15. E.J. Berg, "Backward-Sloping Labor Supply Functions in Dual Economies—The Africa Case," in *Social Change: The Colonial Situation,* ed. Immanuel Wallerstein (New York: Wiley, 1966), pp. 116-18.

16. See Paul C.P. Siu, "The Sojourner," *American Journal of Sociology* 58 (July 1952): 34-44.

17. H.A. Millis, *The Japanese Problem in the United States* (New York: Macmillan, 1915), p. 45.

18. Masakazu Iwata, "The Japanese Immigrants in California Agriculture," *Agricultural History* 36 (January 1962): 27.

19. Millis, p. 155.

20. Yamato Ichihashi, *Japanese in the United States* (Stanford: Stanford University Press, 1932), pp. 172-76 and Millis, pp. 44-45.

21. Sojourners often use their political resources and low price of labor to enter business for themselves (a process which will be fully analyzed in another paper). This does not remove the split in the labor market, though it makes the conflict more complex.

22. Harris.

23. Cf. Emilie J. Hutchinson, *Women's Wages* (New York: Ams Press, 1968), pp.

59-61; and H. G. Heneman and Dale Yoder, *Labor Economics* (Cincinnati: Southwestern, 1965), pp. 543-44.

24.   It is, of course, no accident that color and resources have been historically related. Poverty among nonwhite nations has in part resulted from European imperialism. Nevertheless I would argue that the critical factor in the development of ethnic segmentation in a country is the meeting that occurs in the labor market of that country. The larger economic forces help determine the resources of entering parties, but it is not such forces to which workers respond. Rather, they react to the immediate conflicts and threats in their daily lives.

25.   I.N. Moles, "The Indian Coolie Labour Issue," in *Attitudes to Non-European Immigration,* ed. A.T. Yarwood (Melbourne: Cassell Australia, (1968), p. 41.

26.   Cox, p. 411n.

27.   Roger Daniels, *The Politics of Prejudice* (Gloucester, Mass.: Peter Smith, 1966), p. 29.

28.   Ibid., p. 9.

29.   Leo A. Despres, "Differential Adaptations and Micro-cultural Evolution in Guyana," *Southwestern Journal of Anthropology* 25 (Spring 1969): 14-44.

30.   James W. Loewen, *The Mississippi Chinese* (Cambridge, Mass.: Harvard University Press, 1971), p. 23.

31.   Cox, pp. 417-18.

32.   Cf. H.M. Blalock, Jr., *Toward a Theory of Minority-Group Relations* (New York: Wiley, 1967), who uses this model of labor competition.

33.   Willard, pp. 51-57.

34.   A.T. Yarwood, *Asian Immigration to Australia* (London: Cambridge University Press, 1964), pp. 151-52.

35.   Cameron H. King, Jr., "Asiatic Exclusion," *International Socialist Review* 8 (May 1908) :665-66.

36.   Thomas A. Baily, *Theodore Roosevelt and the Japanese-American Crises* (Stanford: Stanford University Press, 1934).

37.   V.I. Lenin, "Imperialism and the Split in Socialism," in *Collected Works, vol. 23, August 1916-March 1917* (Moscow: Progress, 1964), pp. 105-20.

38.   Cf. Berg.

39.   Such a split was not found in the early Cape Colony, where business was one ethnicity—white, and labor another—nonwhite. Actually, in neither case was the ethnic composition simple or homogeneous; but the important fact is that, among the laborers, who included so-called Hottentots, and slaves from Madagascar, Mocambique and the East Indies [cf. Pierre L. van den Berghe, *South Africa: A Study in Conflict* (Berkeley: University of California Press, 1967), p. 14], no element was significantly more expensive. The early Cape is thus structurally similar, in terms of the variables I consider important, to countries like Brazil and Mexico. It is also noted for its "softened" tone of race relations as reflected in such practices as intermarriage.

40.   G.V. Doxey, *The Industrial Colour Bar in South Africa* (Cape Town: Oxford University Press, 1961), p. 18.

41.   Ibid., pp. 23-24.

42.   Sheila T. Van der Horst, "The Effects of Industrialization on Race Relations in South Africa," in *Industrialization and Race Relations,* ed. Guy Hunter (London: Oxford University Press, 1965), pp. 117-18.

43.   Ibid., p. 118.

44. Ethnically-based labor aristocracies are much less sensitive about cheap labor in any form than are systems that do not arrive at this resolution because they are protected from it. Thus Sutherland and Cressey, *Criminology,* (Philadelphia: Lippincott, 1970), pp. 561-62, report that both the deep south and South Africa continue to use various forms of prison contract labor, in contrast to the northern U.S. where the contract system was attacked by rising labor organizations as early as 1880.

45. For example, Reich.

46. Davis, et al., p. 480.

47. Yarwood, pp. 16, 42.

48. Roger Daniels and Harry H.L. Kitano, *American Racism* (Englewood Cliffs, N. J.: Prentice-Hall, 1970), p. 43.

49. John Higham, *Strangers in the Land* (New York: Athenium, 1965), pp. 47-48.

50. Carl Wittke, "Immigration Policy Prior to World War I," in *Immigration: An American Dilemma,* ed. Benjamin M. Ziegler (Boston: Heath, 1953), p. 10.

51. Carey McWilliams, *Prejudice: Japanese-Americans* (Boston: Little, Brown, 1945), pp. 82-83.

52. Mason, p. 64.

53. Daniels and Kitano, p. 45.

5

The Structure of the Working Class and the Working Wife

Gabriel Kolko

As capitalism develops so too does its transformation of the structure of the working class. This evolution of the system can under certain historical circumstances accelerate the emergence of a subjective class consciousness in the proletariat, but capitalism's revolutionizing impact is far better understood than those economic forces which retard the emergence of a radicalized working class ready to move from an objective class to an articulate political force seeking to attain socialism. These inhibiting, opaque economic factors may merely set the stage for later, perhaps even deeper, crises—and in fact are likely to do so. But without an appreciation of the changing structure of the working class over the past half-century, one cannot understand adequately the main influences defining that class, its character today, and its condition in the future.[1]

In varying ways, the history of the American working class has been indelibly shaped by major, usually insufficiently comprehended trends which mark its specific historical character. Mass immigration from 1880 until 1924 was one such structural factor, as was the quite distinctive application of capital and technology that the unique working class in the United States made necessary. If this combination produced a long period of growth and capital accumulation, by 1929 it was also a major contributor to the depression of the 1930s. After 1946, changing facets of U.S. and Western capitalism, ranging from the explosion of the "service" industries to demographic and social factors, merged with inflation, unemployment, and the structural dilemmas of capitalism to produce a major shift in the composition of the American—and even world capitalist—working class in the form of the rising importance of working women and, above all, the working wife. We are today probably reaching the end of a long period of change and transformation in the American working class, the economic and social meaning and consequences of which are perhaps no less crucial than those which accompanied the 1880-1920 epoch. Moreover, this phenomenon is not merely a characteristic of the U.S. but also of a large part of the industrial capitalist world.

The fact that capitalism alters dynamically the structure of the working class by calling upon it to perform new functions essential to the health of the economy is one that radical analysts have often noted, though in the U.S. one can point only to C. Wright Mills and Harry Braverman as having made important contributions to comprehending such trends. But however insightful the valuable seminal ideas of these and other writers, systematic effort devoted to defining the magnitude of the role of working women in the working class in some of its more tedious but essential detail has not been sufficient, and much more has yet to be done to explore the full significance of this question. And, except for Braverman's brilliant but quite brief observations, the phenomenon of the working woman is relegated erroneously to the often false question of the nature and meaning of the "white-collar" occupations rather than the exact social character of these workers and their quite fundamental relationship to working men, whom they marry, and the forces which push them into the labor market. Far better understood, of course, is how capitalism's needs modify the demand for labor to produce new occupational classes, but the linkages between what is known in this respect and what has been insufficiently appreciated are crucial to any structural analysis of today's working class. Here I propose mainly to perform the drudgery of outlining certain of the main facts—some old and some new—regarding these problems, and only to briefly explore the analytic conclusions one can reasonably draw from them.[2]

GROWTH OF THE WOMEN WORKFORCE

At the beginning of this century, under one-fifth (18 percent) of the American workers were women; in 1974, 39 percent of the employed workforce was composed of women.[3] While the causes and fundamental significance of this vast transformation of the American working class can only be understood in its more complex context, suffice it to say that this far-reaching change is a vital key to comprehending the condition of the working class in the U.S. as well as in much of the capitalist world over the past three decades.

Fully 62 percent of the increased employment in the U.S. from 1950 to 1976 was accounted for by women—a figure that is not altered when unemployed workers are included.[4] This great shift was due to the fact that while only one-fifth of the women in 1900 were in the labor force, by 1940 that figure had risen to 29 percent and by 1976 to 47 percent.[5] Striking as these numbers may be, shorn from their larger setting one can easily distort their real meaning. For, in reality, the growth of the working woman in the proletariat after 1947 is very largely explained by the crucial role of the working wife who lives with her husband.

The labor force participation of single women has not altered significantly since 1940, and from 1950 to 1960 actually dropped. Today, as in 1940, about one-half of the women in this group work, though mainly part-time. Much the same stable pattern holds since 1940 for married women whose husbands are "absent"—deserted, in the military, etc.—as well as widowed and divorced women. In 1940, 11 percent of all families were headed by women and still only 13 percent were in 1975. In 1940, these three categories accounted for well over two-thirds of the women workers, but by 1975 the percentage in these categories had fallen to 42 percent.[6] Today the typical woman worker is increasingly the married woman whose husband is present—wives. Only 15 percent of the women in this category worked in 1940, but in 1975 it was 44 percent, and it is the working wife who is the cause of the post-1950 rising component of women in the working class and the main focus of this essay. Fully one-fifth of all full-time workers and 36 percent of the part-time workers in 1975 were working wives, though in fact about three-quarters of the wives who go to work do so on full-time schedules.[7] This vast growth in the work-force participation of wives is of prime significance to the condition of the working class today.

The causes of this trend are both simple and complex, touching on fundamental questions of the nature of capitalist development I do not pretend to resolve here. The subtle relationship between demographic factors which make it possible for wives to voluntarily enter the labor market, and structural forces which compel them to do so, is a tangled skein of interactions that defies simplifications.

On the one hand, we have the mechanical devices that have greatly reduced the types of work obligations the home historically imposed on wives, and even if housework has not declined in terms of time invested, its nature has altered so as to create options for a wife. Assorted washing machines and the vacuum cleaner partially "liberate" the wife from the nonprofit-creating labor in the home so that she can be exploited in the market sector, producing neither leisure nor freedom but more work—paid and unpaid—as a part of women's lives. On the other hand, there is the greatly increased life expectancy of women, which rose 47 percent between 1900 and 1950 and then far more slowly after 1950 (a mere 5 percent); this factor was a precondition to the later entry of women into the workforce, but *not* its immediate cause.[8]

The generally declining fertility rate as well as the falling number of children under five years per 1,000 women is another of those complex elements which undoubtedly made possible the growing numbers of women workers without necessarily directly causing it. The U.S. fertility rate, in common with most Western capitalist countries, has tended to drop greatly in this century, though the two decades—from 1940 to 1960—during which this longer-term historical pattern was reversed also witnessed a sharp increase in wives entering the labor market. Despite an 18 percent increase in the fertility rate from 1950 to 1960, the participation rate of wives in the workforce also grew 28 percent. It is much more likely that demographic and economic factors operate in conjunction as causes, with the former allowing the pressures and developments within capitalism to eventually find expression in new ways.[9]

EXPANSION AND TRANSFORMATION
OF THE LABOR SUPPLY

Those factors within contemporary capitalism which bring into existence a larger woman proletariat are not wholly self-evident. Simple to comprehend is the impact of immediate and variable economic conditions—depressions or recessions and inflation. Far more difficult is the changing nature of the capitalist process of accumulation, its structure and balance of economic activity between the so-called service and production sectors, and the manner in which a labor force and technology interact.

It is no accident that the rate of entry of women into the labor force is greatest during periods of crises and stagnation in the capitalist economy, and this basic reality imposes a decisive limit on the extent to which one assigns weight to the importance of demography or other structural changes in a capitalist economy. From 1930 to 1940, the percentage of the entire woman population in the workforce grew 22 percent, the greatest single decadal increase in American history—one which was nearly matched only by the 19 percent increase from 1965 to 1975. In fact, despite higher rates of unemployment, more and more women throw themselves at any price into the capitalist labor market and become an ever greater share of the workers at these critical junctures—the growth in their participation rate accelerating rather than falling during periods of high or rising unemployment.[10]

Put another way, when unemployment or economic adversity strikes families traditionally dependent on the income of male workers, the women in the family are driven into the capitalist labor process. Whether this fact accelerates or is caused by the structure shift in the capitalist economy from production to service employment can be debated, but that it is integral to the development of the modern capitalist economy is clear. Suffice it to say that the combination of rising inflation and general unemployment after 1965 is a better explanation—though not the only one—of the recent exceptional upsurge in the unceasing growth of working women and of why the demographic context witnesses this, rather than another, option. In any case, the most recent official study on why wives work showed that even in the noninflationary, relatively full employment year of 1963, 42 percent worked for reasons of "financial necessity" and another 17 percent to "earn extra money."[11]

Hence the question of whether women are being pulled into the labor force by the new openings in services, clerical posts, or the like cannot be divorced from the undeniable fact that economic pressures push them into the labor market more frequently during economic stagnation than during growth periods. How the very availability of cheaper and less-skilled labor at such times makes possible the further transformation of the structure of capitalist activity is one of those fundamental and exceedingly complex issues of socialist analysis which I do not pretend to answer here.[12] The fact that women labor is absorbed to a greater extend during stagnation and depression and ends as a greater proportion of the labor force tentatively reaffirms that the transformation of the organization of capitalist activity will occur more readily in response to a cheap, surplus labor supply than would otherwise be the case.

Here the theoretical problems to be resolved are immense. The fact is that American capitalism after 1929 lost its access to a relatively cheaper labor supply with the termination of mass immigration and the partial exhaustion of the surplus labor from South and rural areas. While an abundant labor supply still often existed among men, especially during the 1930s, the reality that women cost less to hire under virtually all circumstances meant that their future utility was linked to factors—children, home obligations, or social customs—which made them less efficient instruments of labor. That they have since 1962 been substituted both relatively and absolutely for men in the semiskilled operatives class is a reflection on their growing advantages as a lower-wage surplus labor army, as well as on the impact rising capital and technological intensity have on the falling demand for male labor. Availability of ample numbers of women workers, like the comparable function of abundant immigrants at the turn of this century, means a falling labor share in the costs of production and a slower growth of real incomes than otherwise might be essential.[13]

That women are absorbed as a proportion of the capitalist work process more quickly during periods of recession or depression, or difficulties for businessmen as well as workers, is aided by the fact that there are still more women ready to work than there are jobs for them. Their abundance when necessary, and at wages far lower than those for men and still declining relatively, means that both the capitalist "service" as well as the production sectors can have the best of all possible worlds, since the impact of women on both must be taken into account.[14]

The very broad "services," including wholesale and retail trade, finance, insurance and real estate, and personal and professional services (ranging from medical and health to education and servants), grew from 36 percent of the wage and salary workers in 1947 to 46 percent in 1976—while all government employees also increased from 12 to 19 percent of such workers over the same period.[15] Employment in the "production" sector has grown far more slowly over this period (22 percent in manufacturing), and actually fallen in mining. But these industrial designations are far less meaningful than occupational class categories—which I discuss later. Suffice it to say that no one can state with total assurance what might have occurred in the service sector had a cheap labor supply *not* been available to it. The mere fact that services, at least until recently, were generally far less subject to capital investment and technology in the administrative and clerical sector meant that access to cheap labor, overwhelmingly in the form of women, was critical to the further expansion of administrative and clerical posts consistent with the larger efficiency and profitability of the capitalist system.

In short, to some vital though not wholly measurable extent, it has been the availability of cheap labor that has made possible the expansion of the so-called "white-collar" occupations within the context of a relatively low capital investment for most of them. While there is no question that the managerial problems of running modern industrial capitalism have required both an absolute and a relative increase in many of these occupations, the fact that women are available and hired most quickly during periods of economic adversity raises the fundamental question of why such occupational changes occur more rapidly in some periods rather than others. This relation could also explain why the administrative functions of capitalist management were far less subject to capital investment than classic production functions dominated by higher-cost male labor.[16]

These trends are hardly exceptional to the U.S., but to some vital extent are increasingly a characteristic of Western industrial capitalist states. Among fourteen such nations, the participation rate of women in the work force is higher than the U.S. in five cases, and the average rate for all fourteen is almost the same as in the U.S. women's share of the workforce in ten of fifteen nations grew during 1974 and 1975, and the working wives' share of this group has, in particular, accounted for this expansion in most of the nations for which data are available.[17] Indeed, the questions and problems in this paper are largely relevant to the nature of the working class in contemporary world industrial capitalism.

The correlations to this emergence of the working wife as so crucial to the growth of the post-1947 working class are fairly self-evident, but even the obvious must be studied more closely. It is well-known that the labor force participation of women is linked in general to the age and number of their children under eighteen years. The fact that the more children a woman has the less education she has received automatically skews the more highly educated womens' share of the workforce. For example, in 1974 wives in the 25-54 age category with husbands present had a 34 percent workforce participation if they had children under six years but 60 percent if they had none under eighteen years. The usual explanation of this cycle is one of a figure "M," with the woman working until she bears children and then, after a period of some years, increasingly filtering back into the labor force as the children grow up. This general pattern holds in all capitalist nations and is not a great surprise. While the proportion of American wives with children under six has dropped from 33 percent in 1950 to 26 percent in 1975, the employment of even these burdened women in the labor force has risen much more rapidly since 1950. In fact, the pressure of economics has exceeded the responsibilities to child rearing that once were decisive before World War II—above all to the working class.[18]

It is only when one looks at the income of the husband that one learns something more vital about how the presence of children under six, or from six to seventeen, affects the wives' likelihood of working. In 1967, the women with children under six whose husbands earned under $7,000 the preceding year were over twice as likely to work as women with infants whose husbands earned over $10,000.[19] In fact, for wives with children the economic difficulty of their husbands is the most fundamental factor pushing them into the labor market.

GROWTH OF AVAILABLE LABOR MASS

Due almost wholly to the changing role of women in the labor force and the sharp increase in life expectancy, the total mass of potential human labor available to capitalist exploitation has increased significantly since 1900. In 1900, 67 percent—or 32 years—of the average man's life was devoted to participating in the capitalist work process, though the greater agricultural nature of the economy of that period meant that much less of the potential human labor time was accessible to an industrial-commercial economy as we today know it. With the prolongation of life, the average man by 1970 could expect to work 40 years, or 60 percent of his life expectancy. Even though the absolute number of years increased sharply, retirement at that point in their lives when the economy generally no longer regarded them as productive reduced the relative intensity of the exploitation of men as measured in life-year terms *only*. Such a calculation ignores the 28 percent decrease in the average male's work week from 1900 to 1948, though the decline of weekly hours of men until 1948 (it has remained constant at around forty-two hours since then) in no way affected labor productivity—which has gone up by any criterion one uses. Still, the involvement of work life in terms of years is one measure, of many, in perceiving the question of the mass of labor time potentially available to capitalist use, whether or not the intensity of it grows. And after 1948, it is the most meaningful of all possible measures.

In 1900, 12 percent of the life of the typical woman was consumed in the capitalist work process—meaning that precisely 38.8 percent of all human life-years, male and female, were then exploited (save for the exploiters) in the labor process. But whereas the share of male lives spent in this manner declined slightly, for women it has grown so that by 1970, 31 percent of their lives were consumed in the labor process. Taking men and women together, the share of available life-years at work had grown from 39 to 44.4 percent. Despite rising education, child labor laws, and the rest, the intensity and duration of exploitation grew as life became longer—and thereby more productive.[20]

The key to this expanding available labor mass is the woman worker, and the fact that most of it has occurred since 1950 (when it was 41.5 percent) after a period of decline means that it is an important and real phenomenon after 1948 whether one uses hours, weeks, or years as measures—and all are valid. While it cannot expand in the future at the same rate of increase simply because the growth in the number of women workers and longevity must slow down sharply, if not entirely, it suggests the degree to which human existence has over the past three decades been incorporated into the social process of exploitation, and the extent to which labor time in the aggregate has become an ever larger source for the generation of capital accumulation. This is more so the case because the growing women's share of the labor force and labor time, along with the persistence of, if not widening in, the overall male-female average income gap, makes possible a greater exploitation of the working class.

STRUCTURE OF WOMEN'S OCCUPATIONS

The demand for women's labor is overwhelmingly in the mushrooming "white-collar" and service occupations, above all the clerical jobs, of which women's share of the total has grown from 53 percent in 1940 to 78 percent in 1974. In fact, to some critical extent the growth of the white-collar class is synonymous with the entry of the wife into the labor market (see Table 1, columns h-i). Seen in this context, the traditional dichotomy of blue-and white-collar classes in the occupational structure—as well as the theoretical conclusions drawn from their alleged separation—can be seriously misleading. For the key question is not only the separate class position of this or that occupation, but the *family* income, as well as the economic and demographic developments that have caused the flood of new workers from among the wives of male blue-collar workers, and set a much larger context for judging their economic status and consciousness. The problem of class and occupation, in brief, must be seen as an overall field in which a skein of linkages ties major parts of relatively stable, as well as expanding, occupational categories together by marriage and creates common economic strengths and weaknesses among them that have been ignored far too long.

Because women workers are absorbed where the jobs are, and to some unknown but critical extent make these jobs more practical to capitalist enterprise by virtue of the cheapness and availability of their labor, the traditional blue-collar occupations absorbed a scant 12 percent of the increase in the women's workforce between 1962 and 1974.[21] Despite the growth of women's share of all of the semiskilled operatives class from 26 to 31 percent from 1962 to 1974, all blue-collar occupations and private household workers (servants) today comprise less that one-fifth of the women labor force (Table 1, columns o-q). Women as of 1970 have been absorbed mainly into the clerical and service occupations (52 percent), and their proportion of the sales occupations, while having increased slightly since 1962, has not risen above the 8 percent it was in 1940. Even today a woman is twice as likely to be on a factory assembly line as behind a sales counter. And women workers who head families (though the black-white distinctions are sharp) are, despite their very high poverty rate, also occupationally distributed much like all the rest of their sex.[22]

A closer look at these occupational categories reveals very great differences between the types of employment men and women find. In the sales occupations, a woman is likely to be a counter employee under

TABLE 1

Occupational Class	Relative Income Position of Occupational Classes, by Sex and Combined (100 = income of clerical workers)					Percentage Growth of Occupational Class		Female Share of Growth of Occupational Class	
	1962 Male (a)	1962 Female (b)	1974 Male (c)	1974 Female (d)	1974 Combined (e)	1900–70 (f)	1962–74 (g)	1900–70 (h)	1962–74 (i)
Professional, technical & kindred	136	127	129	140	163	837%	53%	41%	49%
Self-employed	231	187+	140						
Salaried	132	127	127	141					
Managers & administrators, exc. farm	123	98	134	126	179	281	20	21	34
Self-employed	106	45	61						
Salaried	135	111	134						
Sales workers	111	68	76		123	330	24	47	53
Clerical & kindred workers	100	100	100	100	100	1520	50	77	95
Craft & kindred workers	111		104	95	151	262	25	6	12
Foremen of blue-collars	131		100						
Craft workers, exc. foremen	108		92						
Operatives	95	82	88	84	101	285	6	31	31
Service workers, exc. private household	78	58	75	74	84	764	63	59	68
private household		58							
Laborers, exc. farm	78		86		106	4	23	114	
Private household workers	30	30	71	39	36	-31		68	31

Cols. a–d are median annual earnings of full-time workers and calculated from Statistical Abstract of the United States, 1976, p. 383; col. e is based on median weekly earnings of employed workers and calculated from U.S. Dept. of Labor, Bureau of Labor Statistics Sept. 12, 1975 release 75-493, table 1.

Cols. f–i are calculated from Monthly Labor Review, Nov. 1975, p. 32, and U.S. Department of Commerce, Historical Statistics of the United States: Colonial Times to 1970 (Washington, 1975), series D 182-232.

TABLE 1 (cont'd)

Occupational Class	Female Earnings as Percentage of Males in Same Occupational Class		Females as Percentage of Employed Workers in Occupational Class			Occupational Distribution of Female Workers, Exc. Farm		Occupational Distribution of Employed Wives, 1975
	1962 (j)	1974 (k)	1940 (l)	1962 (m)	1974 (n)	1940 (o)	1970 (p)	(q)
Professional, technical & kindred	64%	64%	45%	36%	41%	13.3%	15.4%	17.6%
Self-employed	66	65						
Salaried	54	56						
Managers & administrators, exc. farm			12	15	19	3.4	3.6	5.6
Self-employed	29	33						
Salaried	56	57						
Sales workers	42	41	28	39	42	7.7	7.5	6.8
Clerical & kindred workers	68	59	53	69	78	22.4	34.8	35.0
Craft & kindred workers		54	2	3	5	1.1	1.8	1.6
Foremen of blue-collars		51						
Craft workers, exc. foremen		53						
Operatives	59	57	26	26	31	20.3	15.1	12.5
Service workers, exc. private household	51	58	40	54	59	11.8	16.7	16.6
private household		72						
Laborers, exc. farm			3	3	8	1.1	1.0	.8
Private household workers			94		98	18.8	3.9	2.2
Average:	59	57						
% of total employed:			25	34	39			

Cols. j-k are calculated from <u>Statistical Abstract</u> 1976, p. 383. The comparison is for full-time workers.

Cols. l-n taken from U.S. Women's Bureau, Dept. of Labor, 1969 Handbook on Women Workers (Washington, 1969), p. 10, and <u>Monthly Labor Review</u>, Nov. 1975, pp. 28-29.

Cols. o-p taken from <u>Historical Statistics</u>, series D 216-32.

Col. q taken from <u>Monthly Labor Review</u>, May 1976, p. 16, and adjusted to exclude 1.2% of the women in the farm sector.

twenty years but not an insurance agent. Women clerical workers are most numerous in secretarial, typist, and bookkeeper posts, and those clerical tasks in which they are not dominant are generally the most remunerative. The largest groups among women service workers are waiters, hospital workers, and cooks. Indeed, the service class as a whole is mainly composed of the kind of women who forty years ago usually became household servants, and both in terms of income and job function, it must be seen as an unequivocal extension of classic working-class jobs—now wearing white hats but not white collars. Women operatives are most typically "checkers" and "packers," but much else besides. Among professional and technical occupations, teachers and nurses alone account for about two-fifths of the women in this class, and the more lucrative professions are overwhelmingly held by men. In varying degrees, all of the above trends are applicable to most of the industrial capitalist nations for which data are available.[23]

Because women's earnings in the same general occupational classes are so much lower than for men, a gap that has grown since 1962 as women flood into poorer paying jobs, the importance of distinguishing carefully the economic effects of these structural changes among working-class men and women is critical. For the problem of the economic relationship of the broad classes—"white collar" and others—is now largely an issue of accurately defining the role of women in the work structure as well as the approximate symbiotic economic and social relations between various kinds of occupations. It is impossible to judge the relative economic class position of various occupational classes save by sex, and then one *must* know how these working men and women are related outside the immediate work context.[24] Family income and economic position is today often far more relevant than the individual income standing of this or that occupation.

If one takes the relative income position of the broad occupational classes without sexual differentiation, it would superficially appear that the traditional "white-collar" classes—sales-clerical—have fallen behind the blue-collar class's economic status, a proposition that has fed social theory in the industrial capitalist world with a rich harvest of misconceptions for over a half-century.[25] Yet if one perceives the working class by sexual divisions, in which the occupations are compared to others in the same sex as well as to those of the other sex, the differences are more exact, and occupational class relations appear in a wholly different light (Table 1, columns a-e). In any case, the satellite economic functions that women increasingly play vis-à-vis husbands and the now more crucial family income, and the complex way working-class wives are compelled to move into nonblue-collar jobs, require one to judge the field of economic stratification as a whole, with precise occupational designations being less important than economic divisions which, in effect, include many of the white-collar and service tasks as integral extensions of the postwar growth of employment among families in which blue-collar men usually provide the larger part of the income.

Among men, however, the economic differences correlated to occupation appear in a radically altered perspective than if one mixes male and female earnings together. Male sales workers are today well ahead of skilled "craft" workers (excluding foremen), and this economic lead over all blue-collar occupations has grown significantly since 1962. As opposed to 1962, the male clerical worker is now economically as well off as the skilled worker, and his lead over the poorer blue-collar occupations has increased. Indeed, most of the traditional white-collar male occupations are today relatively more affluent vis-à-vis the blue-collar class than in 1962. The internal female economic class structure is no less inequitable than among men, and the superior economic position of women professional-technical and managerial personnel relative to poorer workers in their own sex is quite as great as among men and perhaps even growing. The woman sales worker, as opposed to men in that field, is the most poorly paid of the major women categories.

It is, of course, also a fact that professional-technical workers in the highest income tenth of female occupations generally receive what male workers earn in the middle third of their income-occupation rankings. The gap between the average earnings of men and women increases greatly with age in all countries for which data are available, a fact that reflects sexual discrimination, but also the additional skills and seniority men accumulate by virtue of not dropping out of the labor force for long periods—as women are usually compelled to do.[26]

THE EXPANSION OF THE PROLETARIAT

The increase of women workers to two-fifths of those employed represents an expansion of the working class rather than a transformation of the class structure, since the economic status of the large majority of women places them among the society's lowest income earners regardless of their type of work. The key to their economic position for the now preponderant working wives is not merely their own mediocre income but that of their husbands as well. In fact, that women especially choose periods of economic adversity to enter the labor market confirms that this new, rising class is the working-class families' adaptive personal response to deepening economic difficulties they cannot resolve singly or collectively. The manifold consequences of this adjustment process are crucial to understanding the postwar economic experience, and it is a process that has compelled the women of the working class to play the role of the surplus labor army in providing ample, cheap labor for new or expanded kinds of work that can only be regarded as satellite functions of a classic proletariat, but not as its transformation into a "new class." Such changes as have indeed occurred in the lives of the working class in capitalist society are linked to the income effects of working wives on families in which blue-collar men usually earn the larger share of their income, with such additional occupational roles as wives play being secondary if not unimportant for many or most of them.

The question of precisely which wives work must be determined through a number of oblique but perfectly conclusive measures, since I know of no comprehensive correlation of the distribution of women workers by their husbands' occupations. Suffice it to say, that women family heads are among the very poorest income groups and are not the topic here.

First, wives of unemployed men in virtually every capitalist country are the most likely to be in the labor market, a simple fact which favors the influx of blue-collar family wives into the largely white-collar low-income occupations. Wives of self-employed professionals are the least likely to work, with personal "satisfaction" the most likely motive for employment in their cases.[27]

When wives do go to work, however, they largely re-create among themselves their own economic class structure which parallels that among men—the two reinforcing each other so as to leave intact over time the existing income and wealth distribution structure. For the working wife's occupation is closely correlated to that of her husband. Forty-two percent of the employed wives of professional-technical men are also classed in that category, and such wives of professionals are four times more likely to work in a professional-technical occupation than the working wives of skilled workers—and six times more likely as those of semiskilled. The semiskilled male's wife is eight times more likely to work in his class than the wife of a professional is likely to become an operative. Eighty-three percent of the working wives of professional-technical men are employed as professional-technical, managerial, and clerical workers. Operatives, service workers, and household workers among wives are overwhelmingly married to blue-collar or "white-hat" (service) men.[28] It is only in the clerical category that the wives of the different major male occupational categories meet for statistical purposes, but even here it seems probable that the generally higher educational attainment of wives of white-collar men means that they also dominate the better paying clerical and sales jobs. For in reality the poorer clerical and sales working wives, and virtually all of the blue-collar and white-hat wives, appear to be married to the classic proletariat, making these occupations—both in pay and function—an integral aspect and extension of the structure of the modern working class in industrial capitalist societies.

In 1967, to employ yet another measure to confirm this thesis, 29 percent of the wives of men earning over $10,000 in 1966 were in the labor force. Among those whose husbands were in the much more numerous $3,000-7,000 income category, the wives' participation rate was 42 percent. Fully 61 percent of the working wives in 1967 had husbands whose incomes the preceding year were under $7,000.[29] It is this lower and lower-middle income category that has continued to provide the greater part of the influx of working wives since then.

INCOME OF THE WORKING CLASS

The major consequences of these structural alterations in the working class are not in the changing nature of the occupational distribution, which is largely the effect of economic trends rather than their causes, but in what these developments mean to the economic position of the working class, as well as the fundamental impact it has on this class and on capitalist economies. For today, the working class families with only the husband in the labor force are far outnumbered by those families in which both husbands and wives work. This overriding reality has three quite different and paradoxical consequences worth detailing: (1) it raises the consumer unit income of most working-class homes; (2) it puts a floor under many family incomes during periods of unemployment; and (3) it introduces a new form of volatility into the larger capitalist economy and, to a somewhat lesser degree, into the economic position of working-class families. In short, the rise of the working wife has both stabilizing and destabilizing implications.

In 1950, the median income of families with wives in the paid labor force was 21 percent higher than those without, but by 1974 this gap had increased to 40 percent. In 1974, if the wife worked full-time the whole year, she contributed 38 percent of the family's income, or 12 percent if she worked under 26 weeks or part-time.[30] But these national averages gloss over the fact that the employed wife is married to a worker far more often than not, and that the main effect of her labor is to push blue-collar and lower-income families in which the husbands are blue-collar workers into the higher—but not the highest—income classes. From an income viewpoint, such collective work-sharing creates an addition to the middle and upper-middle income categories without changing the economic position of occupations and classes individually.[31]

The way to comprehend the economic status of the working class, given these developments, is to focus also on the family income unit rather than the individual only, since this in reality becomes the way workers increasingly perceive it. The blue-collar class, with its satellite income white-collar occupations, has in this fact produced something economically more complex than the classic proletariat of blue-collar labor, as well as something less benign than a new "deproletarianized" class of white collars. Economically, socially, and perhaps politically these symbiotic occupational elements are now interlinked by ties of family, not just in the U.S. but perhaps also in most of the industrial capitalist world.

This development explains much of the post-1950 prosperity of the working class, because the rise of the working woman was a direct response to the inability of the traditional male-dominated working class to thrive and meet its obligations with its own participation alone. Unemployment, inflation, and a slow and often nonexistent rise of real income, installment debts which threatened to compel a retrenchment of consumer spending—all these and other structural dilemmas of postwar American capitalism were temporarily resolved by the working class as wives entered the labor market. Postwar American prosperity was not the consequence of the traditionally male-dominated working class's rising fortunes so much as that class's capacity to find solutions to problems which it could not resolve with its traditional means. This influx of wives fueled the entire American economy, and perhaps much of the international capitalist economy, since spending behavior in the past has always meant that after a certain point, additional family income goes much more disproportionately into durables and housing than into basic daily essentials.[32] In this one simple cause of recent prosperity we have a force that, on the one hand, tends to tranquilize the working class and, on the other, threatens capitalism with greater instability in the future.

The manner in which these trends partially alleviate the crises of the working class is illustrated by the impact of the post-1973 recession, for the economic condition of many of the married unemployed is now directly linked to their working wives. Surely the penurious $70-a-week unemployment compensation issued during 1975 for a maximum of twenty-six weeks in most cases cannot explain the absence of much more misery since 1973—since that sum starves a family. The fact is that in 1974, over one-half of the unemployed male heads of families who worked at least one week that year—or the vast majority—also had employed wives who in most cases worked full-time at least twenty-seven weeks. This pattern of entering the labor force when men are unemployed appears by 1976 to have increased the percentage of families in which women worked full-time when their husbands were out of work—thereby doing far more than unemployment compensation to insulate the recession's economic blow.[33]

Women in the U.S., and in half of a sample of eight other industrial capitalist states, during periods of business growth or decline, generally have a higher rate of unemployment than men. But in most countries, the U.S. included, during the 1974-75 recession the percentage increase in the rate of male unemployment grew more rapidly than for women—leaving women with a higher share of the labor force. The female share of total U.S. employment increased from 38.6 percent in the fourth quarter of 1973 to 39.8 percent in the fourth quarter of 1975, while their share of official unemployment dropped from 48.1 to 43.4 percent over the same period. These patterns of recession hitting men relatively harder hold even if one uses the considerably higher true jobless rate.[34] Hence, women are better able to insulate their families' economic fortunes. At the same time, the mere fact that their overall participation rate has gone up immensely despite their still higher rate of unemployment has produced a long-term danger to the capitalist system, just as it produced an intermediate source of strength.

As even some business analysts now admit, the post-1960 decline in the birth rate unexpectedly produced not fewer future workers but more over the past decade, as wives were better able to leave the home and enter the labor market. The U.S. Bureau of Labor Statistics repeatedly failed to accurately project the size of the recent labor force because of its myopia on this phenomenon. So long as the economy expanded until 1974, such worker growth was beneficial in holding down labor's real income and adding to consumer demand at the same time.[35] By changing the composition of the labor force to enlarge employment of the most poorly paid, it made possible a greater rate of profit accumulation than would have otherwise been possible. But today there are many more millions of workers than the economy can absorb, and large-scale permanent unemployment is the outcome—and this fact produces a major new contradiction for capitalism to resolve.

A working-class family that has two earners, given at least as high an overall rate of unemployment for wives, is about twice as subject to some shock from layoffs as those with one. Two earners insulate the extent of unemployment impact, but it also doubles the likelihood of it occurring. At the least, this affects discretionary consumer spending first of all, a fact that business elements already acknowledge as holding back consumer buying after the alleged post-1975 "recovery."[36] Because it is now far more difficult for the working class's future problems to be resolved by the further entry of yet more wives into the labor market—and a slower growth and leveling off in participation rates is much more likely over the next decade—this greater stability in family income also means stability or, yet much more likely, a decline in future consumer demand. Given the surplus labor which has not accumulated, only a much greater cheapening of the cost of women labor is likely to stimulate a significant continuation of its further absorption to fuel the economy as it has in the past.

In brief, the rise of the working wife was an absolutely fundamental change in the structure of the working class that played a major compensatory role in the economy when not much more than military spending was available to capitalist political planners. Having expanded the occupational and income structures to produce a larger and more prosperous working class for some decades, this process is now unable to continue indefinitely having finally approached a plateau in its growth and created conditions which, in the end, have only increased the insecurity of the new labor force. First, it has swollen the absolute and relative size of the working class and its satellite occupations by vastly increasing the potential labor resources being exploited, but for which capitalism cannot produce sufficient new employment—leaving a long-term prospect of permanently unemployed job-seekers. Next, it has made increased consumer spending both possible and also more vulnerable to unemployment in the same families, but capitalism cannot cause spending to grow at the same rate—if at all—to solve the problems of consumer debt, declining real income, and such, which remain both larger as well as structurally integral to the capitalist economy. Last, capitalism has exhausted the recuperative effects of a major technique of postwar economic adjustment—with no options to it readily at hand—and brought us to the end of a long period in which very significantly increased volatility in mass unemployment and spending is the outcome. The means by which the capitalist economy was stimulated for decades have now become another source of its future instability. If the social and political outcome of this dilemma is not easy to predict in the U.S., in the other nations of the capitalist world its potentially basic significance is not so obscure.

NOTES

1. I am grateful to Patricia V. Schulz for valuable research assistance
2. The starting points of all radical discussion on this topic are C. Wright Mills, *White Collar: The American Middle Classes* (New York: 1951), and Harry Braverman, *Labor and Monopoly Capital* (New York: 1974), ch. 15-17. I have touched on certain of the above questions in "Economic Mobility and Social Stratification," *American Journal of Sociology* (July 1957): 30-38, and *Main Currents in Modern American History* (New York: 1976), chs. 3,5.
3. See Table 1 and U.S. Women's Bureau, Department of Labor *1969 Handbook on Women Workers* (Washington: 1969), p. 10. By the end of 1975, 40 percent of all employed were women. See Ralph E. Smith, "The Impact of Macroeconomic Conditions on Employment Opportunities for Women," (a study issued by U.S. Congress, Joint Economic Committee, 94:2, January 3, 1977), p. 9.

4. Calculated from U.S. Council of Economic Advisers, *Economic Report of the President—1977* (Washington: 1977), p. 220.
5. *1969 Handbook on Women Workers*, p. 10; U. S. Department of Labor release 76-994, July 2, 1976, Table A-l. Data is for fourteeen years and over in 1900, sixteen and over from 1940.
6. U. S. Department of Labor, *Monthly Labor Review* (hereafter *MLR)*, June 1976, p. 4; August 1976, p. 4; *1969 Handbook on Women Workers*, pp. 10, 24, 26; U.S. Department of Labor release 75-493, September 12, 1975, Table 3.
7. *MLR*, May 1976, p. 13; release 75-493, Table 3; *1969 Handbook on Women Workers*, p. 26.
8. U.S. Bureau of the Census, *The Population of the United States, Trends and Prospects; 1950-1990* (Washington: 1974), p. 44; *MLR*, February 1976, p. 32.
9. Calculated from *Population of the United States*, pp. 17, 44; *1969 Handbook on Women Workers*, p. 10; *MLR*, May 1976, p. 13; *Le Monde*, March 29, 1977, p. 18.
10. *1969 Handbook on Women Workers*, p. 10; release 76-994, Table A-1; OECD (Organization for Economic Co-operation and Development), *The 1974-1975 Recession and the Employment of Women* (Paris: 1976), p. 13. I have not compared any year to World War II, since that event was an exception that proves nothing.
11. *MLR*, May 1976, p. 14. One recent Labor Department study suggests that greater family labor time is now essential to pay for the growing relative costs of raising children, though in fact inflation's impact on real income after 1965 is probably an additional and more crucial factor. *MLR*, August 1976, p. 6.
12. I have touched this matter briefly regarding blue-collar labor in *Main Currents in Modern American History*, pp. 72-74, 163-65.
13. Ibid., pp. 169-72; Table 1, columns i and n.
14. See Table 1, columns j-k.
15. *Economic Report of the President*, p. 224. This larger "service" designation also subsumes the much smaller occupational class of "service workers."
16. Kolko, *Main Currents in Modern American History*, p. 171; Braverman, *Labor and Monopoly Capital*, passim.
17. OECD, *The Role of Women in the Economy: A Summary Based on Ten National Reports* (Paris: 1975), pp. 10-12; *1974-1975 Recession and Employment of Women*, pp. 9-16.
18. *MLR*, November 1975, p. 11; OECD, *Role of Women in the Economy*, pp. 14-15, 24-27, 33; *MLR*, May 1976, pp. 14-15; *1969 Handbook on Women*, pp. 40-41
19. *1969 Handbook on Women*, p. 33.
20. All data calculated from *MLR*, February 1976, p. 32; August 1976, pp. 3-5. I assume a 50 percent distribution for each sex. If one calculates labor time in the capitalist process from 1900 to 1948 in terms of hours it has remained about stable per person.
21. Calculated from *MLR*, November 1975, p. 32.
22. *MLR*, June 1976, p. 7.
23. *MLR*, November 1975, pp. 6, 32; OECD, *Role of Women in the Economy*, pp. 21-22, 55-57; *1974-1975 Recession and Employment of Women*, pp. 24-26.
24. I committed this error, in common with others, in my *Wealth and Power in America* (New York: 1962), pp. 82-83.

25. These I mention in "Economic Mobility and Social Stratification," pp. 30-31, 36.
26. *MLR,* August 1974, pp. 38-47; OECD, *Role of Women in the Economy,* pp. 60-61.
27. OECD, *Role of Women in the Economy,* p. 28; *MLR,* May 1976, p. 18.
28. All calculated from *MLR,* May 1976, p. 17.
29. *1969 Handbook on Women,* pp. 33-34.
30. *MLR,* May 1976, pp. 15-17.
31. *1969 Handbook on Women,* p. 35.
32. Kolko, *Wealth and Power in America,* pp. 125-26, 140-41.
33. U.S. Department of Labor release 76-913, June 14, 1976, p. 12; *MLR,* May 1976, p. 18.
34. Smith, "Impact of Macroeconomic Conditions...," p. 9; OECD, *1974-1975 Recession and Employment of Women,* pp. 14-15; *Role of Women in the Economy,* p. 37.
35. Citibank, *Monthly Economic Letter,* September 1976, 9-12; Smith, "Impact of Macroeconomic Conditions, " p. 23.
36. *Business Week,* April 11, 1977, pp. 80-83.

6

Working Women and Their Membership in Labor Unions

Edna E. Raphael

Labor union membership affects the status of women in many ways. Perhaps most important is the fact that the large and pervasive income disparities between employed men and employed women are less when the women are union members. On the whole, this advantage probably derives less from union membership as such than from the fact that women are more likely to be union members when employed in industries where men predominate—where, by and large, wages are higher than in industry where women predominate.

Despite advantages which accrue to women through union membership, however, between 1966 and 1970 the proportion of working women who were members of labor unions declined, even as women's participation in the labor force increased. The proportion of working men who were union members also declined, but the decline was greater among women.

The following discussion documents the difference in earnings of women who are union members and those who are not, as well as the recent proportional decline in union membership. Other sections review the current status of legislation to guarantee equal rights for women, and the

114

stance of labor unions with respect to equal employment opportunities for women.

EARNINGS DIFFERENCES

Recent government surveys provide evidence of the higher earnings of union members, both men and women. However, and without exception, in all broad occupational categories and in both 1966 and 1970, the earnings of men were disproportionately higher than those of women. This held for union members and nonmembers, for the country as a whole, and for its four major regions.[1]

In the aggregate, among women who by occupation of longest job held in 1966 and 1970 were employed as private wage and salary workers (including both full-time and part-time workers), union members had higher earnings than nonmembers. The advantage was greater for women than for similarly employed men. The median income of women union members was roughly 80 percent higher in 1966 and 70 percent in 1970 than that of nonunion women (Table 1). The comparable advantage for male union members was only 30 percent in both 1966 and 1970.

TABLE 1
Ratio of Earnings of Private Wage and Salary Workers, by Union Membership and Sex, 1966 and 1970

Occupation group of longest job	Ratio of median earnings								Labor union membership							Women private wage and salary workers (in thousands)	
	Men to women, by union membership				Union member to non-member, by sex				Percent with union membership				Percent change, 1966-70				
	Union		Nonunion		Men		Women		Men		Women		Men	Women			
	1966	1970	1966	1970	1966	1970	1966	1970	1966	1970	1966	1970	Direct	Direct	Adjusted[1]	1966	1970
Total..................	2.0	2.0	2.8	2.5	1.3	1.3	1.8	1.7	31.4	28.5	12.9	10.3	−2.9	−2.6	−5.5	26,065	28,632
White-collar workers..........	(²)	1.8	2.8	2.8	1.0	0.9	(²)	1.4	12.7	10.4	7.8	6.4	−2.3	−1.4	−2.3	13,517	15,352
Blue-collar workers..........	(²)	2.0	2.2	1.9	1.6	1.6	(²)	1.5	45.4	43.0	31.8	28.2	−2.4	−3.6	−5.2	³ 5,780	³ 5,749
Operatives..............	1.9	1.9	2.0	1.8	1.6	1.6	1.7	1.5	48.7	46.9	35.2	29.4	−1.9	−5.8	−8.0	5,444	5,002
Service workers, including private household...........	1.8	1.7	2.1	2.2	2.5	2.6	2.9	3.3	19.3	17.3	4.5	4.6	−2.0	.1	.4	6,195	7,129

[1] Adjusted values represent change in percent of women with union membership from 1966 to 1970 which would obtain if, in 1966, the percent of women in each occupational group who were union members had been the same as the percent of men who were union members:

$$\frac{\text{Percent of men with union membership, 1966}}{\text{Percent of women with union membership, 1966}} \times \text{Change in percent of women with union membership, 1966-70}$$

[2] The 1966 data on earnings were not published by white-collar and blue-collar

categories. Data on earnings of union women by specific occupational groups cannot be aggregated to blue-collar and white-collar totals, because data are not published if the base is less than 100,000.

[3] In 1966, nonfarm laborers and farm workers are combined into a separate category. In 1970, nonfarm laborers are reported as a separate blue-collar category.

SOURCE: For 1966 computations, Labor Union Membership in 1966, Current Population Reports, Series P-20, No. 216 (Bureau of the Census, 1971); For 1970 computations, unpublished background materials for Selected Earnings and Demographic Characteristics of Union Members, 1970, Report 417 (Bureau of Labor Statistics, 1972).

For both men and women, the earnings advantage of union members was greater in blue-collar and service occupations than in white-collar occupations. In 1970, white-collar women union members had a 44 percent income advantage over nonunion women, but among white-collar men, union members earned 8 percent less than nonunion workers.

Comparisons between men and women reveal that whether in unions or not, and in 1966 as well as in 1970, men earned more than women. In 1970, the earnings gap between men and women was narrower among union members who are white-collar or service workers, but wider among union members who are blue-collar workers. For example, among white-collar workers in 1970, nonunion men earned 180 percent more than nonunion women; union men earned 80 percent more than union women. Similarly, among service workers in 1970, nonunion men earned 120 percent more than nonunion women, union men 70 percent more than union women. Among blue-collar workers, income disparities between men and women were higher for union members than for nonmembers. In 1970, among nonunion blue-collar workers, men earned 90 percent more than women; among union members, men earned 100 percent more. This pattern holds when the comparison is limited to operatives (where women are more likely to be employed): among nonunion operatives in 1970, men earned 80 percent more than women; among union members, 90 percent more.

Since larger proportions of women than of men work part time, the earnings gap between men and women was less among full-time year-round private wage and salary workers than among all wage and salary workers. Nevertheless, marked disparities in earnings remain, and here again union membership was not always associated with reduction of the disparity. Among year-round full-time blue-collar workers in the Northeast and South, in both 1966 and 1970, income disparities between men and women were greater among labor union members than nonmembers. This disparity between men and women increased in 1970 (Table 2). In the North Central region, on the other hand, the income disparity between men and women union members in blue-collar jobs was reduced in 1970 so that it was lower than among nonunion men and women.

Within industries, men were more likely than women to be labor union members (Table 3). This finding holds equally for white-collar and blue-collar workers and, where adequate data are available, for service workers as well. Both men and women were more likely to be labor union members if employed in industries predominantly composed of male workers. Or, to put it another way, an industry is more likely to be unionized if most of its workers are men.

Among white-collar workers, men and women were equally likely to be union members in the transportation, communications, and public utilities industry group, where 30.1 percent of white-collar men and 30.1 percent of white-collar women were union members. In public administration, 27.7 percent of the men and 10.7 percent of the women in white-collar jobs were members. In the same industry group—transportation, communica-

TABLE 2
Ratio of Earnings of Year-Round Full-Time Private Wage and Salary Workers, by Union Membership, Sex, and Region, 1966 and 1970

Region and occupation group of longest job	Ratio of median earnings								Labor union membership						
	Men to women, by union membership				Union member to non-member, by sex				Percent with union membership				Percent change, 1966-70		
	Union		Nonunion		Men		Women		Men		Women		Men	Women	
	1966	1970	1966	1970	1966	1970	1966	1970	1966	1970	1966	1970	Direct	Direct	Adjusted [1]
NORTHEAST															
Total	1.6	1.6	1.8	1.7	1.0	0.9	1.0	1.0	35.5	34.8	22.3	19.8	−0.7	−2.5	−4.0
White-collar workers	1.3	1.4	1.9	1.9	.8	.8	1.2	1.1	12.3	16.7	12.9	12.8	4.4	−.1	−.1
Blue-collar workers	1.8	1.9	1.7	1.8	1.1	1.1	1.1	1.1	54.6	53.6	53.9	44.4	−1.0	−9.5	−5.6
Operatives and kindred workers	1.6	1.7	1.6	1.6	1.1	1.1	1.1	1.1	60.1	59.2	56.8	45.9	−.9	−10.9	−11.6
Service workers, including private household	(²)	1.7	1.6	1.6	1.2	1.2	(²)	1.1	30.6	37.0	22.9	20.3	6.4	−2.6	−3.5
NORTH CENTRAL															
Total	1.8	1.6	2.0	1.8	1.0	.9	1.1	1.1	41.0	37.5	18.4	16.5	−3.5	−1.9	−4.2
White-collar workers	1.7	1.4	2.1	2.0	.9	.8	1.1	1.1	13.8	14.3	8.7	10.7	.5	2.0	3.2
Blue-collar workers	1.8	1.7	1.7	1.8	1.2	1.1	1.1	1.2	61.2	59.1	49.3	45.9	−2.1	−3.4	−4.2
Operatives and kindred workers	1.7	1.6	1.6	1.7	1.2	1.2	1.1	1.2	64.1	66.9	51.8	49.2	−2.6	−3.2	−3.2
Service workers, including private household	(²)	1.8	1.5	1.8	(²)	1.2	(²)	1.2	38.7	37.8	7.4	12.1	−.9	4.7	24.6
SOUTH															
Total	1.6	1.6	1.7	1.7	1.2	1.1	1.3	1.2	21.5	81.4	9.3	6.8	−3.1	−2.5	−5.8
White-collar workers	(²)	1.5	2.0	1.8	1.0	1.0	(²)	1.2	8.9	7.9	6.6	5.1	−1.0	−1.5	−2.0
Blue-collar workers	1.7	1.7	1.8	1.6	1.4	1.3	1.2	1.1	31.3	29.2	21.3	16.3	−2.1	−5.0	−7.3
Operatives and kindred workers	1.6	1.8	1.4	1.5	1.4	1.3	1.2	1.1	32.9	30.2	21.4	16.1	−2.7	−5.3	−8.1
Service workers, including private household	(²)	(²)	1.7	1.8	(²)	1.4	(²)	(²)	17.7	12.8	1.0	3.7	−4.9	2.7	47.8
WEST															
Total	1.7	1.5	1.9	1.6	1.0	1.0	1.1	1.1	36.1	31.6	17.6	13.9	−4.5	−3.7	−7.6
White-collar workers	1.8	1.5	2.1	1.8	.9	.9	1.1	1.1	15.9	15.1	11.7	11.5	−.8	−.2	−.3
Blue-collar workers	(²)	(²)	1.8	1.7	1.2	1.2	(²)	(²)	57.0	52.2	46.9	26.0	−4.8	−20.9	−22.5
Operatives and kindred workers	(²)	(²)	(²)	1.5	1.2	1.2	(²)	(²)	61.0	57.4	42.9	27.3	−3.6	−15.6	−22.2
Service workers, including private household	(²)	(²)	2.2	1.8	(²)	1.1	(²)	(²)	36.3	34.0	17.9	16.4	−2.3	−1.5	−3.0

[1] See footnote 1, table 1.   ² Data not published for fewer than 100,000 members in 1966 or 75,000 in 1970.

tions, and public utilities—among blue-collar workers who are operatives, men are more likely than women to be labor union members (58.6 and 11.2 percent, respectively). In other industries as well, relatively large proportions of male blue-collar workers were union members. Among women in blue-collar jobs, this was characteristic only of manufacturing.

With few exceptions, membership in labor unions declined between 1966 and 1970. For the country as a whole, for all private wage and salary workers, and for blue-collar workers, the declines in union membership were greater among women than among men. Membership gained slightly (0.4 percent) among women service workers. The decline was about the same (−2.3 percent) among men and women white-collar workers. Among women workers, the decline was greatest among operatives (−8.0 percent).

Some of the gains and losses in labor union membership by sex and occupational class are more sharply differentiated in data by region and on year-round full-time private wage and salary workers. The gains and losses were not uniform in size or direction. Among both men and women, losses in union membership were greatest in the West. In that region, losses were greater among women than among men, and among women blue-collar workers (–22.5 percent) than among women white-collar or service workers. While losses were not so large in other regions, nevertheless, declines were greater among women in blue-collar jobs than among male blue-collar workers. This loss of union membership among women blue-collar workers was lowest in the North Central region (–4.2 percent). Marked gains appeared among women service workers in the North Central region (24.6 percent) and South (47.8 percent). Gains in union membership among men service workers appeared only in the Northeast.

These findings suggest that the large and even increased disparity in wages between men and women union members in blue-collar occupations was associated with the greater decline in labor union membership among

TABLE 3
Union Membership of Private Wage and Salary Workers, by Occupation of Longest Job, Industry, and Sex, 1970 (in thousands)

[Numbers in thousands]

Sex and occupation of longest job	Total		Industry											
			Manufacturing		Transportation, communications, public utilities		Wholesale trade		Retail trade		Services		Public administration	
	Number of workers	Percent union members	Number of workers	Percent union members	Number of workers	Percent union members	Number of workers	Percent union members	Number of workers	Percent union members	Number of workers	Percent union members	Number of workers	Percent union members
MEN														
Total	48,621	27.8	15,589	38.4	4,353	49.4	2,223	13.6	6,616	12.6	10,059	11.7	3,143	27.7
White-collar workers	18,442	12.5	4,429	11.1	1,278	30.1	1,309	6.1	2,845	9.1	6,004	8.0	1,812	26.5
Blue-collar workers	24,356	42.1	10,695	49.9	2,923	58.6	893	24.4	2,711	17.7	1,985	16.2	517	29.2
Operatives and kindred workers	9,914	46.4	5,844	53.7	1,233	57.7	412	27.4	1,115	17.9	540	22.0	83	37.3
Service workers	4,646	20.1	466	35.2	152	34.2	31	16.1	1,060	9.0	2,070	17.8	813	29.5
Farm workers	1,188	1.8												
WOMEN														
Total	35,624	10.4	6,914	23.3	1,289	29.2	814	5.2	7,115	7.4	17,056	5.4	1,619	11.3
White-collar workers	20,962	7.4	2,231	6.1	1,096	30.1	656	4.1	4,580	7.4	10,546	5.3	1,492	10.7
Blue-collar workers	5,936	27.8	4,634	31.7	124	12.9	151	9.3	424	13.9	536	15.1	(¹)	(¹)
Operatives and kindred workers	5,154	29.0	4,226	31.8	116	11.2	122	9.8	265	17.0	398	18.3	(¹)	(¹)
Service workers	8,324	5.7	(¹)	(¹)	(¹)	(¹)	(¹)	(¹)	2,111	6.2	5,974	4.8	(¹)	(¹)
Farm workers	402	1.0											108	17.6

¹ Data not published for fewer than 75,000 workers.

SOURCE: Unpublished data from the Bureau of Labor Statistics. Data on agriculture, mining, and construction not presented because of small numbers of women workers.

women blue-collar workers. Some of the same data indicate that, among women workers in general, where labor union membership increased, the disparity in wages decreased. For example, in the North Central region and among white-collar workers, labor union membership increased between 1966 and 1970 by 0.5 percent among men and 3.5 percent among women. During the same period, among labor union members, the ratio of men's to women's median earnings declined from 1.7 to 1.4. In the United States as a whole, among service workers, labor union membership increased for women (0.4 percent) and the ratio of men's to women's earnings declined from 1.8 to 1.7. Some of these declines are probably associated with relocation of industry to smaller towns and rural areas where wages are lower than in large urban areas. Data is not sufficient to indicate whether there is any causal relationship between the declines, or in which direction causation flowed.

THE LEGISLATIVE APPROACH

The labor movement has been slow to support equal rights legislation, and not until its October 1973 convention did the AFL-CIO go on record in support of the Equal Rights Amendment. As of March 1974, thirty-three of the fifty states had ratified this amendment (thirty-eight are required for passage).

Until recently, many unions vigorously opposed state laws passed in recent years to supersede long-established "protective" legislation for children and women—concerned with hours, lifting, nightwork, and so on. The women's liberation movement should be credited with alerting labor unions, and women generally, to the fact that state protective laws have often been used by employers, and by some labor unions, to prevent women from holding better paying jobs, from working overtime, and from accumulating plantwide security and seniority by limiting their right to open access to the better jobs.

The Equal Employment Opportunity Commission has expressed concern that such laws do not take into account the capacities, preferences, and abilities of individual women and therefore are discriminatory on the basis of sex. The removal of even one such discriminatory practice, hours restrictions, may combine with other factors to introduce profound changes in the sexual composition of the American labor force, particularly in the blue-collar and service occupations, and to modify modes of operation in labor unions.

Labor union women, however, seem reluctant to resort to resources outside of the labor movement for help with problems resulting from discriminatory practices. Caucuses of women are emerging in several unions—though as yet hardly visible—some in combination with other unions and some confined to one union, across cities, states, and regions. A few skirmishes have taken place at national conventions and under special circumstances, but remain out of the public's eye.

Union women, concerned with the protection of the labor movement's achievements, may hesitate to place these in the jeopardy, which might attend conflicts brought into the courts or before the public. There is always the chance that the courts which test the legality of discriminatory practices may entertain the notion that collective bargaining agreements which perpetuate discriminatory practices are themselves illegal. Legal actions already are being brought by employers to invalidate collective bargaining agreements with labor unions in some of the printing trades where separate locals for men and women have obtained for a long time. Some women unionists, also, may see constraint in the use of courts as a means to reach higher rungs of the union leadership ladder, reasoning that once there, they could help women as a whole to make strides in the blue-collar sector.

Recent guidelines of the Equal Employment Opportunity Commission have almost obligated labor unions to support Title VII of the Civil Rights Act. On April 5, 1972, the commission issued guidelines holding that sex-oriented state employment laws, such as those requiring special rest and meal periods or physical facilities for women, are in violation of Title VII. An employer now is:

> deemed to have engaged in an unlawful employment practice if (i) it refuses to hire or otherwise adversely affects the employment opportunities of female applicants or employees in order to avoid provision of such benefits, (ii) it does not provide the same benefits for male employees.[2]

The Commission requires that to do otherwise the employer must prove that his business necessarily precludes extending these benefits to both. If so, it cannot provide them to either sex. Cases which involve interpretation of these guidelines are in the courts.

A number of national organizations other than labor unions currently subscribe to the view that the motivation for protecting child and female labor was more the protection and advancement of the male's status at work than a humanitarian attitude. The National Safety Council, for example, describes unreasonable statutory limitations and tacit unfair employment practices as a deliberate attempt to exclude the possibility that a large group of workers (women) may enter into competition with those already in the trade (men).[3]

Susan Deller Ross points out that the so-called protection of the state laws has been very uneven. Further:

> It is no accident that labor unions are often co-defendants with employers in suits charging sex discrimination under Title VII, since they engineer collective bargaining agreements which clearly dis criminate against their women members. In a number of recent cases the collective bargaining agreements reserved the highest paid jobs for men only. A few examples are illustrative of the way unions through adherence to State laws, or independent of these laws in collective bargaining agreements, have contributed to job discrimina-

tion. In one case an employer denied a woman's application for a job and gave it to men with less seniority because a union contract required two 10-minute rest periods for women....Such benefit laws hurt women by denying them job opportunities and hurt men by denying them the 'benefit.'[4]

Despite legal and contractual obligations imposed on the unions to provide equal treatment, women have turned to the Equal Employment Opportunity Commission rather than to their unions for redress of alleged grievances. Of approximately 400 such cases before the commission in 1970, the majority concerned seniority and layoff, rates of pay, demotions, and transfers.

Cases brought by the commission often involve adherence by the employer and the union to state laws which still restrict women's employment; for example, a case brought against National Venders, a division of U.M.D. Industries, and International Association of Machinists regarding overtime, in view of a Missouri state law which forbids women to work more than nine hours out of twenty-four.[5] Suits against company and union have become relatively frequent; while these generally refer to one state or region, they effectively introduced change in national practices of large firms and labor unions.

THE WOMEN'S MOVEMENT

In view of women's increasingly large role in the labor force, her small role in the labor movement is discouraging. Some 20 percent of AFL-CIO membership is female, but only a few women hold top-level jobs in American labor unions. Labor organizations—even those with the largest female membership—have few, if any, women in executive positions, and labor feminists consider these few a form of token representation.

In the areas of protective legislation and equal opportunity the interests of the women's liberation movement and women in the labor movement have begun to join. But it is a tenuous friendship, limited to shared interest in law as an instrumentality for change in women's job rights. Beyond this joining of forces over legislative issues, it is doubtful that the liberation movement will ever gain a large following among women blue-collar workers, whether or not they are union members.

The middle-income woman's interest in work as a career, or as a device for self-actualization, is something only remotely related to the blue-collar worker's interest in improvements to the quality of her work life. Further rapprochement between the two forces for change seems as yet very remote. But the liberation movement has had an important if only indirect effect on women in the labor movement, through the encouragement it has given to all women to accept themselves as capable and competent to engage in all action on all fronts.

Overtures to working-class women by the women's liberation movement still largely are met with rebuffs. Mistrust on both sides explains the rebuff, but there are other problems as well. Women in the middle-income group, who largely compose the liberation movement, have choices which working-class women do not have: to work or not to work, the kind of work, part-time or full-time work, to further her education and thus upgrade her occupational level, and so forth. Most women employed in blue-collar jobs have no choices; they work because they must do so. To them, many of the issues so important to the women's liberation movement seem removed and even frivolous compared with their own bread-and-butter issues.

The liberation movement is further separated from women union members by its frequent hostility to labor unions. Some of the recent court actions in behalf of women's job opportunities—brought by organizations affiliated with the liberation movement—have pitted the women plaintiffs against the employer *and* the union; and the unions repeatedly have been on the employer's side in such cases.

In a recent review of women in unions, Alice Cook claimed that unions are paying less attention to special problems of women now than sixty years ago, a time when the Trade Union League and the Labor Education Services held important places in the American labor movement. She noted too that women's pages in labor journals are almost exclusively devoted to consumer problems, recipes, and household hints.[6]

A few labor unions, on the other hand, have established women's departments with much wider concerns than those reflected in the labor journals. The most notable is that of the United Automobile Workers. While the Auto Workers "is an overwhelmingly male union, the 200,000 women members [in 1970] of the UAW exceed in number the total membership of many International Unions."[7] The union has an official position on women, recorded in convention proceedings. Its women's department has worked effectively and cooperatively with women in some of the organizations affiliated with the liberation movement. It is staffed by full-time paid workers; its first director now is a vice-president of the international, one of the few top-level union executive positions held by women in the United States. Through its women's department, the Auto Workers has been aggressive in the use of and support given to legal instrumentalities for women available through the offices of government. It has supported amendments to legislation which would extend coverage or otherwise improve conditions pertinent to all working women, not only its own members. It was in the vanguard of the battle to remove from state statutes the so-called protective laws for working women. Other international unions, the Electrical Workers (IUE) in particular, have also established women's departments which are beginning vigorously to pursue women's interests.

Some other labor unions—such as the International Ladies Garment Workers' Union, the Amalgamated Clothing Workers, and the Textile Workers—which have predominantly women members and which earlier had actively combatted discrimination, are relatively inactive in these areas.

Within the labor movement however, women union activists are on the move. The first state AFL-CIO women's conference was held in Wisconsin in March 1970. By the end of 1972, similar conferences had been held in Illinois, Arkansas, California, and Iowa,[8] and by several internationals, specifically the Auto Workers, Communications Workers, Electrical Workers (IUE), American Federation of Teachers, and American Newspaper Guild. The Wisconsin conference called attention to the small role women play in the labor movement. Emphasis was directed toward women becoming more aware of their rights under Title VII. By passage of resolutions, the conference recognized that:

> protective laws for women passed in 1900 may well have met the needs of the time, but today serve only to limit opportunity in employment for women and discriminate against both men and women.[9]

The conference went on record as favoring passage of the Equal Rights Amendment.

An organization called WAGE (Women's Alliance to Gain Equality) has been established among union women in California. In the summer of 1973, 200 women—rank-and-file members and staff and officers—representing twenty national and international unions in eighteen states met in Chicago to set the stage for a national meeting.[10] Similar regional meetings of union women on the East and West coasts were planned in preparation for the national conference. These women intend to pursue their organizational goals within the existing structure of the labor movement.[11] The Chicago conference moved cautiously. It passed no resolutions and established no policies. It perhaps was a second step, beyond the state conferences, to gain access to top leadership positions and thus to more effective representation of women's interests through labor union organization.

NOTES

Reprinted with permission from *Monthly Labor* Review, May 1940.

Note: More recent data from the Bureau of Labor Statistics biennial report on membership in labor unions and employee associations indicates that the proportion of working women who were union members was the same in 1972 as in 1970, despite the increase in the number of working women. More detailed information is presented in the BLS Bulletin, *Directory of National Unions and Employee Associations, 1973.*

1. *Labor Union Membership in 1966.* Current Population Reports, P-20, no. 216 (Bureau of the Census, 1971); *Selected Earnings and Demographic Characteristics of Union Members, 1970,* Report 417 (Bureau of Labor Statistics, 1972); *Directory of National Unions and Employee Associations,* 1971, Bulletin 1750 (Bureau of Labor Statistics, 1972).

2. *Guidelines on Discrimination Because of Sex,* Part 1604 (Washington: Equal Employment Opportunity Commission, Office of the General Counsel, 1972).

3. "Sex Discrimination in Private Employment: The Conflict Between the Civil Rights Act of 1964 and State Labor Laws for Women," an advanced study project in industrial relations for the degree of Master of Business Administration, 1967; quoted in Susan Deller Ross, *Sex Discrimination and "Protective" Labor Legislation* (New York: New York University Law School, 1970).

4. Ross, *Sex Discrimination and "Protective" Labor Legislation.*

5. *Daily Labor Report,* June 5, 1972.

6. Alice Cook, "Women and American Trade Unions," *Annals* (January 1968): 124-32.

7. Dorothy Haener, "What Labor is Doing About Women in the Work Force," in Mildred E. Katzell and William C. Byham, eds., *Women in the Work Force* (New York: Behavioral Publications, 1972), p. 44.

8. "Women Workers: Gaining Power, Seeking More," *U.S. News and World Report,* Nov. 13, 1972.

9. Proceedings, Women's Conference, Labor Temple, Wisconsin Rapids, Wis., Mar. 7, 1970.

10. *AFL-CIO Federation News,* July 1973.

11. In late March 1974, more than 3,000 women members of 58 unions voted into existence a national organization to work for women's rights within the trade-union movement. The Coalition of Labor Union Women (CLUW) will be headed by Olga Mader, a vice-president of the United Automobile Workers, with Addie Wyatt, director of women's affairs for the Amalgamated Meat Cutters and Butcher Workers Union, as vice-president.

     Among the organization's stated objectives are increased union efforts to organize women workers; increased participation of women in union affairs, particularly in policymaking positions; positive action by unions against sex discrimination in pay, hiring, job classification, and promotion; support of legislation to provide adequate child care facilities, a "livable" minimum wage, improved medical and pension benefits, improved health and safety laws, and better enforcement of these laws; and mass action in behalf of ratification of the Equal Rights Amendment and for legislation to extend to all workers the protection of statutes originally aimed at protecting women, such as maximum-hours limitations, breaks in the workday, and seating of workers.

     A critical problem left unresolved is whether membership should be limited to women union members or opened to other women who work. This and other organizational problems are under study by a national coordinating committee of over 200 members and a 25-member steering committee.

7

Blue-Collar Women in Low-Wage Industries: A Dual Labor Market Interpretation[1]

Robert Bibb

Over the past decade, social scientists have attempted to discern what, if any, substantive changes have occurred in the relative socioeconomic position of women. That women continue to suffer harsh disprivileges throughout the class structure is by now widely recognized. Yet sociologists have been preoccupied with documenting structured sex discrimination in the professions, particularly in academe[2] and have neglected discrimination in the larger population of working-class women in the industrial labor force. This paper argues that a sexually stratified dual labor market exists for substantial numbers of women in the low-wage sector of manufacturing.

Although the gap in economic rewards accruing to men and women varies by major occupational group, it is greater for women in the lower status blue-collar slots. While the gap among full-time year-around professional and technical workers stood at 67 percent in 1970, the median wage income of full-time year-around women operatives amounted to about 59 percent of the yearly income of male operatives, i.e., $4,510 as compared to $7,632.[3] A recent study in Oregon discovered that "depressed occupational areas," including unskilled and semiskilled operatives in low-wage industries, have significantly more women saddled with the additional responsibilities of supporting dependents single-handedly.[4]

It is well known that women perform a disproportionate share of menial labor in the service industries as, for example, domestics laundresses, and personal service workers. Although the manufacturing sector is thought to offer better economic opportunities, the thesis of this paper is that women workers in this area operate in a different market than men, and that those industries which attract female labor form the rock-bottom rungs of manufacturing. Thus, although women workers in factory jobs occupy essentially a "middle stratum" between men in manufacturing and workers in less desirable service jobs, even in this industrial sector the dual labor market phenomenon endures. I will argue that even where conditions are relatively favorable in the manufacturing sector, women occupy a special estate and suffer multiple discrimination—discrimination imposed by the market position of the industry and discrimination resulting from women's special lower status.[5]

Dual labor market theory has not confronted these problems. It has appeared primarily in the radical economics literature dealing with discrimination against other sectors of the labor force, notably urban blacks.[6] These studies have been largely limited to descriptions of different markets, their effects on individuals, and implications for manpower policies. A sociological emphasis explaining the articulation of market sectors with other, nonmarket institutions has been conspicuously absent in this literature. This paper addresses, from the sociologist's point of view, important questions dealing with the intersection of market forces, organizational power, social recruitment processes, and nonlabor market forms of discrimination. I shall first review dual labor market theory, subsequently applying important concepts from this perspective to the particular situation of women workers in manufacturing. Second, the inadequacy of marginal productivity explanations for sex discrimination in industry will be discussed. Third, I shall show that segmented labor markets described by the economists can be explained by referring to the structural location of low-wage industries, the male supremacist character of labor unions, and sex discrimination outside the economy. Finally, I will say something about the impact of recent federal legislation aimed at reducing discriminatory barriers which confine women in manufacturing to low-wage jobs.

DUAL LABOR MARKET PERSPECTIVE

The dual labor market perspective in blue-collar employment suggests that opportunities do not form a graded continuum of jobs uniformly accessible to equally qualified workers. Rather, it posits the existence of two essentially distinct job structures and corresponding labor markets, one providing employment chiefly for white male workers, another catering to blacks and other minorities.

Piore has identified six attributes which differentiate primary from secondary industries and around which the dual labor market has been elaborated. Among other things, primary workers—predominantly males—enjoy (1) high wages, (2) good working conditions, (3) employment stability, (4) equity and due process in the administration of work rules, (5) opportunities for advancement, and most importantly, (6) union organization.[7]

As a paradigm for the analysis of modern productive relationships, the dual labor market thesis has been cogently applied in explaining the persistence of racial discrimination in industry.[8] Baron and Hymer, for instance, drawing upon a recent study of black workers in Chicago, have contended that de facto barriers exist which effectively bifurcate the labor market into racially distinct compartments.[9] They argue that, in particular, (1) firms are cognizant of this division and have different conceptions of the two labor forces when they shop for labor; (2) when shortages of white labor periodically occur, the black labor force typically provides a pool of surplus workers; (3) the existence of segregation in nonlabor market institutions effectively reinforces the segmentation of the labor market into black and white sectors.

The authors believe not only that firms recruit employees on the basis of a dual labor market structure, but that workers themselves have been conditioned to seek out employment in segregated areas, the result of which is that blacks tend to be hired by particular industries and by a definite number of firms within these industries. Furthermore, within any given establishment, segregation can occur on the basis of production units, work sites, or occupational classification. The dual market system is ultimately self-perpetuating in the sense that different patterns of *job seeking* becomes typified responses to discriminatory patterns in the total labor force, i.e., "black job seekers expect automatic rebuff outside of the identified Negro job market".[10] The persistence of a dual labor market is further guaranteed by the fact that minimum wage employers ordinarily fill vacancies by informally soliciting labor among friends and relatives of their employees. Or, less informally, employment agencies, both public and private, often place prospective workers on the basis of a split market.

The principal mechanism, then, by means of which a segmented labor market maintains itself is discrimination.[11] Discriminatory barriers that make movement from the low-wage to the high-wage sectors difficult or impossible perpetuate the "crowding" of minorities into the lowest economic rungs.[12] Major beneficiaries of labor market segmentation and discrimination in the economy include (1) employers in marginal industries who, confronting a swollen captive labor force, are able to pay lower wages than otherwise; (2) organized white male workers, especially in the skilled trades, who enjoy relatively higher wages than otherwise, given a restricted supply of labor in the primary sector;[13] (3) primary employers who, even though paying somewhat higher labor bills, are favored by reduced costs entailed in personnel procedures and applicant screening.

More broadly, the secondary labor market fulfills several critical functions for the primary sector of the economy. First, the existence of a substantial and experienced low-wage labor force makes possible the absorption and rapid deployment of large numbers of workers to areas in the primary sector requiring immediate manpower resources. Industrial expansion during periods of exceptional economic growth, effected by either augmenting existing lines of production or by diverting capital to new product markets, can thus be achieved without impairing the scale of labor resources in other primary spheres. Conversely, during periods of labor market "loosening," the low-wage sector provides a reservoir for the absorption of workers expelled from the primary sector and for individuals unable to obtain decent jobs.

Secondly, the low-wage labor market and its associated industries provide primary firms with innumerable services, products, and materials of production at relatively cheap prices.[14] Frequently, the continued existence of a marginal industry depends upon regularly forthcoming subcontracts from larger enterprises which find the particular activity relatively unprofitable though necessary.[15]

Exceptional capital intensiveness and productivity in the high-wage sector results in the condemnation of one part of the working class to the minimum-wage labor market. The swelling of the secondary sector, and of the industrial labor reserve generally, in turn, exerts pressure on workers in adequate wage industries to sustain increasing productivity in their sector. In this way, the reproduction of the low-wage labor force keeps pace with the advance of social accumulation.[16]

In summary, dual labor market theory contends that workers do not compete to sell their labor power in one market. Discrimination operates to produce distinct but functionally symbiotic labor market segments which variously disprivilege and economically benefit particular groups and individuals.

WOMEN IN BLUE-COLLAR MANUFACTURING JOBS

Women constitute two-fifths of the industrial blue-collar labor force; nearly one-fifth of all women who work are either laborers, operatives, or craftspersons in industry.[17] This is more than the proportion of women who are service workers (16 percent) but substantially less than the proportion of women workers in clerical jobs (34 percent). The percent of female employees in blue-collar jobs fluctuates greatly. For instance, between 1964 and 1968, women in manufacturing industries increased by nearly 21 percent. Yet, overall, the proportion of women in blue-collar manufacturing occupations has been steadily shrinking, although it still constitutes a sizable category. Among employed married women with husbands present, 27 percent were in such occupations in 1947. By 1967, their proportion had fallen to 19 percent.[18] Still, some industries have experienced a rate of increase in blue-collar female employment greater than that for men. Operatives and kindred workers in the manufacturing of miscellaneous wood products, cutlery and hand tools, and hardware are increasingly likely to be females, as are those in canning, meat packing, and primary nonferrous metals.

Although women are almost as likely as men to be factory workers, they are almost never employed as skilled craftsworkers, while one out of five men are.[19] Blue-collar women, unlike their male counterparts, seem to be confined to semiskilled labor, irrespective of their educational attainment (see Table 1.) Males in blue-collar occupations are somewhat more likely to be in better-paying craft jobs than in operative categories when they have completed high school, and nearly as likely if they have not. Women, conversely, are overwhelmingly operatives, irrespective of high school certification.

TABLE 1
Skill Distribution of Blue-Collar Workers by Education and Sex, 1970
(percent)

| | High School | | | |
| | 1-3 years | | 4 years | |
Occupation Group	Men	Women	Men	Women
Craftpersons	40.8	9.0	50.5	12.8
Operatives	43.5	84.9	39.4	81.5
Laborers, nonfarm	15.7	6.1	10.1	5.7

Source: U.S. Department of Labor, Women's Bureau, "The Economic Role of Women." p. 102, Table 27.

Over three-fourths of all female operatives were employed on a full-time, full-term basis in 1967. Yet full-timers earned just under 60 percent of men's incomes in the same category. Moreover, the earnings differential between full-schedule male and female operatives tends to widen throughout much of the work life.[20] Unemployment is another liability associated with blue-collar work; operative and industrial laborer categories reflect the highest female unemployment rates, 8.2 percent and 14.3 percent, respectively.[21] Further, unemployment data on blue-collar women do not report the larger patterns of underemployment and the submergence of women back into the home situation.

SEXUALLY BASED WAGE DIFFERENTIALS: THE MARGINALIST POSITION

Various theories have been advanced to explain or otherwise justify the existence of male-female earnings differentials in industry, the most widely accepted of which alleges that the marginal productivities of women and other low-income workers is deficient relative to that of better paid white male workers.[22] According to this view, employers will continue to increase wages as long as the marginal cost of labor is less than the value of what the workers contribute to total revenue. In the extreme, marginalists assert that, *ceteris paribus,* the distribution of wages is isomorphic with a ranking of productivity components like ability, education, and experience. Thus, Thurow says, "the distribution of marginal products is identical with the distribution of earned income."[23]

Other economists have conceded that the marginal productivity of women workers, black workers, or any other particular work force is linearly dependent upon the stock of reproducible capital in the employer's possession, the character of raw materials, the level of technology, and the skill and training of the labor force—generally in that order.[24] In addition, marginalists cite, as a *residual* cause of income differences, differential prices paid in different employments for units of any given labor resource. These are said to arise from either interferences with the price system or resource immobility or both.[25] Typically, however, when accounting for obvious wage discrimination with respect to sex, only skills and other human capital determinants are explicitly stressed. Thus, inadequate marginal productivity is not seen to be structured into the characteristics of the work role or particular industry, but rather attaches to the individual woman worker herself, to the types and extent of human capital she brings to bear in the work process.[26] Neoclassical economic theory, as in the case of urban blacks, holds working-class women personally responsible for perpetuating the wage discrimination under which they labor. Applied to racially based ghetto employment problems, it was a marginal productivity human capital approach, with its emphasis on the personal characteristics of the poor themselves, which informed most of the ill-fated MDTA antipoverty programs prior to 1973.

Marginal productivity notions run into rocky empirical shoals.[27] It is more reasonable to suppose that workers' incomes and statuses do not uniformly reflect their productivities, particularly in the low-wage labor market where a majority of blue-collar women operatives are found.[28] While some part of the wage differential between male and female blue-collar labor undoubtedly reflects the fact that women are customarily assigned employment in low-skilled, low-paying jobs, it is equally true that when skill categories are commensurable, women workers are still paid substantially less.

Thus, in the manufacturing of men's and boy's suits, women routinely work as hand finishers and sewing machine operators at an average hourly rate less than $2.70 while male finish pressers and cutters earn from $3.50 to $4.25.[29] Yet the amount of human capital required in performing the "women's jobs" in this industry—as gauged by length of traineeship—is as great or greater than that required of male employees. Education, as another human capital input, does not differ substantially by sex among factory workers either.[30] An Oregon Bureau of Labor survey discovered that 82 percent of women with dependents who were employed as factory workers were high school graduates.[31] Nationally, the median educational attainment for female operatives approximates that of male operatives and for craftsworkers is somewhat higher.[32]

Apologists for the marginal productivity perspective often argue that sex-determined wage differentials merely reflect women's sporadic attachment to the labor force, their lack of cumulative experience, and thus, *long-term* human capital relative to men. Yet even among women who have worked continuously since leaving school, a sizable gap is evident, pointing toward direct discrimination. After assessing the relative significance of numerous factors reputed to produce this wage differential, the 1973 Economic Report of the President concluded that: "A differential, perhaps on the order of 20 percent between the earnings of men and women remains after adjusting for factors such as education, work experience during the year, and even lifelong work experience."[33]

Marginal productivity explanations generally insist, in addition, that discrimination in industry, whether racial or sexual in nature, represents a monetary loss for the employer, in the sense of diminishing efficiency, yet privileges white male workers as a group.[34] By extension, male workers are seen to be responsible for crowding blue-collar women into the low-wage labor market. The employer, conversely, is pictured as either (1) concerned about the circumstances of female employees but unable to act in the face of working-class male chauvinism and restrictive union policies or (2) willing to pay for discrimination—as a "luxury tax"—because he likes it.[35]

That short-run economic benefits, resulting from segregated labor markets, have accrued to organized craftworkers cannot be denied. Unions of skilled workers have traditionally influenced the economic opportunities of minorities in a negative way through exclusion by formal and informal means, by maintaining segregated locals, by upholding discrimination in the building trades, by job referral systems, and so on. Various writers have documented the persistence of widespread exclusionary practices among local skilled trade unions.[36] With these studies in mind, Bergmann attempted to estimate the economic consequences of discrimination to primary employers and to workers of both races. She determined that the crowding of Negroes into a small number of menial occupations produces modest, yet real, wage gains for white craftworkers—perhaps on the order of ten percent.[37]

However, with respect to industrial-type unions, the ability of labor representatives to exclude women is somewhat more difficult to demonstrate. That discriminatory practices result more from the demands of industrial unions than from employer-initiated hiring policies is questionable. On the one hand, sexual exclusion can strengthen union bargaining power when occupational entry is constrained and valued skills controlled. Industrial unions, generally, have not been able to substantially monopolize skilled labor resources. Still, it can be argued that certain contractual arrangements fostered by industrial unions—say, seniority, nightshift work, and providing overtime in lieu of hiring extra help—have discriminatory implications with respect to women. The resolution of this issue awaits further evidence. While the short-run consequences of sexually segmented labor markets may mean monetary loss for an individual primary employer and somewhat higher wages for his workers, in the following section it is contended that the long-term results point toward a strengthening of the employing class as a whole.

BENEFICIARIES OF SEXUALLY SEGMENTED LABOR MARKETS: AN ALTERNATIVE VIEW

The dual labor market thesis has been brought forth in opposition to the notion that unemployment and low wages are a function of the characteristics of the working poor. Recently reformulated by Doeringer and Piore,[38] dual labor market theory denies that the types and extent of human capital workers bring to bear in industry crucially affect their economic destinies. Instead, the authors argue that low-wage workers are often artifically confined to the secondary labor market precisely because they have economic value there: discrimination swells the labor force that is restricted to the low-wage sector, thus reducing the wages secondary employers must pay in order to maintain a work force.[39] The existence of a marginal sector, moreover, produces an alleged dampening effect on the wage demands of organized primary workers in two ways: first, by posing the realistic threat of replacement, and secondly, by providing a comparative reference group which serves to convince better paid workers that their objective conditions are indeed enviable. The dual labor market stands as an institutionalized set of productive relations which function to guarantee higher profits for the managerial class taken as a whole.[40]

The blue collar labor market is segmented and hierarchically structured along yet another axis, namely, with respect to sex. Blue-collar women, most of whom are employed in the secondary sector, are accustomed to poverty-level wages, hazardous conditions, authoritarian or paternalistic supervision, and open shops. Often, they recognize that certain industries, and particular firms within them, hire almost exclusively female labor while other enterprises hire males for similar work at vastly greater wage rates. Thus, working class women tend to seek employment in a relatively bounded, sexually segregated network of blue-collar occupations and industries typified by poverty-level wages.

Thirty-nine percent of the working poor are women engaged in blue-collar industrial jobs.[41] Women disproportionately staff the assembly lines and shop floors of the low-wage "secondary" sector of industry while white males are overwhelmingly located in the "primary" sector. Goldberg and others suggest that the economic exploitation of blue-collar women is functionally analogous to race discrimination, in the sense that both jeopardize the bargaining strength of the working class as a whole, eventuating in low wage structures.[42] She contends that women, like blacks, have been used perennially as a marginal work force to smooth over cycles in the economy. Typically, working-class women are recruited under conditions of labor scarcity and expelled when alternate sources of cheap labor are plentiful. Minimum wage employers have dealt with women as a greatly flexible and readily available labor pool willing to work for cheap wages.

That women, like blacks, have come to fulfill an important role in supporting particularly marginal industries, is suggested by data in Table 2, which compares labor force sex composition and wage structures for eleven major industries. Almost without exception, industries with disproportionately female work force are overwhelmingly low-wage industries. Conversely, where women comprise only a small fraction of the total labor force—notably, iron and steel, pulp and paper, and auto parts—are unlikely to be low-wage employers. A product-moment correlation of .89 summarizes the association between sex composition and wage structure obtaining in these eleven industries.

TABLE 2
Percent Low-Wage Employment and Sex Composition of Labor Force in Selected Industries, 1961-66

Industry	Year	Male Employment	Female Employment	Percent Low-Wage*
Work Clothing	1961	6,134	45,460	77.1
Laundries	1963	96,744	322,139	75.4
Cotton Textiles	1965	136,641	82,836	35.1
Wood Furniture	1965	106,810	13,190	48.1
Footwear	1965	70,597	103,206	50.6
Structural Clay Products	1964	47,577	3,747	20.8
Meat Packing	1963	114,770	17,195	10.0
Motor Vehicle Parts	1963	151,756	34,928	6.1
Paints and Varnishes	1965	24,684	1,463	4.7
Iron and Steel Foundries	1962	151,071	1,857	2.2
Pulp and Paper	1962	160,614	6,155	2.4

*Average hourly wage below $2.25   r = .89

Source: Barry Bluestone, "Lower Income Workers in Marginal Industries," in Ferman et al., Poverty in America, pp. 288, 290, Table 5.

Unionization appears to be one of the crucial explanatory variables in this situation. Industries in which women constitute a sizable portion of the shop-level work force are, with the exception of clothing and apparel, less likely to be organized than industries having a negligible female labor force. An inverse relationship obtains between proportion female work force and extent of unionization across census classified industry groups, a pattern typified by the leather and leather products industry (see Table 3).

If only industries in which unionized women workers predominate are considered, the expansion of the blue-collar female work force has not been accompanied by an expansion in union membership. For instance, from 1958 to 1968 in the clothing industry, increases in the female labor force have been six times as great as increases in female union membership.[43] Where unions have not penetrated and where women make up a majority of the work force, men are frequently paid more than women performing similar or identical work. Thus, the average hourly earnings of women in the raw textile industry in 1965 amounted to $1.63. Men averaged $1.82. Discrepancies by sex were evident in *all* intraindustry job categories.[44] By region, the average hourly differences were: Southeast 16 cents; New England, 25 cents; and Mid-Atlantic, 36 cents.

TABLE 3
Women as a Percent of Manufacturing Labor Force and Extent of Union Organization by Industry, 1968

Industry group	Women as percent of labor force	Extent of Unionization %	Rank
Ordinance and accessories	26	75 and over	1
Food and kindred products	25	50-75	5
Tobacco manufacturers	45	50-75	6
Textile mill products	45	Below 25	19
Apparel and fabrics	80	50-75	14
Lumber and wood products	10	50-75	7
Furniture and fixtures	23	25-50	15
Paper and allied products	22	75 and over	2
Printing and publishing	31	50-75	8
Chemicals and allied products	20	50-75	9
Petroleum refining	9	75 and over	3
Rubber and plastics	32	50-75	10
Leather and leather products	56	25-50	16
Stone, clay, glass products	16	50-75	11
Primary metal industries	7	50-75	12
Fabricated metal industries	18	25-50	17
Electrical machinery, equipment	40	50-75	13
Transportation equipment	11	75 and over	4
Scientific, professional instruments	36	25-50	18
Miscellaneous Manufacturing	45	Below 25	20

Spearman's rank-order correlation = .489

Source: Lucretia M. Dewey, "Women in Labor Unions," Monthly Labor Review 94 (February, 1971): 45, Table 4.

Even more discrepant are the average hourly earnings of female operatives in the women's and misses' dress industry for eleven major metropolitan areas (see Table 4). In Dallas, 38 percent of full-time female dress industry employees earned hourly rates below the minimum wage prevailing at that time, that is $1.40.[45]

TABLE 4
Average Hourly Earnings in the Women's and Misses' Dress Industry, by Sex for Eleven Metropolitan Areas, 1966

Metropolitan area	Average Hourly Earnings	
	Women	Men
Boston	$2.05	$3.44
Chicago	1.94	2.86
Dallas	1.60	1.88
Fall-River, New Bedford	1.97	2.16
Los Angeles and Vicinty	2.07	2.84
Newark, New Jersey	2.30	3.01
New York City	2.46	3.50
Patterson, N.J. and Vicinity	2.30	4.19
Philadelphia	2.08	2.70
St. Louis	2.00	2.64
Wilkes-Barre, Hazelton	1.88	2.01

Source: U.S. Department of Labor, Women's Bureau, Handbook on Women Workers 1969, p. 152, Table 68.

One would think that working-class women would increasingly eschew poverty wage factory work. Yet, Seifer maintains that as more women enter the labor force and as work itself becomes increasingly automated, competition for low-skilled low-wage employment has been intensified, with the result of higher levels of unemployment and lower wage increases.[46] Accordingly, in August, 1973, while 4 percent of all blue-collar men were unemployed, women in blue-collar jobs recorded a 7.1 percent unemployment rate,[47] a differential which has widened uniformly through-out the 1960s. In Oregon, blue-collar working women with dependents holding down full-time jobs (90 percent do) had a median monthly income in 1968 amounting to only $283.40 or about $3,400 annually.[48] Nearly half of these women earned less than $250 per month and a fifth earned wages so low they required public welfare as a source of additional income.

Presumably, Oregon women, like blue-collar women elsewhere, continue to work because the alternative of public assistance is an even worse fate.[49] Employer demand is often predicated upon the cheapness and availability of female labor, two of the principal factors promoting the development and persistence of sexually segmented labor markets and segregated jobs within industries.

Illustrative in this respect is Grace Hutchins's classic investigation of wage differentials paid to men and women in identical manufacturing occupations.[50] The author estimated that for 1950, "extra profits" coming from the output of women at lower pay rates formed nearly a quarter (23 percent) of the *total* U.S. manufacturing company profits. On the women's jobs in the electrical industry, she found that companies made a profit 70 percent greater than from the plants where few women were employed. At General Electric skilled female assemblers were paid less than male floor sweepers.

In industries hiring large numbers of new female production workers, the jobs and wages of male employees are often higher than those paid to women doing the same jobs. Thus, Hutchins discovered that at Westinghouse's East Pittsburgh plant, women were assigned to jobs at $1.30 an hour which were formerly performed by men at $1.50.[51] In numerous industries, the process of expanding the female blue-collar work force vis-à-vis men continues to be a strategic management policy for keeping down male wage increases and upholding profits. In Table 5, I compare the percent increase in the female labor force with percent increase in average hourly wages among operatives in the U.S. Census's twenty major industry groupings for the decade 1960-70. A product-moment correlation of −.606 obtains between wage gains and increases in female staff. Industries recording only nominal female labor force expansions reached or exceeded median yearly wage hikes throughout the ten-year period. In fact, two industries which decreased their relative proportions of women workers experienced the most dramatic wage increases. On the other hand, many industries whose female staff expanded by 60 percent or more witnessed only meager hourly wage gains, generally less than 50 percent, increments which, by virtue of inflation over the last decade, actually represent a reduced standard of living for the recipients. To arrive at an adequate sociological understanding of these relationships, however, requires that we now deal with the structural location of those industries which disproportionately hire females.

only meager hourly wage gains, generally less than 50 percent, increments which, by virtue of inflation over the last decade, actually represent a reduced standard of living for the recipients. To arrive at an adequate sociological understanding of these relationships, however, requires that we now deal with the structural location of those industries which disproportionately hire females.

CHARACTERISTICS OF MINIMUM WAGE INDUSTRIES: STRUCTURE AND EFFECTS

Piore emphasizes that the distinction between primary and secondary jobs is not necessarily based on technological differences: "Work normally performed in the primary sector is often shifted to the secondary through subcontracting, temporary help services, and the recycling of employees."[52] In general, however, low-wage industries *are* technologically less developed, even though they may require skills similar to workers in primary industries.

Average hourly wages in the secondary sector have generally lagged behind those provided in the primary sector, and the wage gap has widened over the last decade.[53] For most marginal industries, it does not seem that an increasing labor demand reflects a rise in wages offered, as neoclassical economics would have us believe. Bluestone has argued that—particularly in apparel, furniture, and fixtures—substantial advances in employment have occurred while poverty wage scales were retained. Parenthetically, the percentage of female workers in the category "furniture and fixtures" has nearly doubled over the past ten years (see Table 5).

Similarly, that meager wages are a function of low productivity seems to be a questionable assertion. Overall, marginal industries have been characterized by productivity *gains* consistent with those elsewhere in industry, yet wage increases have not kept abreast either absolutely *or* relatively.[54]

Whether the increasing discrepancy between productivity and wages reflects an intensification of exploitation in marginal industries remains an unresolved issue. Tyler suggests that it does not, since the high degree of competitiveness in the secondary sector prompts a general lowering of prices rather than escalating profits.[55] Big, oligopolistic industries, operating under a system of "administered prices," can and do pass on increased labor costs to the consumer.[56] A comparison between size of firm and profitability, represented in Table 6, lends support to this argument. Marginal industries which, by definition, are relatively insubstantial in terms of combined capital assets, are characterize by depressed profit rates generally.

The connection between corporate size and the ability of a firm to capture a substantial share of its product-market is intuitively obvious.

TABLE 5
Women Operatives in Experienced Blue-Collar Labor Force and Average Hourly Wage Rates, 1960 and 1970 (full-time, full-term workers)

Manufacturing Group	Percent female*			Average hourly wages**		
	1960	1970	% increase	1960	1970	% increase
Ordinance and accessories	16.4	26.0	58.2	$2.60	$3.61	38.8
Food and kindred products	31.5	34.8	10.0	2.02	3.16	56.4
Tobacco manufacturers	54.9	51.6	-6.0	1.67	2.92	74.9
Textile mill products	53.2	54.8	3.0	1.56	2.45	57.1
Apparel and fabrics	74.0	75.5	2.0	1.56	2.39	53.2
Lumber and wood products	11.4	15.1	32.5	1.82	2.96	62.6
Furniture and fixtures	15.6	28.1	80.0	1.82	2.77	52.2
Paper and allied products	25.5	23.7	-7.1	2.15	3.44	60.0
Printing and publishing	42.5	45.5	7.3	NA	3.92	NA
Chemicals	12.4	17.0	37.1	2.43	3.69	51.9
Petroleum refining, etc.	5.6	9.0	60.1	2.82	4.28	51.8
Rubber and plastics	26.4	35.1	33.0	2.26	3.20	41.6
Leather, leather products	43.9	57.6	31.2	1.61	2.49	54.7
Stone, clay, glass	15.1	18.7	23.8	2.20	3.40	54.5
Primary metal industries	3.8	7.1	86.8	2.75	3.93	42.9
Fabricated metal products	19.7	22.9	16.2	2.36	3.53	49.6
Machinery, except electric	11.8	16.0	35.6	2.47	3.77	52.6
Electrical equipment	18.3	32.7	78.7	2.23	3.28	47.1
Transportation equipment	10.7	16.1	50.5	2.65	4.06	53.2
Instruments, etc.	42.6	48.8	14.6	2.26	3.35	48.2

$r = -.606$

* Source: U.S. Department of Labor, Women's Bureau, "The Economic Role of Women;" reprinted from Economic Report of the President 1973, pp. 157-158.

** Source: "Current Labor Statistics;" Monthly Labor Review, 84, July, 1961 and 94, July, 1971.

Low-wage industries which lack capital are unable to achieve economies of scale in production comparable to those enjoyed by larger establishments, and they are subject to raging market competition. In turn, profit as a proportion of equity is directly related to the degree of oligopoly within

TABLE 6
Profit Rates by Corporate Size for all Corporations, 1961

Asset class (lower limit)	Profit Rate*
$ 0	1.4%
50,000	6.4
100,000	8.2
500,000	9.5
1,000,000	9.5
2,500,000	10.5
5,000,000	10.6
10,000,000	11.1
25,000,000	11.1
50,000,000	11.7
100,000,000	11.3
250,000,000	11.6

*Profit before taxes divided by equity.

Source: U.S. Treasury Department, Internal Revenue Service, Statistics of Income, Corporation Income Tax Returns for 1961-62.

manufacturing sectors. Thus, Table 7 depicts a strong positive association between profitability and concentration among twenty major industrial groupings. And if data from Table 7 are assessed in relation to the relative size of the female work forces within these industries, correlation coefficients can be estimated between percent female and profit rate ($r = -.37$) and between percent female and the index of industrial concentration ($r = -.58$).

These associations immediately point toward a syndrome of interlocking traits surrounding the low-wage, marginal industries: meager capital assets, intense market competition, limited profit capability, and disproportionately female labor forces. This characterization suggests that working-class women in the marginal sector are not paid inadequate wages because they "deserve" no better, nor even because secondary employers are unusually exploitative (the profit picture in these industries would suggest they are not). Instead, poverty-level wage rates are a direct consequence of the marginal firm's precarious structural location in the economy. Saddled with even modestly higher labor bills, it is questionable

TABLE 7
Profit Rates and Concentration Ratios by Industry Group for All Manufacturing Corporations in 1954

Industry group	Concentration ratio*	Profit rate**
Motor vehicles and parts	98.1	27.1
Tobbacco	91.5	20.3
Transportation equipment	75.6	29.8
Rubber	74.2	17.8
Primary metal	70.8	13.0
Chemicals	63.3	19.9
Electrical machinery	60.8	20.7
Petroleum and coal	57.7	7.7
Instruments	56.1	23.9
Stone, clay, glass products	55.0	19.9
Food and beverages	45.7	14.4
Machinery, except electrical	44.4	16.2
Fabricated metal	40.3	15.6
Paper	39.4	17.3
Textile mill products	37.1	5.1
Leather, leather products	33.7	11.4
Furniture and fixtures	23.8	12.8
Printing and publishing	21.5	15.1
Apparel and fabrics	20.5	7.6
Lumber and wood products	15.5	12.2

r = .655

* Percent of sales by eight largest sellers.

** Profit before taxes divided by stockholders' capital

Source: Howard Sherman, <u>Profit Rates in the United States</u>. p. 85.

r between profit rate and % female = -.370
r between % female and degree of oligopoly = -.584

whether many of these establishments could in fact survive. The entrapment of women and other minorities serves to prolong the survival of inefficient and "infirm" industries.

A continual supply of inexpensive labor and, hence, a reprieve from likely financial dissolution is provided by the presence of an industrial reserve army. The inability of high-wage capital intensive primary industries to absorb all individuals compelled to sell their labor power stands behind the generation of this human productive factor. By no means have the tremendous output increases in the mass production industries been accompanied by increases in their blue-collar work forces. The maintenance of public welfare standards ordinarily below officially defined poverty thresholds assures that at least some portion of the industrial surplus population will seek out minimum wage employment.[57]

That women are disproportionately found in the low-wage industries does not arise from employer preferences. The sex composition of the work force is essentially a matter of indifference. Rather, it results from (1) direct market discrimination in the primary sector and (2) other nonlabor market sexual discrimination which produces differential mobility potentials between men and women workers. Concerning the first, the exclusion of females from many jobs in the primary sector and their crowding into a comparatively small number of industrial occupations results in a general depression of wage rates for blue-collar women. Second, resource immobility, a notion familiar to classical economic theory, suggests that women are much more captive geographically than men.[58] Men can and do move to take better jobs, while women are frequently tied to a geographic area, usually of some male's choosing. In this way, a relative "oversupply" of female labor is frequently created. In short, low-wage industries do not persist primarily because women and other minorities are available. They would likely persist as long as an industrial surplus population is present, whatever race or sex composition predominates. Discrimination, however, insures that these industries *will* be staffed by minorities.

In general, the effects of resource immobility in facilitating labor force segmentation are most pronounced under conditions of labor market "loosening." Yet even when labor is scarce, this phenomenon will appear because the rest of the market is so organized that it assures a "free" market for small business people, marginal industrialists, and their employees.

For primary industries operating under monopolistic competition, survival depends upon expanding sales, not on cutting expenses. Big firms in the same industry realize mutual threats when each attempts to expand in the same product markets. Thus, product diversification has evolved as a principal interfirm organizational mechanism for suppressing ruinous competition and transferring the brunt of market forces to the secondary sector. Frequently, big firm diversifications increase competitive relations among secondary industries threatened by possible primary firm intrusion.

Marginal employers lack economies of scale in technology and organization to diversify; instead they are left to compete in narrowing product areas which primary employers choose to ignore.

Vertical integration is another primary sector organizational strategy employed by firms attempting to control their economic environments. Organizing factor suppliers and product distributors through interlocking directorates, satellite control, or outright ownership provide increased security for big corporations, allowing (1) shifts in technical, managerial, and marketing resources to new product expansion during periods of economic growth and (2) capital-for-labor factor substitution when "tight" labor markets persist. Even in the short run, monopolistic pricing power means that primary industries can extend substantial wage increases without laying off workers.[59] Often secondary industries, to the extent that they rely upon means of production supplied by oligopolistic corporations, bear the brunt of administered prices like other consumers. In short, primary firms can and do collude to control their economic environments, and these maneuvers render even more problematic the environment within which marginal employers operate.

These variables—noneconomic sexual subordination, low social and legal income minima, and the differential market organization of primary and secondary firms—have received scant attention by sociologists and labor economists. What I have contended is that the failure of secondary employers to pay women higher wages cannot adequately be explained exclusively on the basis of "normal" supply and demand functions, low marginal productivity, or still less, the personal attributes of blue-collar women. In large measure, low pay results from the structural location of industries in an economic system characterized by differing degrees of interfirm organization. Minimum wage employers, like the women who work for them, confront different economic environments than do high-wage employers and workers.

BLUE-COLLAR WOMEN AND THE UNIONS

Unions are environmental features encountered by primary industries. Blue-collar women in the secondary sector of the dual labor market are, however, typically unorganized. While 40 percent of the adult work force is composed of females, less than 18 percent of all union members are women.[60] Moreover, the increase in female membership has not kept pace with the growth of the female blue-collar labor force in manufacturing. In 1966, there were 107 national unions in which women's membership ranged from none to less than 10 percent, and not a single female member was reported by 45 national unions with a combined membership of nearly

2.2 million.[61] Yet the presence of union organization seems to be crucially related to women's incomes: union women earn approximately $1,500 a year more than unorganized women in the same occupations.[62]

Among blue-collar women who are organized, a majority continue to be represented by a handful of unions with almost exclusively female membership: principally, the International Ladies' Garment Workers Union, Amalgamated Clothing Workers, and the Communications Workers of America, unions whose overall membership is on the decline.[63] Moreover, women, relative to male workers, are disproportionately represented by weak "unaffiliated" and "independent" local unions and underrepresented in powerful AFL-CIO affiliated organizations. Unaffiliated locals in fact account for 70 percent of the total female union membership.

Various theories have been put forth to explain the absence of effective union organization among blue-collar women. Orthodox economists point toward motivational shortcomings among women workers themselves; single women are said to view work as a temporary transitional status before marriage and married women work to provide family luxuries by supplementing their husbands' incomes. Thus, McNally argues that "organization is difficult, if not impossible, where individuals expect to be wage earners but for a short time because of anticipated withdrawal from the labor market."[64] The implication is that organized labor has made substantial and unrelenting efforts to organize women workers, but to no avail.

However, unions have shown scant interest in organizing women. Frequently unions have acquiesced to, or even encouraged, management to redefine and differentially remunerate new jobs on the basis of sex.[65] In those industries in which female workers are organized but aggregated into "women's" occupations, many union negotiating committees have been less enthusiastic in pushing for wage increases for their female than for their male members. Nor have unions been aggressive in pushing for paid maternity leave benefits. In many organized industries, wage discrepancies between the sexes have measurably widened over the last decade. For example when contracts negotiated in 1962 and 1972 by Local 593 of the Amalgamated Meat Cutters and Butcher Workmen (Washington D.C. metropolitan area) are compared, hourly wage increases for wrappers and weighers—comprising an exclusively female work force—have lagged behind the wage gains of male journeymen meat cutters (see Table 8).

Moreover, in the 1972 contract, the job description for "wrapper-weigher" has been broadened to encompass several minor functions previously performed by male meat cutters or apprentices, namely, slicing bacon and lunch-meats, filling display cases, sharpening knives, and

TABLE 8
Hourly Wage Rates by Sexually Segregated Job Category, Negotiated for Washington, D.C. Area Butchers and Allied Workers, 1962 and 1972

Year	Job Category		Wrapper-weigher wages as a percent of journeymen butcher wages
	Journeymen Meat Cutters	Wrappers and Weighers	
1962	$3.12	$2.08	66.7%
1972	6.01	3.61	59.9%

Source: Amalgamated Meat Cutters and Butcher Workmen of North America, AFL-CIO. "Agreement between Local 593 and Washington Metropolitan Area Food Retailers Association." October 1962 and May 1972.

traying fresh meat cuts. With respect to the split labor market thesis, it is also important to note that the overall employment of women relative to men in the meat industry has increased significantly.[66] The conclusion that women workers are increasingly being used in lieu of better paid male butchers in order to drive up industry profits is hard to escape.

Plainly, positions of authority and responsibility within the unions are systematically denied women. In 1972, women officeholders comprised less than 7 percent of all union officials, while women made up about 22 percent of the total union membership.[67] Typical is the Amalgamated Clothing Workers Union which, with a 75 percent female membership, has only *one* female vice president among 28. At the AFL-CIO Executive Board itself, not one woman is presently seated. At the state level, of 173 officers and elected officials comprising AFL-CIO labor councils, only 8 were women in 1972.[68] When women do hold office, if at all, it is usually at the local level, conventionally as recording secretaries and trustees. The underrepresentation of women as members and officials in the labor movement amounts to a quasi-caste situation in the major institutions. The unions are centrally important. They have largely ignored blue-collar women in the minimum wage industries, an otherwise fertile domain for organizing activities; they have excluded women from the most lucrative skilled trades; and finally, they have minimized the participation of women in the AFL-CIO's decision-making apparatus.

DISCUSSION: SEX DISCRIMINATION AND RECENT FEDERAL LEGISLATION

I have contended throughout this paper that the entrapment of working-class women in poverty-wage industries cannot be explained by orthodox theories of wage determination. Rather, we must look toward a structural analysis of discrimination, labor market segmentation, and the position of marginal industries in the overall economy.

Piecemeal federal legislation addressed to sex discrimination in industry has recently been forthcoming. However, its impact on breaking down the dual labor market structure is debatable. On June 10, 1963, after successful lobbying by the International Union of Electrical, Radio, and Machine Workers, President Kennedy signed the Equal Pay Act, which amended the Fair Labor Standards Act. The EPA requires employers to compensate men and women in the same establishment equally for work of "equivalent skill and responsibility." Additionally, Title VII of the Civil Rights Act of 1964 was subsequently broadened to prohibit sex, as well as racial, discrimination in hiring, promotion, and remuneration. Finally, the Equal Employment Opportunity Act of 1972 was passed, giving EEOC officials court enforcement power in cases suggesting sex discrimination. Nevertheless, each of these legislative breakthroughs was limited in scope and effective only to the extent that executive action would be forthcoming whenever necessary.

The persistence of a sexually segmented blue-collar labor market concretely reflects the limited nature of existing civil rights law as well as lackadaisical executive enforcement. The Equal Pay Act of 1963 does not call for job evaluation as a means of determining what jobs are in fact "equal." Determining the existence of wage discrimination is left to customary collective bargaining procedures.[69] Yet as we have seen, the great majority of blue-collar women do not work under union contracts. Moreover, the equal pay protection applies only within single establishments of any particular employer. An "establishment," for purposes of this statute, designates any *physically separate* place of business or manufacture. Employers have been quick to take advantage of this clause.

A more recent controversy surrounds the proposed ratification of the Equal Rights Amendment. It is not clear what the consequences of ERA ratification for working-class women will be. The amendment seems to offer the hope of breaking down barriers which have segregated many blue-collar women into low-wage "female" factory jobs, providing that stringent enforcement measures are undertaken.

I have argued that the entrapment of women in the low-wage labor market reflects a coincidence of supply and demand factors, the structural location of marginal industries, and multiple forms of sex discrimination. In general, policy intended to extend adequate wages, good working conditions, and job security to working-class women must renounce "victim blaming" economics. Only in this way will job opportunities, particularly in the skilled trades, become more accessible to women workers locked into minimum wage industries.

NOTES

1. I am indebted to Joan Huber and William H. Form for extensive critical advice on this and all earlier drafts. I also wish to thank James F. O'Connor, Dennis W. Roncek, Joe L. Spaeth, and John B. Parrish for their helpful comments.

2. Cf. Cynthia F. Epstein, *Woman's Place: Options and Limits in Professional Careers* (Berkeley: University of California Press, 1970); Helen Austin, *The Woman Doctorate in America: Origins, Career, and Family* (New York: Russell Sage Foundation, 1969); and Alice Rossi, ed., *Academic Women on the Move* (New York: Russell Sage Foundation, 1973).

3. U.S. Department of Labor, "Current Labor Statistics," *Monthly Labor Review* 94 (July 1971) : 2.

4. Oregon Bureau of Labor, *They Carry the Burden Alone: The Socio-Economic Living Patterns of Oregon Women with Dependents* (1968), p. 1.

5. Conceptualizing women in manufacturing as essentially a middle stratum in the blue-collar world was suggested by William H. Form.

6. Harold M. Baron and Bennett Hymer, "The Negro Worker in the Chicago Labor Market," in *The Negro and the American Labor Movement,* ed. Julius Jacobson (Garden City, N.Y.: Doubleday, 1968); Daniel Fusfeld, *The Basic Economics of the Urban Racial Crisis* (New York: Holt, Rinehart, and Winston, 1973); and Michael Reich, "The Economics of Racism," in *Problems in Political Economy: An Urban Perspective,* ed. David M. Gordon (Lexington, Mass.: D.C. Heath, 1971), pp.107-13.

7. Michael Piore, "Jobs and Training," in *The State and the Poor,* ed. Samuel H. Beer and Richard E. Barringer (New York: Winston, 1970), pp.53-83.

8. Edna Bonacich, "A Theory of Ethnic Antagonism: The Split Labor Market," *American Sociological Review* 37 (October 1972) : 547-59 (chapter 4 in this volume); A.D. Krueger, "The Economics of Discrimination," *Journal of Political Economy* 71 (May 1963): 481-86; and Reich.

9. Baron and Hymer, p.98.

10. Ibid., p.101.

11. Piore.

12. Fusfeld, p.68.

13. This is not to say, however, that workers in the high-wage primary industries are not adversely affected in the long run by discrimination.

14. Fusfeld.

15. Piore.

16. Karl Marx, *Capital,* vol. 1 (New York: International Publishers, 1967), p.636.

17. U.S. Department of Labor, *Background Facts on Women Workers in the United States* (Washington, D.C.: Government Printing Office, 1970), pp. 13-14.

18. Gertrude B. McNally, "Patterns of Female Labor Force Activity," *Industrial Relations* 7 (May 1968) : 206.

19. U.S. Department of Labor, Women's Bureau, "Women Workers Today" (Mimeo, June 1973), p.5.

148   Robert Bibb

20. U.S. Department of Labor, Women's Bureau, "The Economic Role of Women," in *The Economic Report of the President 1973* (Washington, D.C.: Government Printing Office, 1973), p.104.

21. Tom Kahn, "The Economics of Inequality," in *Poverty in America,* ed. Louis Ferman et al. (Ann Arbor: University of Michigan Press, 1968), pp.240-57.

22. Cf. Lester Thurow, *Poverty and Discrimination* (Washington, D.C.: The Brookings Institute, 1969); Arthur Ross, ed., *Employment Policy and the Labor Market* (Berkeley: University of California Press, 1965); and Gary Becker, *The Economics of Discrimination* (Chicago: University of Chicago Press. 1957).

23. Thurow, p.20.

24. Basil J. Moore, *Modern Economic Theory* (New York: Free Press, 1973).

25. Richard H. Leftwich, *The Price System and Resource Allocation* (New York: Holt, Rinehart and Winston, 1966).

26. Jacob Mincer, "The Distribution of Labor Incomes: A Survey with Special Reference to the Human Capital Approach," *Journal of Economic Literature* 8 (March 1970) : 1-26.

27. A critical discussion of principal theories of wage distribution is provided by Joan Huber, "Mechanisms of Income Distribution," in *The Sociology of American Poverty,* ed. Joan Huber and Peter Chalfant (Cambridge, Mass.: Schenkman, 1974), pp.103-23.

28. Piore.

29. U.S. Department of Labor, "Current Labor Statistics," *Monthly Labor Review* 94 (July 1971) : 4.

30. An excellent discussion of the constraints on education as a poverty-reducing mechanism can be found in S.M. Miller and Pamela A. Roby, "The War on Poverty Reconsidered," in *Poverty: Views from the Left,* ed. Jeremy Larner and Irving Howe (New York: William Morrow, 1969), pp.68-82.

31. Oregon Bureau of Labor.

32. U.S. Department of Labor, *Background Facts on Women in the United States* (Washington, D.C.: Government Printing Office, 1970), p.12.

33. U.S. Department of Labor, Women's Bureau, "The Economic Role of Women," in *The Economic Report of the President 1973* (Washington, D.C.: Government Printing Office, 1973), p.106.

34. Barbara R. Bergman, "The Effect on White Incomes of Discrimination in Employment," *Journal of Political Economy* 79 (March-April 1971) : 294-313; and Becker.

35. Becker.

36. Ray Marshall, "The Negro and Organized Labor," *Journal of Negro Education* 32 (1963) : 375-89; Ray Marshall and Vernon M. Briggs, Jr., *The Negro and Apprenticeship* (Baltimore: Johns Hopkins Press, 1963); and William B. Gould, "Discrimination and the Unions," in *Poverty: Views from the Left,* ed. Neremy Larner and Irving Howe (New York: William Morrow, 1969), pp.103-23.

37. Bergmann.

38. Peter Doeringer and Michael Piore, *Internal Labor Markets and Manpower Analysis* (Lexington, Mass.: D.C. Heath, 1971).

39. Piore, p.63.

40. On this point, see especially Marx's (pp.640-48) discussion of the functional importance of a hierarchially segmented proletariat toward continual accumulation of surplus in the face of falling profits.

41. Laurie D. Cummings, "The Employed Poor: Their Characteristics and Occupations," *Monthly Labor Review* 88 (July 1965) : 828-41.
42. Marylin Power Goldberg, "The Economic Exploitation of Women," *Review of Radical Political Economics* 2 (1970) no. 1.
43. Lucretia M. Dewey, "Women in Labor Unions," *Monthly Labor Review* 94 (February 1971) : 43.
44. U.S. Department of Labor, *Handbook on Women Workers* (Washington, D.C.: Government Printing Office, 1969), p.151.
45. Ibid., p.152.
46. Mary Seifer, *Absent from the Majority: Working Class Women in America* (New York: National Project on Ethnic America, 1973), p.26.
47. Ibid., p.32.
48. Oregon Bureau of Labor, p.47.
49. Cf. Francis F. Piven and Richard A. Cloward, *Regulating the Poor: The Functions of Public Welfare* (New York: Random House, 1971).
50. Grace Hutchins, *Women Who Work* (New York: International Publishers, 1934).
51. Ibid.
52. Piore.
53. Barry Bluestone, "Lower Income Workers and Marginal Industries," in *Poverty in America,* ed. Louis Ferman et al. (Ann Arbor: University of Michigan Press, 1968), pp.273-302.
54. Ibid., p.293.
55. Gus Tyler, "Marginal Industries, Low Wages, and High Risks," *Dissent* (Summer 1961) : 321-25. In a few instances, however, the alleged competitive situation of minimum wage industries should not be exaggerated. Some of these firms produce highly specialized products for restricted markets or else maintain *regional* monopolies. That there occurs a steady absolute lowering of prices for commodities manufactured by minimum wage industries would seem to be fallacious, at least intuitively, and thus warrants empirical confirmation.
56. Andrew Hacker, *The Corporation Take-Over* (New York: Harper and Row, 1964).
57. Piven and Cloward.
58. John B. Lansing and James N. Morgan, "Effects of Geographic Mobility on Income," *Journal of Human Resources* (Fall 1967).
59. Paul A. Baran and Paul M. Sweezy, *Monopoly Capital* (New York: Modern Reader, 1966).
60. Institute of Management and Labor Relations, *Report of the Conference on Unions and the Changing Status of Women Workers* (New Brunswick, N.J.: Rutgers University, 1964), p.3.
61. U.S. Department of Labor, *Directory of National Unions and Employee Associations* (Washington, D.C.: Government Printing Office, 1972), p.82.
62. Seifer, p.33.
63. Dewey, p.42.
64. McNally.
65. Goldberg.
66. U.S. Department of Labor, Women's Bureau, "The Economic Role of Women," in *The Economic Report of the President 1973* (Washington, D.C.: Government Printing Office, 1973), p.157.

67. Virginia A. Bergquist, "Women's Participation in Labor Organizations," *Monthly Labor Review* 97 (October 1972) : 5.
68. Ibid., p.8.
69. *The American Federationist,* "Equal Pay for Women," July 1964.

8

What is the New Working Class?[1]

Martin Oppenheimer

If there is a ruling class, what is its negation? Is it the traditional blue-collar proletariat? Or have blue-collar workers been coopted, historically replaced by the peoples of the Third World or by their U.S. counterparts? Or have shifts in technology created a new white-collar working class as the leading potentially revolutionary force in Western society?

While the question of which class or grouping is to become the chief agency for fundamental change is not a new one, it has become much more urgent in recent years given the failures of liberalism, on the one hand, and of insurgent movements ranging from civil rights to Black Power to Weathermen on the other. Nor is this an academic issue, for linked to one or another prognosis is a strategy and a set of tactics for one's politics in the next few years.

This essay will assess the arguments for a new working class and its revolutionary potential. While the roots of new working-class theory go back to the late 1800s, it was not until the 1960s in Western Europe that material appeared in which the white-collar strata were depicted as a mass revolutionary force (as opposed to earlier work which had emphasized the role of particular white-collar groupings as revolutionary elites). This conclusion stemmed from the failure of blue-collar formations to accomplish much fundamental change and, related to that, the fact that blue-collar workers were rapidly being displaced as the numerically significant class by white-collar workers. The rise of mass higher education as a training ground for the new proletariat and, in turn, as an arena for insurgency contributed to this new perspective; in the United States, the expulsion of white intellectuals from the black movement created a further motivation to seek new populations which might prove amenable to organizing activity for radicals.

In its most general terms, the new working-class theory states that white-collar workers are displacing blue-collar workers as the major working class grouping in the technologically advanced societies. As the rationalization of their work develops and as they become subject to the economic and social crises of advanced capitalism/imperialism, their political consciousness will develop along lines roughly analogous to their European blue-collar predecessors: from trade unions to social democracy to revolutionism. White-collar workers (in varying combinations with other class groupings, including blue-collar workers generally, skilled and technical strata more particularly, oppressed Third World people, the lumpenproletariat and overlapping significantly with women) will become a revolutionary vanguard class capable of overthrowing the present social order and replacing it with a socialist society.

No discussion of this perspective is possible unless we clarify first of all the boundaries of the "new working class." Up to now discussions of the white-collar strata[2] failed to distinguish clearly between the middle-class, new managerial strata and the large white-collar mass; unless we can isolate a "class" somewhat more successfully from among the white-collar strata, the potential of that class cannot be analyzed.

In the U.S., most labor force data are based on the collection and publication of figures by the federal government. This creates an immediate problem: classifications exist without reference to (and possibly in an attempt to obscure) the question of significance, power, and control: that is, of social class. The concept of "ruling class" does not exist for the government's data collectors, yet the entire ruling class of this country, by whatever one's definition, is subsumed in one broad classification, "white collar occupations." The traditional capitalist ruling class—the owners of the major means of production and distribution—is buried within one category of the "white collar occupations," that of "managers and administrators" (which also includes the Mom and Pop grocery store on the corner). At the other extreme, that of the white-collar mass, job classifications are sufficiently broad that many tens of thousands of white-collar workers are classified in "service occupations." Police officers, for example, are "service workers," but police desk workers, who are more properly white-collar workers in their day-to-day function, are still policemen and are also classified as service.

What this means is that our information on the number of white-collar workers is not precise. Using union figures to find out how many white-collar workers are unionized is also misleading, since many "white-collar unions" (such as the American Federation of State, County and Municipal Employees) have both service and blue-collar members (only about one-third of AFSCME is white collar), and numerous service and blue-collar unions have white collar members, sometimes not counted in separate white-collar units. The Teamsters, Steelworkers, Auto Workers, Electrical Workers, Seafarer Machinists, and a number of others all organize white-collar workers, while such unions as AFSCME and Local 1199 (hospital workers) organize everything from social workers to garbage collectors.

Another problem occurs when we try to pin down white-collar occupations into their four general strata: (1) managers, officials, and proprietors; (2) professional and technical; (3) clerical; (4) sales. First, which broad occupational category (blue, white, or gray collar) is involved? Transportation baggagemen are considered clerical (white collar). Why aren't they listed as "service" workers (gray collar)? Second, which stratum within the broad category of white-collar occupations is involved? Airplane pilots and navigators are considered "professional, technical" but railroad conductors, and ships' officers, pilots, pursers, and engineers are considered "managers, officials, and proprietors." Many "sales workers," such as ad men and real estate brokers, are far closer to being proprietors than they are to being five-and-ten-cent store retail clerks. Third, specific occupations vary widely in their social class content—yet college presidents, professors, and instructors are lumped together on a single occupational line. Presidents should certainly be considered among "managers, officials, and proprietors."

Another problem: neither the armed forces nor housewives are considered "in" the labor force. Nor are part-time workers, seasonal workers, and occasional workers counted fractionally in the labor force, even though they might work longer if the opportunity were available—they are all considered fully "in" while they are working, even though they work only an hour per week. Some temporarily laid off workers (e.g., for retooling) are considered "in" while not working at all. If some fraction of housewives were considered "in" and partially unemployed and part-time workers were considered partially "out," our employment rolls would be staggering. This is all quite apart from the fact that housewives are in some sense in the labor force even though not employed for wages, since they constitute a part of a political/economic unit essential to the functioning of certain strata of employment and its reproduction. Despite all these problems, some overall figures may be useful so that we know what the terms of discussion are (see Table 1).

In terms of the future, several things appear to be clear: first, the employment figure of roughly 103.4 million by 1985 will include many more women, numerically and proportionally. Second, the service-producing sector (trade, finance, government, etc.) will increase by about one-third. Third, there will probably be some 57.6 million job openings in that period (from retirement, death, and employment growth), with some 12.1 million "requiring" a college degree; but there will be some 13.1 million

TABLE 1
Civilian Labor Force

	January, 1978		Projected to 1985	
	number (in millions)	%	number (in millions)	%
Total Employment	92.8	100.0	103.4	100.0
Total White Collar	46.5	50.1	53.2	51.5
Mgrs. & Admin.	10.0	10.7	10.9	10.5
Professional, Technical	14.0	15.0	16.0	15.5
Clerical	16.5	17.7	20.1	19.5
Sales	5.9	6.3	6.3	6.1
Total Blue Collar	30.9	33.2	33.7	32.6
Crafts, Foremen	12.1	13.0	13.8	13.3
Operatives	14.1	15.1	15.2	14.7
Nonfarm Laborers	4.6	4.9	4.8	4.6
Service Workers	12.7	13.6	14.6	14.1
Farm Laborers	2.8	3.0	1.9	1.8

college graduates entering the labor force. Fifty-nine percent of all openings will be in the white-collar occupations; still, the number of blue-collar workers will continue to rise, from 29.8 million in 1974 to 33.7 million in 1985.

Within the white-collar occupations, clerical employment will increase by one-third; only service employees will grow at a more rapid rate. Thus the trajectories of growth among the core strata within the white-collar and blue-collar categories (clericals vs. operatives), which have already crossed, will continue to move in opposite directions as proportions of the labor force: there will be 20.1 million clericals in 1985 (19.5 percent of the labor force), and 15.2 million operatives (14.7 percent of the labor force).

An initial impression, that by 1985 over half the labor force will be "white-collar workers" (leading to a certain illusion as to the size of this new "proletariat") can be corrected and put into a more accurate context only if we exclude white-collar strata which more or less clearly are not, by any reasonable definition, "working class."

We must eliminate from consideration as "workers" some eleven million managers and administrators, many of whom are members of the ruling class, what remains of C. Wright Mills's "old middle class" of small proprietors, and that sector of Mills's "new middle class" of managers and officials whose incomes derive directly from their ability to generate profits at the expense of the workers, or indirectly from their ability to conduct the public sector so that it will respond to the private sector's need to generate profits. This stratum would include such occupations as professional politicians, welfare administrators (but not caseworkers), school superintendents, "neocolonial" administrators, and the "comprador bourgeoisie" of our internal colonies. It would exclude some misclassified workers, such as the previously mentioned railroad conductors plus, perhaps, some union officials.

A second grouping which should be removed from the ranks of the "new working class" are those referred to by Mills as "the new entrepreneur" (promoters, adjusters, foundation, hustlers, research shop operators, public relations people, middlemen between organizations and government). These people hold jobs called professional and technical (professors, engineers, lawyers, natural scientists, personnel and labor relations workers, publicity writers, etc.) and do in fact "sell their labor power on the market for a wage," yet the wage is often incidental to other incomes derived from and linked to profits at the expense of the working class in some direct sense. Such people cannot be considered, objectively speaking, workers. Unfortunately, it is impossible to estimate how many fall into this category, but let us guess that ten percent of professional and technical do, or 1.6 million more. (This may be a low estimate given the character of such professions as law, where nearly everyone is linked to the ruling class.) If we add 1.5 million commission sales people and contractors, the character of whose work far more approximates that of the petty bourgeoisie because they are in some sense self-employed, then we have as our ruling class, its immediate lackeys, and the petty bourgeoisie which shares its consciousness some 14 million people in 1985 (some 13.5 percent of the "labor" force) whose revolutionary potential hovers around zero. Assuming this to be a realistic approach, what is the likely shape of the labor force in 1985?

TABLE 2
Estimated Division by "Class" Definitions, 1985

number
(in millions)

	number (in millions)	
Total Employment	103.4	
The Ruling Class, Petty Bourgeoisie,		
Dependents, Lackeys, etc.	14.0	(13.5%)
New Working Class	40.8	(39.4%)
Old Working Class, Including		
Farm Laborers	35.6	(34.4%)
Service Workers	14.6	(14.1%)
Estimated Officially Unemployed	6.2	(6.0%)
Estimated Unofficially Unemployed	6.2	(6.0%)
Total of Those Who Sell Their		
Labor Power for a Wage, or		
Would if They Could	103.4	

The point of this demonstration is not to play a numbers game; it is to argue that *even* if one pays attention *only* to numbers (which we should not do), no major social change is possible without the concurrence of the blue-collar working class which continues to grow numerically even though declining proportionally. And it is to delimit what we are talking about when we use the term "new working class": most, though not all, professional and technical workers; clerical workers; most, though not all, sales workers; and those "service workers" and others who have been misclassified.

There has been some confusion about whether the "new working class" is a new stratum of the old working class or whether it is to be analytically counterposed to the blue-collar proletariat. The "technical" wing of the "professional and technical" stratum represents a conceptual (and possibly political) bridge between the blue-collar working class and the new working class. One can conceive of the labor force as consisting of people who produce (blue collar), people who directly service those who produce, including some who distribute (gray collar), and people who manipulate symbols about production and service (white collar—from clerical, who

TABLE 3
Women and Men in Different Occupational Strata, 1973 (percent)

	Women	Men
White Collar	60.7	39.8
Mgrs. & Admin.	4.9	13.6
Professional, Technical	14.5	13.6
Clerical	34.3	6.6
Sales	6.9	6.1
Blue Collar	16.2	47.4
Craft, kindred	1.4	20.8
Operatives	13.8	18.8
Nonfarm Laborers	.9	7.7
Service Workers	21.6	7.9
Farm Workers	1.6	4.8

push papers about production, to professors and authors, who push ideas, etc.). The further away from direct production a stratum of workers gets, the less important it is in terms of controlling production, stopping it, and laying hold of it once again under its own terms—which is an argument in favor of the critical significance of blue-collar workers in a revolutionary situation, a point made by Ernest Mandel in 1968, possibly in arguing against a Weatherman/Third World/lumpenproletarian perspective: "Any attempt to transfer that role (revolutionary mission) to other social layers, who are unable to paralyze production at a stroke, who do not play a key role in the productive process, who are not the main source of profit and capital accumulation, takes us a decisive step backwards from scientific to utopian socialism...."[3]

The exception to the above description of white-collar workers is the technical wing—architects, designers, draftsmen, engineers, some scientists, surveyors, technicians, and the like, who often actually work in production directly. In fact, unlike most other white-collar workers, production could not take place for one minute without them. In contrast,

TABLE 4

Percent of All Workers in Occupational Strata Who are Women, 1973

White Collar	48.7%
Mgrs. & Admin.	18.4
Professional, Technical	40.0
Clerical	76.6
Sales	41.4
Blue Collar	17.6
Craft, kindred	4.1
Operatives	31.4
Nonfarm Laborers	6.9
Service Workers	63.0
Farm Workers	17.0

the withdrawal of the labor of most other white-collar workers, while serious after a while, creates only a nuisance in the short run. Service workers, located in between, have an in-between significance, for example, in a sanitation or police strike.

A closely related issue relevant to the technical stratum is the process of automation. Structural unemployment, while increasingly serious, affects either the lesser skilled or those whose overspecialized skills become obsolete. With increasing automation and cybernation there may, in fact, be fewer in a position to "paralyze production at a stroke." It is even conceivable, though remote, that the day will come when successful revolution by the large masses will be possible only with the cooperation of a tiny minority of technical workers who alone will be able to paralyze production and then resume it again under new social rules, a Veblenesque prophecy. Whether a revolution led by such an elite vanguard can lead to a more democratic society is a real question, but it is not presently on the agenda. Suffice it to say that for some purposes, the technical stratum should perhaps be classified as the upper stratum of the blue-collar working class, rather than as part of a "professional and technical" stratum of white-collar workers.

One issue raised by some radical analysts is that the public sector or government employees, because their incomes are derived from taxation (off the backs of the blue-collar working class) and because they administer coercive state mechanisms (welfare, education, the police, etc.) cannot be defined as working class at all; they exploit, rather than being exploited, it has been argued. What is an exploited worker and how does one analyze salary in order to trace its source to the exploitation of others, as against its source as a cost in which salary represents a minor fraction of some product which is being appropriated by an employer?

In classical terms, public sector employees (and, increasingly, white-collar professionals in the private sector as well) sell their labor power on the market for a wage, and at least in that sense are workers, so long as that wage is their primary source of income. It does not matter how much that wage is, except that obviously wages are important in determining life-styles and are thereby related to consciousness (subjective though not objective class). In the public sector, all wages are derived largely from taxes, which are disproportionally garnered from all wage earners (including white collar). Furthermore, there is no measurable "product" which is sold on the market for a "profit." There is a "service" which is "delivered" outside the rules of the market. Thus if we separate the public sector artificially from the private one, it would indeed seem that government employees are simply "drones" and live by the "exploitation" of producing workers.

However, if we conceive of public sector employees as indirect corporate workers (as theorists of the new working class do), then a different picture emerges. Government work represents, in this theory, indirect costs of production which the private sector (through its indirect control of the political state) is enabled to "socialize" or pass on to the general public in the form of taxes. Thus the government, through the educational system, trains corporate workers; through the welfare system, maintains a reserve labor army; through the police system, keeps revolutions under control, etc. Government workers who in this fashion also "contribute" to the productive process, albeit indirectly, are therefore also exploited. In this approach, taxes are simply an indirect cost of production—an indirect form of pricing, one might say, which is not the crux of the notion of exploitation. One cannot say that auto workers exploit garment workers because the price of cars is high; neither can one say that social workers exploit auto workers because the "price" of taxes (welfare) is high. In brief, it is not prices that are the issue: it is wages. It is not the price system that socialists want to do away with—it is the wage system.

It follows from this kind of argument that white-collar "workers," whatever they may be, are not a "new class." Insofar as they are women due to child-rearing duties, the transfers of husbands, and the stultifying nature of clerical jobs leads to higher turnover rates in at least some female dominated jobs and limits the likelihood of becoming related to on-the-job concerns. The sheer economic gain to specific organizations which comes from paying women less than men would receive in the same job must also be considered as a part of the picture.

Thus we have, in the white-collar field, a sex-defined stratum (quasi caste would be more accurate than class) analogous to nonwhites in the overall labor force. One can go so far as to say that within the white-collar strata, the parallels are even closer: at least in the professions, women and blacks tend to be concentrated in similar kinds of jobs, which is a precise reflection of this parallel in certain low-level blue-collar and service jobs. Blacks, who have traditionally done "women's work" (domestic service, dishwashing, restaurant work, hospital orderlies) and who continue to do so at the lower levels, also find that when they make it into higher employment levels they continue to do "women's work": social work, teaching, etc. And the tokenism which affects one group also affects the other at the upper employment levels: showcase blacks and showcase women find that they must both discard many group characteristics and adopt white male behavior patterns in order to "make it."

A crucial question is what the relationship of the women's movement will be to the perspective of white-collar politicization, given the high proportion of women in the white-collar field. Can white-collar workers be organized apart from the women's movement, as blue-collar workers (including women) largely were? Or is the situation such that without the women's movement no real progress can be made by white-collar workers? So far, few long-range efforts have been made by the feminist movement to organize women as white-collar workers, with the exception of women's caucuses in various professional (mainly academic) organizations, and some efforts among clerical employees. There has been considerable discussion about relating to "working-class" women, generally meaning blue collar; to welfare mothers, mainly nonwhites; and to prostitutes, who are indeed white-collar professionals except that illicit occupations are no more considered a labor force category than are those of the ruling class. But so far, very little has been done about relating to 12 ¼ million women clerical workers.

In 1974 only 8 percent of clerical workers were unionized as compared with nearly 42.4 percent of all manufacturing workers. In a 1977 survey of registered nurses, 82 percent reported that their workplace condition was governed by individual bargaining. Only 4 percent of RNs reported they were in a union-covered workplace; 14 percent reported some other form of group agreement.

proprietors, they are the bourgeoisie. If they are officials or managers, they serve the bourgeoisie. The term "new class" should be reserved for societies where certain upper strata of the white-collar grouping (officials, managers, professionals, technicans) have displaced the bourgeoisie, not where they serve it.

A startling fact, true of no other major social class in history since slavery, must accompany any further analysis: one cannot discuss white-collar workers without discussing women in the labor force. By mid-1977, 40 million women were in the labor force—49 percent of all women sixteen and over worked at some point that year. Correspondingly, 41 percent of the entire labor force is female, and that proportion is continuing to climb. Of those women in the labor force, 62 percent were in white-collar jobs by 1974; in turn, of all white-collar workers, 48 percent were women. In 1973, more than 40 percent of all women workers were employed in ten occupations: secretary, retail sales person, bookkeeper, elementary school teacher, typist, cashier, registered nurse (all white collar); and private household worker, waitress, and sewer/stitcher.

Two things are apparent: first, despite women's high rate of participation in the white-collar grouping as a whole, their distribution among the different white-collar strata is inequitable: they are slightly overrepresented in the professional-technical stratum, fantastically overrepresented in the clerical stratum, and considerably underrepresented in the managers/administrators stratum; second, though not obvious from Table 4, they are disproportionally concentrated (within each stratum) toward the lower end of the income, prestige, and power components of white-collar life. In certain professions and in upper management, women are notoriously few in number, and even in higher administrative levels of occupations, in which women dominate overall, men tend to be in command. At the bottom of the income-prestige-power continuum, about one woman in three in the entire labor force is in the "clerical" stratum. In the white-collar area, they constitute 78.7 percent of all clerical workers, 96.6 percent of all registered nurses, 70.9 percent of all elementary school teachers, and 60 percent of all social workers, as of 1976; as numerous observers have suggested, they dominate fields which at least in some ways are extensions of sex-role stereotyped household duties, particularly in middle-class American families. That is, they take care of people or things.

At the same time, discrimination continues. The "reasons" for discrimination that are presented in the literature are complex and interlocking and include at least: competing attachments to family which undermine potential advancement, especially in the professional ranks; concentration in "second-class" fields because they require shorter training—possibly related to early marriage or to reentering the labor market at later age;

career interruption (by child-bearing and rearing) functioning to remove women as competitors for advancement; consequent less tenure functioning to generate lower salaries and less responsibility even in the same job titles; lack of mobility (for job transfers). Less related to the job itself are such (by now well-known) factors as socialization to certain behavioral and occupational roles; the sex-typing of occupations ("when a very large majority of those in them are of one sex and when there is an associated normative expectation that this is as it should be");[4] the linkage of work and prestige, so that "men's work, whatever it is, tends to be most highly regarded in most societies, and that highly regarded work seems to be reserved for men,"[5] or at least for white men. Sex-typing and job segregation is a function of controlling meeting and mating under socially appropriate conditions (that is, conditions under which class and caste barriers are not violated). Underpinning such reasons are more common-denominator reasons which suggest that it is functional to our organizational society to maintain the suburban nuclear family as a logistical-support unit for the mobile white-collar male (even though it may be dysfunctional for *human beings),* hence the need, within our class society, for the promotion of sex-role stereotyping and a general attitude of male chauvinism roughly analogous to white racism.

Finally, this chauvinism both supports, and in turn is supported by, functional (for them) institutional practices of outright discrimination against women (also against blacks and others) which are profitable or practical from the viewpoint of a given organization or institution in terms of its short-run survival or competitive advantage. For example, conscious decisions are made to staff a white-collar office with women to ease the transition of such an office to automatic data processing—on the assumption that A&P (normal attrition and pregnancy) will take care of layoffs which men would fight harder against. In a similar way, it is necessary for governmental units to find large numbers of clerks, typists, and so on whose incomes can be limited for budgetary purposes. The turnover of

Some unions understand the need to organize white-collar women, a necessity if the trade-union movement is to survive.[6] Thus many white-collar unions are beginning to employ women organizers, elevating them to higher positions in unions, orienting their literature and social programs to women's needs, and even seeking special collective bargaining rights for women (e.g., day care centers, clauses protecting job rights after maternity leaves, etc.).

In the context of a changing technology in which ever higher proportions of workers will be in the white-collar strata and in which more of those workers will be women, a radical women's movement confronts unprecedented opportunities to relate to "the working class." This situation, combined with increasing pressures on the American family system, may well become one of the primary contradictions in the American social system.

It is time to summarize the main arguments for and against the new working class as an agent for revolutionary change. One area of discussion has to do with the increasing numbers of white-collar workers and their proportion in the labor force. The fact that half of those workers will soon be women, whose own demands (particularly on the family system) have increasingly radical implications, strengthens the argument for the significance of the new working class. Yet one can also argue that white-collar workers will not seriously outnumber the sum of blue- and gray-collar workers for some time to come. Further, black workers, whose demands have implications in many ways as radical as those of women, are increasing as a proportion of blue-collar workers (and younger black workers are increasing as a proportion of the unemployed). The argument for the continuing importance of blue-collar (together with service) workers remains a strong one even if we look only at sheer numbers.

The increase in numerical importance of white-collar workers must be offset at least in part by considering their role in the productive process. With the exception of technical workers, white-collar workers are far less essential to production than blue- or gray-collar workers and inherently cannot play the "key role in the productive process" so important in a revolutionary situation. Even the critical working-class weapon of the strike loses much of its force when applied to white-collar workers—in the private sector they are easily dispensed with for short periods of time, and in the public sector, where many of them perform nonessential bureaucratic functions, this is no less true. The public sector, moreover, is neither competitive nor accountable in terms of profitability: the pressures on the employer to settle a strike for fear of losing profits and sales to competition simply do not exist. Nor is the "work-in" tactic of much use for, since most white-collar workers produce nothing tangible, they cannot lay hold of their "product" and market it themselves to keep the returns and distribute them as they determine.

A second area of discussion has to do with trends at the workplace which seem to be "proletarianizing," therefore in the long run radicalizing, the new working class. Incomes are becoming more similar to those of blue-collar workers; work is becoming more routinized and segmented and less professional and autonomous; centralized bureaucracies determine product, market conditions, and working conditions in the same way they do in the blue-collar factory; the unemployment rate creeps up; the tax structure disproportionally punishes lower-middle income whites as well as blue-collar workers (threatening their life-style dreams of homeowning). In general the white-collar life-style becomes more and more like that of the blue-collar worker. The much advertised American mobility system turns out to be merely horizontal (from blue- to white-collar as the generations succeed each other, with similar life-styles, insecurities, and problems) rather than vertical (from lower blue-collar life-styles to upper white-collar ones).

Radicalization, or at least social democratization, it is said, will result. The data concerning increasing numbers of unionized white-collar workers and the nature of their demands (going beyond mere bread-and-butter issues into questions of the quality of services and participation in decision making) is cited as evidence.

But the evidence is far from clear when we examine it more closely. Political-type demands are still more the exception than the rule. Radical caucuses exist mainly in academic settings and are very weak there; where radical groups exist elsewhere, it is more often in the form of counterinstitutional groups (e.g., Health-PAC) than as part of a "long march through the institutions" strategy. Even the union data are far from reassuring.

The proportion of the labor force that is unionized decreased from about 23.6 percent in 1960 to 21.7 percent in 1974. Between 1974 and 1976, even the absolute members decreased (to about 22.5 million members). In the meantime, however, white-collar membership in unions increased from 1970 (with 3.35 million) to 1976 (with 3.85 million), so that by 1976, white collarites constituted 18.4 percent of all U.S. union members, and 26.9 percent of all members of unions plus other employee associations. If we look at the particular unions that gained the most members in the decade from 1966 to 1976, it is clear that white-collar unions, or unions with large proportions of white-collar members (especially in the public sector) gained most in percentage (partly because they started off farthest behind): of the top eight gainers, five (American Federation of State, County & Municipal Employees; American Federation of Teachers; Service Employees; Retail Clerks; and Communications Workers) are heavily or largely clerical, sales, and/or professional, technical workers.

Many gains in white-collar unionization, however, came "on the cheap" in federal employment, as the result of President Kennedy's Executive Order 10933 (1962). This permit to unionize forbids federal employees from striking. More important, it came about (as did much of the blue-collar organizing during World War II) with little struggle from the top, which has serious implications for the kind of union and the degree of worker consciousness and militancy that results. Within five years the proportion of federal employees represented by unions had increased from 19.8 percent to 45.3 percent—of these, over 80 percent of the lower-stratum white-collar workers were in four agencies: Defense, VA, Treasury, and HEW.

The assumption that unionization represents progress at all is also open to question. Aronowitz renews a traditional criticism, namely that the trade-union movement continues to function chiefly to help the system rationalize itself.[7] This point may become less true, however, in a time of economic crunch when unions must confront the system more militantly, if only in order to survive.

Another set of factors seems to counter the suggestion that white-collar workers will solidify their interests. These are related to the sheer segmentation of the field. The range of job types within one work unit is at least as wide as in the blue-collar shop. Workers are geographically dispersed (in the suburbs) and their mobility is relatively high (from place to place). Men are divided from women in a caste-like form on the job. Women's after-hours domestic work makes their participation in unions difficult. Finally, confused identities stemming from being a "professional" who is supposedly different from a "worker," creates a job stratum which probably has less "worker consciousness" than any other stratum in history at its inception.

Voting data also do not lend themselves to an optimistic prognosis at present. White-collar workers (though the strata are not clearly differentiated) seem to vote more conservatively than blue-collar workers, though not by very much; their attitudes in surveys concerning racial discrimination are generally worse than their blue-collar counterparts.[8] So far there is nothing to suggest that white-collar workers are not as likely to move in the direction of a right-wing "solution" to a crisis situation than in a progressive or left direction, at least in the United States.

Two further points are sometimes made in arguing for the radicalization of white-collar workers; first, that between university training and the counterculture (which overlap), a certain cultural and antiinstitutional radicalization takes place which affects particularly those populations which will become white-collar workers. Second, when those populations do enter white-collar institutions, this "pre-socialization" will coincide with pressures on those institutions from "client populations" of oppressed people (whom the institutions are supposedly designed to serve). This contradiction will move white-collar workers to cast their lot with their oppressed clients.

But this radicalizing tendency, too, is offset by other realities. The vast majority of students endure the experience and do not become politicized by that alone. Countercultural influences often operate, in fact, to divert radical energies from the political to the cultural sphere, enabling the individual worker to survive the idiocies of bureaucratic routine through "escapes." More significantly, pressure from oppressed "client populations" (e.g., unemployed workers, blacks, Third World people, students) work less to force the white-collar worker to reevaluate his or her stance toward the system than to push the worker into a stubborn defense of white-collar privileges. In short, as Moody puts it:

Many of the professional and semi-professional jobs in public employment are related to the oppressive functions of the state....Often the oppressive nature of the work, as opposed to the official conception of the job as a service, leads to rebellion....(But) the objective nature of the work separates them from other sections of the working class....All of this has had a distorting effect on consciousness....[9]

None of these obstacles to the radicalization of the new working class are insurmountable, given a deepening crisis in the capitalist order. The size of the new working class and its proletarianization in a period of the fiscal crisis of the state combine to begin to overcome its segmentation, its lagging consciousness, and its objective role (especially in the public sector) as an agent of oppression. At the same time, tendencies to mystify remain. Ethnic, racial, and sexual divisions persist to be manipulated by power structures. The fact that the American left is not "together" contributes to a political vacuum in which the new working class has only the choice between impotent statist liberalism, a racist brand of populism, and an antiquated, repressive conservatism. In such a climate, a fascist movement, perhaps initially in the guise of "tax revolt," can thrive.

A strong left, capable of building a coalition of blue- and white-collar workers on the one hand, and between those classes and specially oppressed groups such as women, the poor, blacks, and other Third World groups on the other, is the only alternative.

NOTES

1. This article is an updated version of one which first appeared in *New Politics,* vol. 10, no. 1 (Fall, 1972). © Martin Oppenheimer.
2. For example, C. Wright Mills, *White Collar* (New York: Oxford University Press, 1951); and Lewis Corey, *The Crisis of the Middle Class* (New York: Covici, Friede, 1935).
3. Ernest Mandel, "The Working Class under Neo-Capitalism," *Guardian,* 28 September 1968.
4. Cynthia Fuchs Epstein, *Women's Place* (Berekely: University of California Press, 1971), p.152.
5. Ibid. p.162.
6. Albert Blum et al., *White Collar Workers* (New York: Random House, 1971).
7. Stanley Aronowitz, *False Promises* (New York: McGraw-Hill, 1973), ch. 6.
8. Richard F. Hamilton, *Class and Politics in the United States* (New York: Wiley, 1972).
9. Kim Moody, *The American Working Class in Transition* (New York: International Socialists, 1970).

9

Working-Class Paraprofessionals in Mental Health Fields

Frank Riessman

Our major concern in this article is to document the role of paraprofessionals[1] in promoting service for clients in the mental health and psychiatric fields; that is, we are mainly interested in the practice of the paraprofessional as it relates to the functioning of the patient or consumer.[2] Although he plays other roles, (e.g., social change agent, etc.), our focus is on his input to service delivery. As we shall see, a number of major studies provide considerable evidence that the paraprofessional does indeed play a role in contributing to improved mental health of clients and patients both in hospitals and community settings.

Unlike public schools, where paraprofessionals are relatively new (although a significant minority of the staff), in the mental health programs, they are of long standing and comprise a large majority of the employees.

Consideration of the role of paraprofessionals in mental health must begin first with an identification of just who it is one is discussing. If one defines as professionals those holding post-baccalaureate professional degrees and excludes those engaged in only maintenance and housekeeping activities, one can suggest three types of paraprofessionals.

167

The first type is what might be called the "old" hospital-based worker. He is typified by the psychiatric aide working in a hospital setting, engaged in supportive therapeutic work. He usually does not have a college degree and is not indigenous to the community in which he is working, although he generally comes from a low income background and is frequently black or Puerto Rican.

The new middle-class paraprofessional is typically a woman with a degree who has received special training in mental health skills and is generally engaged in substantive therapeutic work. Margaret Rioch's program is perhaps best known in this area. The women she trained were middle class, mainly white, and held previous college degrees.

Finally, there is what has been called the indigenous paraprofessional who is recruited from the community where he works. He is usually employed, although not exclusively, in mental health centers, does not hold a college degree, and is engaged in therapeutically relevant work.

The first type, the "old paraprofessional," is of course the most common and the heart of the staff of mental health hospital facilities. The "new paraprofessional" is seen in the various efforts of the late 1950s and 1960s to meet professional manpower shortages, while the "indigenous parapro-fessional" is largely the child of the antipoverty and community mental health efforts. It is the last two categories to which we will give special attention.

THE "OLD" PARAPROFESSIONAL

A highly significant well-controlled experiment conducted by Ellsworth indicates that the old type of paraprofessional can play a powerful role in the improved treatment outcome for hospitalized male schizophrenics.[3] "A demonstration project in which the focus was on treatment was the development of the psychiatric aide as the rehabilitation agent," conducted at the Fort Meade, South Dakota Veterans Administration Hospital. Fort Meade is a 600-bed hospital; for the purposes of the demonstration, the patients of one building were used as an experimental group (n = 122) and patients of two other buildings as a control group (n = 214). For patients in both groups, the program was similar in use of medication, use of activity group therapy, the process of reaching decisions as to discharge, assign-ment of new admissions, and patient characteristics.[4]

The demonstration program was designed to raise the level of aide-patient interaction. To do this effectively the role of the aide in the hospital had to be altered, particular as relates to participation in decision making.

A *higher* percentage of the experimental group patients were released to the community during the thirty-month demonstration period, and a *lower* percentage of them had to return to the hospital.[5] Post-discharge outcomes were based upon six indices: (1) level of behavioral adjustment; (2) median days subsequently hospitalized; (3) released versus not released; (4) percent achieved twelve consecutive months in community; (5) good social adjustment; (6) discharge status six years later.

For the twenty-one pairs of comparisons (the experimental and control were each divided into three subgroups each depending upon degree of schizophrenia), the experimental group did better on all twenty-one, in thirteen of them at a substantial level of significance.[6] "Although the chronically hospitalized patients group profited most by the approach used in the experimental program, the acute group of patients also responded significantly."[7]

The key factors in the aides' role seemed to be in the increased interaction with patients and the aides participating more actively in decisions regarding patients. The two factors interconnected "as the active involvement of the aide in the decision-making process was found to be a necessary condition in sustaining aide-patient interaction."[8] Ellsworth concludes: "Our project has shown clearly that the role of a nonprofessionally trained person can be modified extensively in a psychiatric rehabilitation setting. When this modification takes the form of actively involving the nonprofessional in all phases of patient rehabilitation the treatment outcome for hospitalized male schizophrenics is highly significant."[9]

THE NEW PARAPROFESSIONAL

Perhaps best known in this area is the early work of Margaret Rioch[10] and the studies of Carkhuff and Truax. Both these investigations as well as a number of others reported in this section, provide evidence regarding the effectiveness of paraprofessionals as treatment agents.

In 1960, the adult psychiatry branch of the National Institute for Mental Health funded Rioch's Mental Health Counselors Program.[11] It was designed to fill the need for staff to provide low-cost psychotherapy and at the same time provide useful work for women with grown children. The value of these women was seen in their successful child-rearing experience and maturity. Eight women were chosen from among eighty who sought applications. Their median age was forty-three; seven were married, one widowed; they had an average of 2.4 children; all were college graduates, three had post-baccalaureate degrees; six had held professional jobs; four had been psychoanalyzed; all of their husbands held executive or professional positions. Their upper-class status is further shown by their ability to participate in a two-year training program without pay, with no guarantee of a job at the end.

All eight women completed the four semesters of training which emphasized professional breadth, not technician specificity. It was limited to psychotherapy and emphasized on-the-job training. Most of the patients of the trainees were adolescents.

Blind evaluation by outside experts of taped interviews with clients by trainees (not identified as such) were conducted. On a scale from 1 (poor) to 5 (excellent), the rating of the interviews on eight factors ranged from 2.7 (beginning of interview) to 4.2 (professional attitude), with an overall global impression mean score of 3.4.[12]

Evaluation of patient (n=49) progress showed that none changed for the worse, 19 percent showed no change; and 61 percent some change—35 percent slight improvement, 20 percent moderate improvement, 6 percent marked improvement.[13]

As to the counselor's faults, the director reports "they pleasantly reassure, protect and sympathize when it would be better to question more deeply and seriously. A second fault is a tendency to try to deal on a surface, common sense level with problems that are soluble only by eliciting unconscious conflicts."[14]

Similar to the Mental Health Counselors Program in terms of the background of the women trained as counselors, the Child Development Counselors program at the District of Columbia Children's Hospital differed from Rioch's program in that the counselors worked with patients of a different class background.[15] A similar cross-class effort was involved in Davidoff et al.'s Mental Health Rehabilitation Workers project in Albert Einstein College of Medicine, which also used mature women,[16] as did a Rochester, New York program where housewives worked with emotionally disturbed young school children.[17] The many programs using college students as therapeutic agents crossed both class and age lines.[18] Still other programs use peers as therapeutic agents.

In Australia, paraprofessional part-time volunteers (mature adults, successfully married) provide marriage counseling service. Some 270 persons serve approximately 15,000 persons per year. The volunteers receive weekly training for about a year and a half, primarily in a nondirective client-centered Rogerian approach. In about 15 percent of the cases the problem was solved, and in another 25 percent of the cases marital relations were noticeably improved, according to Harvey.[19]

Aides trained in Rogerian "play therapy" worked with six Head Start children diagnosed by a psychologist as in need of psychotherapy due to uncontrollable withdrawn and inhibited behavior. "All six children treated by the aide showed signs of improvement during the treatment period, " as reported by Androvic and Guerney.[20]

Similar to these efforts is the work at the Arkansas Rehabilitation Research and Training Center led by Charles Truax. Here the effort has been to identify those characteristics which make for more effective counseling, and for the use of lay counselors. Two major experiments are of interest. The first compared the work of lay therapists, clinical psychology graduate students, and experienced therapists.[21] It involved

150 chronic hospitalized patients. "The variety of current diagnoses included manic depressive reactions, psychotic depressive reactions, and schizophrenic...."[22] Patients were randomly assigned to lay persons who had 100 hours of training, clinical psychology graduate students, and experienced counselors. "The lay mental health counselors were able to provide a level of therapeutic conditions only slightly below that of the experienced therapists and considerably above that of graduate student trainees."[23]

Earlier work of the Arkansas group had isolated three factors as critical to therapist's effect upon patient; his communicating a high level of accurate empathy, nonpossessive warmth, and genuineness to the patients. There were no significant differences between the three groups of counselors as related to communicating accurate empathy or nonpossessive warmth. On the third factor, communicating genuineness to the patient, the experienced therapists showed significantly higher performance. Summarizing the effect upon patients of the work of the lay therapists, Truax, the project director, wrote: "Reseach evaluation indicated highly significant patient outcomes in *overall improvement, improvement in interpersonal relations, improvement in self-care, and self-concern, and improvement in emotional disturbance*"[24] (emphasis in the original).

The second study conducted at the Arkansas Center addresses more closely the effect of paraprofessional counselors. Some 400 patients at the Hot Springs Rehabilitation Center, a large residential center, were randomly assigned in three different groups: (1) to experienced professional M.A. degree counselors; (2) to experienced counselors assisted by an aide under maximum supervision; and (3) to aides (former secretaries with little if any college but 100 hours of training) working alone under supervision. Within each of the three patterns, caseload was varied at either thirty or sixty; thus, there was a 3 x 2 experimental design. Two-thirds of the patients were male; two-thirds white; all had personalities of behavioral problems, and a sizable number had speech and hearing defects or were mentally retarded.[25]

Performance under the three patterns of staffing was measured based upon the client's: (1) work quantity; (2) cooperativeness; (3) work attitude; (4) work quality; (5) dependability; (6) ability to learn; (7) overall progress. On all measures: "The best results were obtained by the aides working alone under the daily supervision of professional counselors. The professional counselors working alone had the second best results, while the counselors plus the aide had the poorest effects upon clients."[26]

The greater positive effects on client rehabilitation by the aides with their own caseload appeared to be "due both to the somewhat higher levels of warmth and empathy communicated to the clients by the aides and the greater motivation and enthusiasm of the aides."[27] The aides spent more time with clients, especially when they had *high* caseloads. The professionals, when they had high caseloads, spent less time with clients. The aides, in effect, appeared to feel that it was necessary to work hard to get to all the cases, while the professionals seemed to feel that with so many clients to see, what was the use. However, "Overall, neither the total number of minutes spent in contact with individual clients nor the frequency of client contacts was related to the client vocational progress."[28] Carrying their conclusions beyond this project, the authors state: "The findings presented here are consistent with a growing body of research which indicates that the effectiveness of counselling and psychotherapy, as measured by constructive changes in client functioning, is largely independent of the counselor's level of training and theoretical orientation."[29] Summarizing his review of many of the programs described above, Garfield concludes, "The implication of all the programs. . . is that counselors can be trained in a clinical setting, in a reasonably short time, to perform a variety of functions."[30]

The broadest examination of the work of paraprofessionals in mental health is Sobey's study of over 10,000 paraprofessionals in 185 NIMH-sponsored programs.[31] As the data are presented in gross categories, one cannot, for the most part, distinguish the particular type of paraprofessionals being employed, although it would seem that they include persons from all three of the groups we have delineated above—the "old" paraprofessional, the "new" paraprofessional, and the indigenous paraprofessional. The major finding relates to the reason for the use of paraprofessionals: "Nonprofessionals are utilized not simply because professional manpower is unavailable but rather to provide new services in innovative ways. Nonprofessionals are providing such therapeutic functions as individual counselling, activity group therapy, milieu therapy, they are doing case finding; they are playing screening roles of a non-clerical nature; they are helping people to adjust to community life; they are providing special skills such as tutoring; they are promoting client self-help through involving clients in helping others having similar problems."[32]

The basis for the use of paraprofessionals is illustrated by the responses of project directors to the question of whether, given a choice of hiring professionals, project directors would prefer to use paraprofessionals for those functions which professionals had previously performed.[33]

In short, 54 percent perferred to use paraprofessionals over professionals for tasks previously performed by professionals, or to put it another way, only 32 percent preferred to use professionals. As could be anticipated from the above: "Overwhelmingly the project directors felt that the service performed by nonprofessionals justified the expense of training, supervision and general agency overhead."[34] The directors saw paraprofessionals contributing across a broad spectrum of program activities including servicing more people, offering new services, and providing the project staff with new viewpoints in regard to the project population.[35] The response to the last item relating to "new viewpoints" suggests that a significant number of the paraprofessionals were indigenous workers. Also in sixty-nine projects, the directors reported expanding the professional's understanding of the client group through association with the paraprofessionals.[36] The same thrust is to be seen in the comment that "the introduction of nonprofessionals was perceived as infusing the projects with a new vitality, and forcing a self-evaluation which although painful, led to beneficial changes for the field of mental health."[37]

The work-style and personal attributes of the paraprofessionals were important, as they brought "a change in atmosphere within the agency, and more lively and vital relationships among staff and between patients and staff....Improved morale, better attitude toward patients, definite improvement in over-all quality of service were other improvements reported. The addition of youthful, untrained personnel within several hospitals make the older trained personnel re-examine their own roles and the role, structure and function of the entire hospital."[38] In summary: "Nonprofessionals were viewed as contributing to mental health in two unique ways: (1) *filling new roles based on patient needs* which were previously unfilled by any staff; and (2) performing parts of tasks previously performed by professionals, but *tailoring the task to the nonprofessionals' unique and special abilities*"[39] (emphasis added). The value of the use of new paraprofessionals is summarized by Carkhuff, a former staff member of the Arkansas Center: "Indirectly comparable studies, selected lay persons with or without training and/or supervision have patients who demonstrate changes as great or greater than the patients of professional practitioners."[40]

THE INDIGENOUS PARAPROFESSIONAL

The characteristics of the lay counselor, as described by Carkhuff,[41] appear to apply as well to the indigenous worker: (1) the increased ability to enter the milieu of the distressed; (2) the ability to establish peer-like relationships with the needy; (3) the ability to take an active part in the client's total life situation; (4) the ability to empathize more fully with the client's style of life; (5) the ability to teach the clients, from within the client's frame of reference, more successful actions; (6) the ability to provide clients with a more effective transition to more effective levels of functioning within the social system.

One of the earliest uses of indigenous paraprofessionals was at Howard University, where the "Baker's Dozen" project of Jacob Fishman,[42] Lonnie Mitchell,[43] and colleagues was conducted. The team's work has continued both at Howard and at the University Research Corporation, whose many reports include consideration of mental health programs, primarily as part of New Careers efforts.[44]

A 1969 survey of eighty community mental health enters found that 42 percent of all full-time positions were filled by indigenous workers. The figures were higher in drug abuse treatment (60 percent) and geriatric service (70 percent).[45] A study in the same year of paraprofessionals in ten community mental health centers in New York City reported their "actual work as described by administrators varied from unskilled to highly skilled, but more often is of the highly skilled variety."[46] The work included: interviewing, escort service, home visits, manning a storefront office, receiving complaints, collecting information, acting as translators, performing individual and group counseling, organizing community meetings, leading a therapy group, assisting patients in self-care, acting as patients' advocates with other agencies, casefinding, screening applicants, making case conference presentations, doing casework, giving speeches, planning after-care services, and giving supportive psychotherapy to expatients.[47]

Reiff and Riessman make the point that the use of the indigenous paraprofessional is part of the new concern for service to the poor. If the only concern is to meet professional manpower shortages, indigenousness is unnecessary. However, if there is a concern to reach and serve those unreached and unserved, in short, if the propelling motive grows out of a critique of service performance, then the indigenous worker may be needed.[48] The ability of the indigenous paraprofessionals is "rooted in their background. It is not based on things they have been taught, but on what they *are*."[49] They are poor, from the neighborhood, minority group members, their family is poor, they are a peer of the client with common language, background, ethnic origin, style, and interests.[50] They can establish special relations with clients—the paraprofessional "belongs," he is a "significant other," he is "one of us." His life-style is similar to that of the client, especially "the tendency to externalize causes rather than look for internal ones."[51]

Hallowitz, the codirector of the pioneering Lincoln Hospital Mental Health Services Neighborhood Service Center program, describes a range of activities for the indigenous worker in such a setting. These include: expediting, being a friend in need, sociotherapy, supervised work, services to posthospital patients, services to the disturbed in the community, self-help.

The Lincoln Hospital Mental Health Services Neighborhood Service Center program began with an OEO grant of January 1, 1965. Three centers were established, each staffed with five to ten aides. They were seen as "bridges" between the professionals and the community. They are expediters, advocates, and counselors. Something of the power of their impact and the need for services in a community such as the South Bronx is shown by the service figure of 6,500 persons at two of the centers in the first nine months. Since the program offered services to the clients' whole family, it was estimated that over 25,000 persons were affected during that period.[52]

Harlem Hospital has employed indigenous workers in a variety of roles. Harlem residents interested in working with the aged provided outpatient geriatric psychiatric services. They made home visits, provided escort services, observed and reported upon patient behavior, and provided social services. About half of the study group of sixty cases were successfully managed. Especially innovative is June Christmas's Harlem Hospital Group Therapy Program, which uses indigenous aides.[53] The aides work in a half-day treatment program for a small group of chronic psychotic posthospital patients. The aides participate as cotherapists in weekly group psychotherapy sessions, act as participants and expediters in the monthly medication group meetings, are members of the weekly therapeutic community meetings, and lead the weekly client discussion goups. In addition, they perform case services, family services, and home interviews: they survey patient needs and provide community mental health education.[54] The program was expected to hold one-third of the patients; it has held two-thirds.[55] A four-step career ladder—trainee, worker, technician, and specialist—is gained in part through the efforts of local 1199 of the Drug and Hospital Workers Union.[56]

The Temple University Community Mental Health Center has trained indigenous workers as mental health assistants, workers who they describe as "helpers first, then therapists."[57] Over time, a work pattern developed where the mental health assistants "function as a 'primary therapist' providing on-going treatment and continuity of care which would include the procurement of ancillary (professional) services whenever appropriate".[58] The assistant, a title the workers themselves preferred to "aide," worked with 96 percent of the patients in the clinic's first year. Two key factors in their work involved "holding" patients and, by being available, preventing hospitalization. "While the percentage of patients' attrition between initial contact and first appointment is still high, it is a lower rate than that presented for comparable patient aggregates in usual clinic settings. The need to hospitalize patients contacting the crisis center and clinic has decreased by 50 percent due to the Assistants' availability for immediate outpatient care."[59]

The Central City Community Mental Health Center in Los Angeles uses community workers in a program designed to develop additional mental health manpower, train new workers, improve understanding between the disadvantaged and mental health personnel, and increase the available services and create new services appropriate to the disadvantaged. The community workers are used in the mental health facility itself, at a family service center, in various social welfare agencies, in a public health project, and in a public housing program. They also provide crisis intervention therapy in a suicide prevention program.[60]

Among the other uses of indigenous paraprofessionals in mental health programs are: alcoholism counselors in a program of the Baltimore County Health Department; paramedic technicians at a state residential school for the mentally retarded in Hawaii; part of a home treatment team at the Veterans Administration Hospital in Tuscaloosa, Alabama; and in a child guidance clinic component of a comprehensive mental health center in Rochester, New York.

FORMAL EDUCATION AND PERFORMANCE

In a far-reaching study of seventeen state rehabilitation agencies, involving 209 counselors, 50 supervisors, and 1,502 patients, the ratings of supervisors and patients were correlated with four levels of worker education—post-M.A., M.A., B.A., and less than B.A. "Higher levels of academic training of rehabilitation counselors do not result in higher supervisor ratings on the dimension of overall effectiveness of the counselor. Higher levels of academic training for rehabilitation counselors do not result in higher client reports of satisfaction with his counselor."[61]

The lack of correlation between formal education and work performance has been cited in many of the reports described above. It may be that the type of formal education presently offered does not lead to improved paraprofessional performance because, as we have seen, training of untrained people has led to improved performance. New training approaches are beginning to develop at the college level.

Something of a new approach is being developed in the new mental health college programs. An NIMH grant in 1965 inaugurated at Purdue University the first two-year training program for mental health workers.[62] This was followed in 1966 by a Southern Regional Education Board conference on the role of community colleges in mental health training. In 1967, two Maryland community colleges began such programs,[63] and by September 1968, twenty-six community colleges were offering similar programs, and fifty-seven in 1970. The programs emphasize practicum, interviewing skills, counseling, use of community resources, and techniques of behavior modification.[64]

In evaluating the Purdue program, various effects have been noted regarding changes in patient care—"humanizing" the hospital, opening closed wards, establishing patient government, using recreation and work facilities more, and using new treatment modalities such as milieu therapy and sociotherapy.[65]

These developments offer some countervailing tendencies to the finding of the survey of New York City community mental health centers described above, that despite the fact that 70 percent of the center administrators rated the paraprofessional contribution as "essential" and another 22 percent rated it as "highly desirable," there is "little thought given toward developing the paraprofessional job into a worthwhile one."[66]

Perhaps encouraging is the fact that the graduates of the new Purdue program, while working in mental health programs, have chosen not to do so in traditional mental health facilities. It may be, as the authors suggest, that these new workers are disillusioned with the traditional medical model of mental health services.[67]

The tensions involved between new personnel, new training, and traditional mental health practices have been well captured in a far-reaching article by Minuchin. He points out that initially the use of paraprofessionals in mental health grew out of the manpower shortage. "For many professionals, a very important major assumption was implicit in this strategy; that we could maintain intact the traditional conceptualizations of mental illness and treatment, simply fitting the nonprofessional into the already existing structure of delivery of service. But the inclusion of paraprofessionals in the existing structure of delivery of service brought to a head a bipolarity of approaches to mental illness which was already incipient in the field."[68]

At the one pole where sociological thinking dominated, where pathology is seen as coming from the "outside in," paraprofessionals have had less difficulty in fitting in. On the other pole, when the individual is very much a separate human being, the problem of fitting in has been very much greater. The paraprofessionals are seen as doing little more than "implementing the professional's recommendation and their supervision."[69]

Minuchin's answer is that the field itself must be changed, indeed the very relationship of individual and society reconceptualized.[70] As we have seen, the paraprofessional, initially introduced in a narrow framework, has in one way or another become a force for and focus around changes of a basic nature in the field. These changes, rather than minor tinkering within the present structure, may be the shapers of the paraprofessionals' future role in mental health.

SUMMARY

A wide range of data on traditional "old" paraprofessionals working in hospitals, new middle-class paraprofessionals, and indigenous paraprofessionals all indicate in various ways that paraprofessionals can play a role in the rehabilitation and treatment of patients. Probably no single study is conclusive by itself, although a number of them, such as the Ellsworth study, are well controlled and offer rather powerful evidence. The point is that the multiplicity of evidence derived from a great variety of different sources, stemming from different investigator biases, and using diverse methods and indices leads to the conclusion that paraprofessionals play an important role as treatment agents and contribute to the improved mental health of clients and patients in highly significant, often unique, ways.

NOTES

1. Many terms have been used for the noncredentialed worker: nonprofessional, subprofessional, new professional, paraprofessional, aide, auxiliary, allied worker, community professional, community worker, new careerist, etc. Recently, the term paraprofessional seems to be most widely accepted and is the one we shall use throughout the article, although many of the workers themselves are beginning to prefer "new professional." See Roberta Boyette, "The Plight of the New Careerist," *American Journal of Orthopsychiatry* 41 (1971): 237-38.

2. There is a huge and rapidly growing literature concerning paraprofessional programs in general, as well as mental health programs in particular. Illustrative is the recent publication of a bibliography on paraprofessional programs which contains well over a thousand items: National Institute for New Careers, *New Careers Bibliography: Paraprofessionals in the Human Services* (Washington, D.C.: University Research Corporation, 1970).

3. Robert Ellsworth, *Nonprofessionals in Psychiatric Rehabilitation*(New York: Appleton-Century-Crofts, 1968).

4. Ibid.,p.87.

5. Ibid.,p.162.

6. Ibid., p.161.

7. Ibid.,p.164.

8. Ibid.,p.165.

9. Ibid.

10. Margaret Rioch et al., "National Institute of Mental Health Pilot Study in Training Mental Health Counselors," *American Journal of Orthopsychiatry* 33 (1963): 678-98.

11. Ibid., pp. 683-84.

12. Ibid., p. 685.

13. Ibid., p. 688.

14. Francine Sobey, *The Nonprofessional Revolution in Mental Health*(New York: Columbia University Press, 1970).

15. Carl Eisdorfer and Stuart E. Jolann, "Principles for the Training of 'New Professionals' in Mental Health," *Community Mental Health Journal* 5 (1969): 357.

16. Ida F. Davidoff, "The Mental Health Rehabilitation Worker: A Member of the Psychiatric Team,"*Community Mental Health Journal* 5 (1969): 46-54.

17. Melvin Zax et al., "A Teacher-Aide Program for Preventing Emotional Disturbances in Young Schoolchildren,"*Mental Hygiene* 50 (1966): 406-15.

18. Emory L. Cowen et al., "A College Student Volunteer Program in the Elementary School Setting," *Community Mental Health Journal* 2 (1966): 319-28; Jules D. Holzberg et al., "Chronic Patients and a College Companion

Program,"*Mental Hospitals* 15 (1964): 152-58; S.F. Kreitzer, "The Therapeutic Use of Student Volunteers" in *Psychotherapeutic Agents: New Roles for Nonprofessionals, Parents, and Teachers,* ed. Bernard F. Guerney, Jr. (New York: Holt, Rinehart & Winston, 1969); William E. Mitchell, "Amicatherapy: Theoretical Perspectives and an Example of Practice,"*Community Mental Health Journal* 2 (1966): 307-14; Frank Reissman and Emanuel Hallowitz, "Neighborhood Service Center Program," A Report to the U.S. Office of Economic Opportunity on the South Bronx Neighborhood Service Center, December 1965, pp. 1-7.

19.   L. V. Harvey, "The Use of Non-Professional Auxiliary Counselors in Staffing a Counseling Service,"*Journal of Counseling Psychology* 11 (1964): 348-51.

20.   Michael P. Androvic and Bernard Guerney, Jr., "A Psychotherapeutic Aide in a Head Start Program, Part 1, Theory and Practice,"*Children* 16 (1969): 16.

21.   Charles B. Truax, *An Approach toward Training for the Aide-Therapist: Research and Implications* (Fayetteville: Arkansas Rehabilitation Research and Training Center, 1965), p. 10.

22.   Ibid.,p. 9.

23.   Ibid., p. 12.

24.   Charles B. Truax, *The Use of Supportive Personnel in Rehabilitation Counseling* (Fayetteville: Arkansas Rehabilitation Research and Training Center, n.d.).

25.   Charles B. Truax and Janus L. Lister, "Effectiveness of Counselors and Counselor Aides," *Journal of Counseling Psychology* 17 (1970): 333.

26.   Ibid., p. 334.

27.   Ibid.

28.   Truax, "The Use of Supportive Personnel."

29.   Robert M. Vidaver, "The Mental Health Technician: Maryland's Design for a New Health Career," *American Journal of Orthopsychology* 34(1969): 1015.

30.   Sol L. Garfield, "New Developments in the Preparation of Counselor's Level of Training and Job Performance,"*Journal of Counseling Psychology* 17 (1970): 524.

31.   Sobey, p. 6.

32.   Ibid., pp. 155-56.

33.   Ibid., p. 154.

34.   Ibid., p. 159.

35.   Ibid., p. 161.

36.   Ibid., p. 175.

37.   Ibid., p. 160.

38.   Ibid., p. 174.

39.   Truax, "An Aproach toward Training for the Aide-Therapist."

40.   Robert E. Carkhuff, "Differential Training of Lay and Professional Helpers," *Journal of Counseling Psychology* 15 (1968): 119.

41.   Ibid., pp. 121-22.

42.   Jacob R. Fishmen and John McCormack, "Mental Health without Walls: Community Mental Health in the Ghetto,"*New Careers Perspectives* 4 (1969); Jacob R. Fishman and Lonnie E. Mitchell, "New Careers for the Disadvantaged," a paper presented at the annual meeting of the American Psychiatric Association, May 13, 1970, San Francisco, California.

43.   Lonnie E. Mitchell et al., "Baker's Dozen: A Program for Training Young People as Mental Health Aides," in National Institute for Mental Health,

Mental Health Program Reports 2 (1968): 11-24; Lonnie E.Mitchell et al., *Training for Community Mental Health Aides: Leaders for Child and Adolescent Therapeutic Activity Groups; Report of a Program* (Washington, D.C.: Institute for Youth Studies, Howard University, 1966).

44. National Institute for New Careers, *An Assessment of Technical Assistance and Training Needs in New Careers Projects Being Sponsored by the United States Training and Employment Service, Manpower Administration, U.S. Department of Labor* (Washington, D.C.: University Research Corporation, 1969); National Institute for New Careers, *New Careers in Mental Health: A Status Report* (Washington, D.C.: University Research Corporation, 1970).

45. National Institute for New Careers, *New Careers in Mental Health,* pp.14-15.

46. Harry Gottesfeld et al., "A Study of the Role of Paraprofessionals in Community Mental Health,"*Community Mental Health Journal* 6 (1970): 286.

47. Ibid.

48. Robert Reiff and Frank Riessman, *The Indigenous Nonprofessional: A Strategy of Change in Community Action and Community Mental Health Programs* (New York: National Institute of Labor Education, 1964), p.6.

49. Ibid., p.8.

50. Perhaps the ultimate in the use of the indigenous worker is an NIMH-funded project to train twelve Navajo males as medicine men. They are to learn the fifty ceremonies of tribal traditions for treating illness and to work with the Public Health Service doctors in referrals and assistance.

51. Reiff and Riessman, pp. 9-10.

52. Reissman and Hallowitz, pp. 1-7.

53. June Jackson Christmas, "Group Methods in Teaching and Action: Non-Professional Mental Health Personnel in a Deprived Community,"*American Journal Of Orthopsychiatry* 36 (1966): 410-19.

54. Ibid., pp. 413-14.

55. Ruth Wade et al., "The View of the Professional," *American Journal of Orthopsychiatry* 34 (1969): 678.

56. National Institute for New Careers, *New Careers Bibliography.*

57. Mary Lynch et al., "The Role of Indigenous Personnel as Clinical Therapists," *Archives of General Psychiatry* 19 (1968): 428.

58. Ibid., p. 429.

59. Ibid., p. 430.

60. National Institute for New Careers, *New Careers in Mental Health,* p.12.

61. James R. Engelkes and Ralph R. Roberts, "Rehabilitation Counselor's Level of Training and Job Performance," *Journal of Counseling Psychology* 17 (1970): 524.

62. Alfred Wellner and Ralph Simon, "A Survey of Associate Degree Programs for Mental Health Technicians,"*Hospital and Community Psychiatry* 20 (1969): 166.

63. Vidaver, p. 678.

64. Wellner and Simon, pp. 166-67.

65. John Hadley et al., "An Experiment in the Education of the Paraprofessional Mental Health Worker: The Purdue Program,"*Community Mental Health Journal* 5 (1970): 42.

66. Gottesfeld et al., p. 289.

67. Wellner and Simon, p. 168.

68. Salvador Minuchin, "The Paraprofessional and the Use of Confrontation in the Mental Health Field," *Journal of Orthopsychiatry* 39 (1969): 722-29.

69. Ibid., p. 724.

70. Ibid., p. 725.

10

The Ideology and Methodology of Employment Statistics

John C. Leggett and Claudette Cervinka

Puppet shows are generally thought of as a harmless form of entertainment for children. The puppeteer pulls the strings, the puppets dance, and the kids are entertained. But when the puppeteer is the United States Department of Labor's Bureau of Labor Statistics and the puppets are the figures on unemployment in the United States, this manipulation becomes a deadly serious game.

The unemployed in this country, particularly racial minorities, are systematically undercounted. By arbitrarily deciding who should and shouldn't be counted, how they should be counted, who is or isn't unemployed and even passing off comparisons of "oranges to apples" as valid statistical practice, the Bureau of Labor Statistics (BLS) sounds the call that the government would like us to believe—that the picture is rosy and things are getting better all the time.

The BLS statistics purport to show that the welfare state takes care of its own. And the executives of this state publicly pose as helpers of the down and out. But just who are they helping by hiding large numbers of unemployed workers—and who are they harming? What does it mean when the *New York Times* reports that New York state unemployment was 5.7 percent in August 1971, down from 6.1 percent in July? Few nonprofessional persons have the time or resources necessary to piece together the true picture. Most of us have been content to let the puppeteer weave his illusion, vaguely aware that some sort of behind-the-scenes manipulation is involved. The time has come to cut the strings and take a harsh look at the real figures.

A new peak of statistical obfuscation was reached in January of 1971 when the Department of Labor changed certain of its counting procedures. Harry Brill, a sociologist at the University of Massachusetts and a skilled interpreter of labor statistics commented in *The Nation:*

> President Nixon recently told the press and the public that the actual unemployment rate averaged lower in 1970 than during the recession years of the 1960s. He is, unfortunately, mistaken. Actually, the current estimate of unemployment would read higher had the Department of Labor not changed its counting procedures. Until 1967, the Department in its monthly survey counted as unemployed all those who volunteered that they were too discouraged to look for work. According to its own study, the rate then would have been 50 percent higher if it had solicited the reasons for not actively seeking work. Despite these findings, the Department of Labor decided to assume that anyone not actively looking for work must therefore not be interested in working. So now even those who volunteer their despair—and more are despairing—are no longer regarded as unemployed.
>
> The Department counted as unemployed until recently (1967) those who were actively seeking a job within the last sixty days. This too was drastically changed—to four weeks. Altogether dropped from the calculations of the unemployment rate are the youngest members of the labor force, ages 14 and 15. Since their chances of being out of work are extremely high, excluding them from the labor force count further reduces the official rate of unemployment. Formerly tallied as unemployed were workers who had jobs, but for various reasons were not working and were looking for work. For example, workers laid off because of weather conditions, such as those in the construction trades, fall into this category. Those belonging to this group are now counted as employed even though they are not receiving pay and are actively in pursuit of work.

Most importantly, this reshuffling of categories was accompanied by an unadjusted comparison. The Bureau of Labor Statistics drew a comparison between the unemployed of the early 1970s with those of the early 1960s without telling us how if at all the BLS had removed the recently deleted categories from the earlier estimates to allow for a fair comparison. No such statistical control was applied—tantamount to comparing oranges without peelings (1971) against oranges with peelings (1961) while forgetting to inform the general public how the comparison has been made. Rather than providing adjusted figures, the BLS supplies separate figures on dropped groups so that the researcher must compute an adjusted figure himself.

TABLE 1
Race, Employment Status, Sex, and Age: 1969-70 (in thousands)

(In thousands)

Employment status, sex, and age	Total		White		Negro and other races	
	1970	*1969*	*1970*	*1969*	*1970*	*1969*
Both sexes, 16-19 years:						
Civilian labor force	7,246	6,970	6,439	6,168	807	801
Employment	6,141	6,117	5,568	5,508	573	609
Unemployment	1,105	853	871	660	235	193
Unemployment rate	15.3	12.2	13.5	10.7	29.1	24.0

Before we can go any further in our analysis we must acquaint ourselves with the way in which the BLS does in fact gauge three things: (1) being a member of the labor force, (2) being unemployed, and (3) being employed.

First, who is in and who is out of the labor force? According to "How the Government Measures Unemployment" (BLS Report Number 312, June 1967):

> Persons under 16 years of age are excluded from our count of the labor force, as are all inmates of institutions, regardless of age. All other members of the civilian non-institutional population are eligible for the labor force by our definitions. Therefore, persons age 16 and over who have no job and are not looking for one are counted as "not in the labor force." For many who do not participate in the labor force, going to school is the reason. Family responsibilities keep others out of the labor force. Still others suffer a physical or mental disability which makes them unable to participate in normal labor force activities.

Most of these situations are quite clear: Bob Jones reports that he is attending college; Barbara Green feels that her two young children need her care; or Stephen Smith would like to work, but his doctor told him that he must not because he recently suffered a heart attack.

All three of these people are not in the labor force and are classified accordingly, in their respective categories: "in school," "keeping house" and "unable to work."

There is a fourth group of persons who are not in the labor force. They are classified "other," which includes everyone who did not give any of the above reasons for non-participation in the labor force. Such persons may be retired and feel that they have made their contribution to the economy throughout the course of their lives, they may want to work only at certain times of the year, or they may believe that no employment is available for workers with their experience or training.

The illustrations are less than wholly inclusive. The category of labor force excludes, for example, hundreds of thousands of prison inmates who labor in our prisons and asylums. In addition, the labor force category also excludes millions who have tired of looking for work. Even if these people had earlier sought work with no results, by some strange twist of logic the fact that they failed to look for work in the last month mysteriously removes them from the ranks of the unemployed. They are shoved into some sort of limbo beyond the labor force.

Whom in fact does the BLS count (in its monthly survey of 50,000 Americans) as unemployed? By 1967 the definition of unemployed had become what it is today:

Persons are unemployed if they have looked for work in the past four weeks, are currently available for work, and, of course, do not have a job at the same time. Looking for work may consist of any of the following specific activities: registering at a public or private employment office; meeting with prospective employers; checking with friends or relatives; placing or answering advertisements; writing letters of application; being on a union or professional register.

There are two groups of people who do not have to meet the test of having engaged in a specific job seeking activity to be counted as unemployed. They are: a) persons waiting to start a new job within 30 days and b) workers waiting to be recalled from layoff. In all cases, the individual must be currently available for work.

Finally, who are the employed?

There is a wide range of job arrangements possible in the American economy, and not all of them fit neatly into a given category. For example, people are considered employed if they did any work at all for pay or profit during the survey week. This includes all part-time and temporary work as well as regular full-time year-round employment. Persons are also counted as employed if they have a job at which they did not work during the survey week because they were on vacation; involved in an industrial dispute; prevented from working by bad weather; or taking time off for various personal reasons. These persons are counted among the employed and tabulated separately as "with a job but not at work," because they have a specific job to which they will return.

These specifications require a closer look. Missing from the unemployed, but counted among the employed, are people who work ten, twenty, or thirty hours a week. In fact, all forms of part-time help count as employed. But that isn't all. Finding their way into the employed category are short-and long-term strikers, regardless of whether or not they have an income. The short- and long-term ill (noninstitutionalized), and those on vacation, with or without pay, are also considered employed. Being employed, then, is not the same as being engaged at work. And even if you don't have an income, you can still be employed. Think about it.

On the other hand, people also tend to overlook the narrow criteria used for computing who is unemployed. They also forget that the category "unemployed" does not include those beyond the labor force. These two considerations are important since the percentage unemployed is computed by dividing the number of employed. More precisely, the unemployed are the numerator of the ratio, and since many of the objectively unemployed have been pushed into the limbo of "not in the labor force" by the BLS, they are not considered as part of what would otherwise be a fairly large numerator. Furthermore, since strikers, the ill, and the vacationers count as officially employed, we have in effect an unduly puny numerator peering down at a bloated denominator. The BLS has created a Kafkaesque situation where a sudden and numerous increase in strikers (hospital patients and/or vacationers) would inadvertently contribute to the immediate minimization of the official figure on unemployment. Think about that one, especially in communities such as Detroit.

Perhaps more puzzling than the "mistaken ratio" of the employed to the unemployed is the periodicity of the count. Even if we were to assume that monthly reports, corrected for their underestimation, would be useful, we could nonetheless use a more demonstrative measure of unemployment-one in fact computed by the BLS but inadequately publicized by it. From the point of view of at least some unemployed, far more important than a monthly rate is the aggregate unemployment rate. This BLS rate refers to the number of people who are unemployed over a period of one year. Harry Brill makes clear why he thinks this yearly rate is more important:

> If on the average, four million people are jobless each month, that does not necessarily mean that the individuals who are counted as unemployed in one month are the same who are counted as

unemployed a month later. Turnover among the unemployed occurs, and thus the total percentage, or number, of those who have been unemployed during each year must exceed the average monthly count.

This is not news to the Department of Labor. According to the testimony delivered by Secretary of Labor Wirtz before the Senate Committee on Employment and Man Power, "approximately 14 million men and women were unemployed at some time during the year of 1962." Fourteen million individuals are roughly 20 percent of the total "labor force"! Therefore, the total annual rate (20 percent) is 3.77 times the average monthly rate (5.3 percent) of that year. To that must be added millions of unemployed persons who are not counted by the Departments of Labor, and the figure soars to represent 18 or 20 million individuals.

Contrast the average monthly gross figures of four million with a yearly number of approximately 14 million persons unemployed for an average of eight to ten weeks (with an increasing proportion out of work for about fifteen weeks), even if we discount the frictionally unemployed (those people between jobs) for that length of time suggests that the unemployment picture is not as rosy as the government would have us believe.

The BLS has come under criticism from various sources because of its slanting of unemployment news. Perhaps in part because of these external criticisms, the BLS has experimented with measures which have in fact more clearly indicated the true number of people without work but with the desire to work should a job become available. In 1964, during the rosy days of Lyndon Johnson's administration, the Department of Labor published statistics which indicated that total monthly unemployment might be considerably higher than the 4.5 million specified in the official figures. The experimental-statistical measure on unemployment did in fact include those not in the official labor force. Specifically, the unemployed category for the first time included (1) those who had worked part time but wanted full-time jobs, as well as (2) those who had given up the search for work, plus (3) all of the others found beyond the pale of labor force participation (that is, those who had never searched for work). The BLS appeared to be on its way to evolving a measure of work force, one with a more realistic and humane definition than "labor force." The impact of the additional categories was clear according to a story in the March 11, 1964 *San Francisco Chronicle:*

The figures show that among white men aged 45 to 54 with four years of education or less, 221 of every 1000 are not working. Of these, 84 are listed as unemployed and 137 as "not in the labor force." Among those with college degrees, the corresponding figure shrinks to 39 who are not working, including ten unemployed and 29 not in the labor force.

Curiously enough, this more representative measure was dropped by the BLS soon after its introduction. The much needed innovation on work force measurement was erased, and the BLS opted for continuation of the traditional labor force categorization.

Some groups have suffered more than others from the consequences of undercount. And it's not too difficult to guess who they are. Blacks (and women) are cases in point. Many of their objectively unemployed fail to get counted. Hence their cases fail to get the publicity warranted by their circumstances. On January 8, 1971, the *Wall Street Journal* reported:

> What's more, experts say, the administration view overlooks what has been happening to the black labor force. As of November, it has shrunk somewhat despite population growth and the return of more black veterans from Vietnam. In the 16 to 19 age group, for instance, the black male force slumped 12 percent to 396,000 for the 12 months ending last November; the percentage of eligible blacks in this group working or seeking work dropped to 40.5 percent from 48.4 percent a year earlier. (Meantime, the white male teenage work force was swelling, in both size and participation rate.)
>
> But while fewer black teenage males were working or seeking work, the group's jobless rate was holding at 21 percent to 25 percent of the total work force. "Some people become so depressed they simply drop out of the labor force," explains Dale Hiestand, associate professor of business at Columbia University's graduate school of business. "But when they do, they aren't counted as unemployed—even though they really are."

It's the same old story. While unemployment among blacks is actually worsening, official figures hide the seriousness of the problem.

The official number of black unemployed has increased sharply in the last several years as the economy has slid into a recession. In an article in the *Monthly Labor Review* for February 1971 Paul Flaim and Paul Schwab document this point (see Table 1). The simple fact is that the number of young blacks beyond the labor force and officially unemployed is several times greater than the number of those officially employed.

The BLS can make certain unemployment situations seem less serious than they really are by skillfully juggling just where the figures are recorded. For instance, there is no separate category for Chicanos and Puerto Ricans. Obviously this means there is no way to gauge the seriousness of the unemployment problem for the Spanish-speaking population. But even beyond that, including this figure in the "white unemployed" category can obscure even further the incidence of black unemployment. This is particularly true in areas with large Chicano or Puerto Rican populations—New York City, for example. By inflating the number of white unemployed with the high rate of Spanish-speaking unemployed, the overall ratio of white/nonwhite unemployment becomes smaller. Blacks then must compare their situation with unreal, inflated figures on white unemployment.

Along the same lines, the BLS counts people of Asiatic background in the nonwhite category. This can obscure black unemployment in the San Francisco bay area and Hawaii, for example, where the unemployment rates for Japanese-Americans are extremely low. When these figures are lumped into the nonwhite statistics in a city like San Francisco, the general incidence of unemployment among nonwhites is lowered. Since "nonwhite" is generally read as "black," the black unemployment situation is obscured once again.

The solution is clear and simple. Unemployment figures must be broken down further than white and nonwhite. Statistics on separate racial minorities must be readily available so that each minority group can demand and get the separate help which it deserves. As a beginning step toward clearing up the confusion, we can strive to develop a typology of those whom the BLS refuses to count as unemployed. Fortunately, progress has already been made in this area. Harry Chester, research associate for the international union offices of the UAW, has developed a most useful four-part typology on workers now counted as "nonparticipants" in the labor force:

The discouraged workers. (This group is counted by BLS, but classified as "persons not in the labor force.") These are workers who, even though they desired work, were not engaged in job-seeking activities within the past four weeks because they thought that jobs in their line of work were not available, because they thought that employers would refuse to hire them due to their age or their race, or simply because they had been job hunting prior to the most recent four-week period and had given up in despair.

According to BLS, this group of discouraged workers amounted to 807,000 in the first quarter of 1971 and to 685,000 in the second quarter of 1971. Actually the number of discouraged workers is probably much larger. Various studies in depth have shown that because of the pressure of public opinion, workers are reluctant to admit that they have stopped looking for work because they can't find a job. Many pretend instead that they stopped seeking work because they are disabled or are chronically sick.

The nonpersons. Checks on the population census have shown that government surveys are unable to enumerate persons who are without a fixed residence (persons who sleep in condemned buildings, on park benches, at railroad stations). This group of persons is not represented in the BLS labor force sample, and we don't know anything about this group except that it is very clear that the group's unemployment rate is much higher than the national average.

Unemployed workers who are temporarily sick. In order to be counted as unemployed, a person must be available for work in the survey week. Consequently, unemployed workers who, in the survey week, are temporarily sick are counted as persons not in the labor force even though they need a job and even though, except for their temporary sickness, they would have been seeking work and would have been available for work.

In addition to causing a serious undercount of unemployment, this rule also causes the following anomaly: a worker with a job who is temporarily sick is considered a member of the labor force. But an unemployed worker who is temporarily sick is classified as a person not in the labor force.

Workers enrolled in government training programs. The enrollees of government training programs are classified either as employed, even though they don't have a regular job, or as persons not in the labor force, even though they need a job and engage in a job-seeking activity by getting themselves trained for a job.

Prior to 1965, this group was classified as unemployed. The magazine *Human Resources* (Fall 1969) which first raised this point estimated that this reclassification had the effect of reducing the overall unemployemnt rate by 0.4 percentage points.

Can we expect professional BLS statisticians to move to include these people in the category of unemployed? Current events would suggest the possibilities are indeed slim. Unfortunately, professionals employed by the BLS are apparently not in a position to do much about it. Any mild efforts to be objective in the monthly BLS press briefings and written reports were curtailed by a Nixon administration bent on allowing only the president's own immediate political emissaries the right to handle the important task of releasing statisics on unemployment.

On September 30, 1971, the *New York Times* most clearly indicated the degree to which the Nixon administration and top BLS administrators were bringing pressure to bear on the BLS professionals. In an editorial entitled "Politicizing the B.L.S.?", the *Times* states:

> Two ranking economists are reportedly planning to leave the bureau on the eve of a reorganization that would considerably reduce their

areas of authority. Administration spokesmen insist that the sha-
keup, part of a general overhaul of Federal statistical services
announced last July, has nothing to do with politics. The initial list
of new appointees rushed out by the White House yesterday had
done a little [*sic*] to dispel reports of political maneuvering in
connection with B.L.S. restaffing.

Three extensive reports reprinted in the *Congressional Record* indicate that
more is involved than press briefings. A thoroughgoing reorganization of
place, with business-oriented officials supplanting career officials in key
posts dealing with statistical analysis. So it now appears, regardless of the
consequences, that we are in for still more manipulation and illusion by
the puppet master.

Part III
The Working Class in an International Context

11

Organized Labor and American Foreign Policy

Henry Berger

During the course of the 1972 presidential election campaign in which he refused to support George McGovern, AFL-CIO President George Meany took the occasion to restate the foreign policy of the nation's largest union federation. In an article for the official journal of the labor organization over which he presides, Meany reaffirmed the commitment of the federation to the post-World War II foreign policy of the United States and denounced his critics as neo-isolationists whose proposals "would endanger the national security of the United States, jeopardize the freedom of our allies and hurt the prospects for world peace."[1]

In contrast, Meany declared that the "basic policy pursued by Democratic and Republican Administrations in the last 25 years has demonstrated its success in preventing major war and the expansion of communist totalitarianism." Those who seek limitations on American commitments abroad, to reduce American military expenditures, or to reach detente with Russia and China he dismissed as unwitting contributors to communist efforts to "seek world conquest and domination through political blackmail, subversion, military threats and aggression." By 1974 Meany had even managed to put President Nixon into this category. "I'm anticommunist," Meany told *Washington Post* columnist Haynes Johnson. "In fact if I remember right, Mr. Nixon claimed some years ago that he was the number one anticommunist...but if he was number one, I felt that I was number two. But he's no longer the number one anticommunist, I can assure you."[2]

Meany and other defenders of AFL-CIO foreign policy argue that organized labor's primary goal in foreign affairs has been and must continue to be the consistent defense of freedom against all forms of totalitarianism. But for some time now, liberal and radical critics of the AFL-CIO have condemned labor's conduct of foreign policy. The federation's rigid anticommunism, its interference in labor affairs abroad, its support of conservative and authoritarian foreign governments (as in Brazil and Vietnam), the assistance which it received in the past from the CIA, the unsavory alliance which it is claimed to have formed with the United States government and American business firms (particularly in underdeveloped nations), its quarrel with the International Labor Organization (ILO), its withdrawal from the International Confederation of Free Trade Unions (ICFTU), its unyielding approval of America's intervention in Vietnam, and its opposition to the Chilean government of Salvadore Allende are specific actions which the critics say demonstrate the cold war and even imperialist character of AFL-CIO foreign policy.

The reaction of the executive council of the AFL-CIO to President Nixon's Chinese and Russian policies illustrate this continuing posture. Upon the announcement of the President's decision to visit Peking, the executive council, which is the chief decision-making body of the 13.5 million member labor federation, voted twenty-four to four to oppose Mr. Nixon's "sudden, abrupt, and complete change of U.S. policy towards Communist China." Meany characteristically had gone further previously and suggested the dangers involved in Nixon's planned visit to China could result in another Munich. He reminded the president that during the 1930s the League of Nations "abandoned its principles and sacrificed Ethiopia and gave support to the fascist Mussolini and his friend Hitler." Similarly, Meany and the council blasted the notion of detente with the Soviet Union as a "fraud." The Soviet Union has not changed its objectives; only its methods. Detente has merely served as a smoke screen for a continuing Soviet military buildup, for the expansion of Soviet power abroad, and for the tightening of repressive rule at home and in Eastern Europe. Moreover, claims Meany, detente has produced results which have been far more beneficial to the Communist countries than to Western nations. It's a "one-way street," the labor chieftain bluntly declared. The United States makes concessions but the Soviets make none.[3]

These views concerning recent developments in United States foreign policy were ratified without recorded dissent at the AFL-CIO's 1973 national convention. The federation thus maintained its historical tradition of stringent opposition to communism or accomodation with Moscow and Peking. At the same time, the AFL-CIO persists in arguing that there is a communist ideological, military, and political threat to American security at home and abroad, that few differences in world objectives exist between the Soviet Union and Communist China, and that most international crises (including the conditions which created the Chilean coup of 1973 and the Middle Eastern Yom Kippur war) have been created or exploited by "international communism."[4]

How did it come about that the strongest and largest labor organization in America has followed a consistently "cold war" foreign policy? Who makes that policy, how representative of the rank and file are the views and actions of the leadership, and how effective is labor in achieving its aims overseas? Is the defense of freedom against totalitarianism the only objective of labor's foreign policy and has it always been a consistent effort? Why and how is organized labor's foreign policy different from the current strategies and tactics of official American foreign relations? Finally, to what extent does the foreign policy which labor spokesmen articulate contradict the interests and needs of the American working class?

The centrality of foreign policy to American society today is obvious. In virtually every significant respect, domestic and foreign concerns are closely related—as the current economic crisis illustrates. American workers are very much affected by and involved in those concerns as they touch their personal lives.

At the outset, it is important to establish a proper perspective. Unions, both affiliated and nonaffiliated with the AFL-CIO, represent about a fourth of the total work force in this country. At no time have more than about a third of the workers outside agriculture been organized, and for much of our history, those enrolled in unions totaled less than 10 percent. The bulk of union membership today consists of manual workers engaged in manufacturing, mining, construction, and transportation. Large numbers of blacks, other racial minorities, and women have in the past remained outside the ranks of organized labor.[5] Moreover, unions are winning fewer representation elections than ever before, their share of the work force is declining, and organized workers represent a shrinking percentage of the electorate (18 percent as opposed to 28 percent in 1964).[6]

Even so, like most groups in America, it is not sheer numbers alone which determine power or influence. More important are the quality of organization, the location of the particular organizations within the structure of the society, and the ability of such groups to maximize pressure at crucial times and in critical places. The building trades, the teamsters, the unions of the mass production and mining industries, railroad labor, and those unions engaged in defense production have been the powerhouses of American labor. Service employees and government workers are gaining a strong voice. These organizations influence decision making in the United States. Since most of these unions are affiliated with the AFL-CIO, that organization's leaders have commanded the attention of those who formulate and direct American foreign policy, and those union leaders have been identified with labor's activities abroad.

Any effort to examine the nature of labor's foreign policy must take account of these factors. Unfortunately, most of what is published is either largely descriptive in nature or of the exposé type, emphasizing cloak-and-dagger operations of such celebrated personalities as Jay Lovestone, recently retired director of the AFL-CIO's Department for International Affairs. The "who, what, when, and where" are important. But it is not enough to say that personalities have always played a dominant role and leave it at that. That kind of assessment tells us little about why American labor leaders hold the particular views they do or what historical influences have shaped labor's international perspective.[7]

Some commentators argue that workers in general are not concerned with foreign affairs; they are concerned with more immediate matters such as bargaining grievances. In the absence of such interest from the rank and file, the leadership has devised and executed foreign policy. But this description is nothing more than an adroit attempt to explain away the elitist character of decision making in the AFL-CIO. These same writers argue that those who make labor's foreign policy do so largely in accordance with the wishes of most unionists, and that these unionists would approve the attitudes and actions of the leadership if they were asked their views. There is significant evidence to the contrary.[8]

Studies of worker attitudes do indicate opinions. The Gallup polls from 1966 to 1969, for instance, indicate a generally growing opposition to the war in Vietnam among manual workers (see Table 1).[9]

But the usefulness of this data is limited. There is no distinction made between union and nonunion workers. Most important, there is no breakdown of the category of manual laborers into skilled, unskilled, service workers, and day laborers. The Roper surveys, however, do provide such data (see Table 2).[10]

The Roper figures show that skilled workers have supported American involvement in the war far more than other groups of workers; but among

TABLE 1
In View of the Developments Since We Entered the Fighting in Vietnam, Do You Think the U.S. Made a Mistake Sending Troops to Fight in Vietnam?

Manual Workers:

		Yes, Mistake	No	No Opinion
1966	March	22%	63%	15%
	May	35	49	16
	September	36	47	17
	November	30	52	18
1967	May	36	49	15
	July	39	49	12
	October	44	47	9
1968	February	42	46	12
	March	45	46	9
	April	43	45	12
	August	50	37	13
	October	49	40	11
1969	February	49	43	8
	October	56	34	10

TABLE 2
Do You Think It was a Mistake for the United States to Get Involved in Vietnam?

March 1966

	Yes	No	No Opinion
Skilled Workers	16.6%	71.0%	12.2%
Unskilled Workers	26.7	59.3	13.8
Service Workers	21.5	57.3	21.0
Laborers	30.8	50.2	18.8

February 1967

	Yes	No	No Opinion
Skilled Workers	32.2	57.9	9.7
Unskilled Workers	36.3	54.1	9.4
Service Workers	38.5	45.9	15.5
Laborers	45.3	45.3	9.2

April 1968

	Yes	No	No Opinion
Skilled Workers	41.8	48.3	9.8
Unskilled Workers	44.5	41.9	13.5
Service Workers	39.2	47.6	13.0
Laborers	57.1	38.0	4.7

all workers antiwar sentiment grew at a rate not reflected by the succession of prowar statements issued by the AFL-CIO during the same period. A Harris poll taken in 1968 provided different data concerning views on Vietnam among union members only, but without any breakdown by trades (see Table 3). The results show that two-thirds of the AFL-CIO members asked either favored a more aggressive policy in Vietnam or supported the present involvement.[11] On the other hand, when public opinion pollsters asked in 1968 and 1969 if defense spending should be increased, decreased, or remain the same, workers supported a decrease in such expenditures in significant percentages (see Table 4). However, no breakdown between the union and nonunion members was provided.[12]

The Harris polls of 1970-72 do distinguish between unionists and the rest of the population on this issue. Union members, the veteran pollster discovered, favored cutting defense spending 60 percent to 29 percent. This figure compared with a similar 58 percent to 30 percent for the rest of the country. Indeed, the Harris polls for the years 1968 to 1973, over a whole range of issues, domestic and international, support the general view that organized labor's views, *taken as a whole* do not differ significantly from those of the rest of the population. In short, the hard hat image of rank and file labor unionists as being more conservative than other

TABLE 3
Which Statement about Vietnam Do You Agree With Most?
(Harris Poll, April 16, 1968)

	Total queried	Union members	AFL-CIO	Teamsters
I disagree with our present policy. We are not going far enough. We should go further, such as carrying the war more into North Vietnam.	21%	23%	27%	31%
I agree with what we are doing, but we should increase our military effort.	38	41	37	44
I agree with what we are doing, but we should do more to bring about negotiations, such as stop bombing North Vietnam.	17	21	15	15
I disagree with our present policy. We should pull out our troops now.	15	10	13	11
Not sure.	9	6	8	-

Americans is sharply overstated. More significantly, Harris found that while AFL-CIO leaders supported militant anticommunism, rank and file trade unionists opposed the renewed bombing of North Vietnam in December 1972, 52 percent to 37 percent, favored the recognition of Cuba, 50 percent to 33 percent (early 1973 poll), and endorsed closer relations with the Soviet Union and China, 77 percent to 12 percent (1972 and 1973 polls). "In short," Harris concluded, "it appeared that George Meany was playing status quo politics; while his own members were far more inclined to opt for change."[13]

TABLE 4
December 1968, Should Defense Spending Be:

December 1968

Should defense spending be:

	Decreased	Increased	Stay the Same	No Opinion
Skilled workers	51.3%	19.8%	22.9%	5.8%
Unskilled workers	47.3	26.8	18.0	7.8
Service workers	57.1	20.2	20.2	2.3
Laborers	43.7	22.9	25.0	8.3

July 1969

Is government spending for defense:

	Too little	Too much	Just right	No Opinion
Skilled workers	8.9%	39.9%	35.6%	13.3%
Unskilled workers	7.5	39.0	37.5	14.0
Service workers	3.7	50.6	34.1	11.3
Laborers	7.8	36.8	44.7	10.5

These polls, of course, do not cover all foreign policy issues or even all aspects of the questions which were asked. The time period is limited and the information does not provide explanations for the answers workers give to such questions. Nor do they tell us why differences exist between various categories of workers, including race and income. But they suggest very strongly that the question of rank and file thinking on foreign policy matters is much more complicated than is usually depicted by the defenders and detractors of official AFL-CIO policy on the subject.

We do know that the building trades are the power base of George Meany's position in the AFL-CIO, and they have been the strongest supporters of anticommunism and the Vietnam War for a variety of mixed reasons. We also know that 10 percent of the entire labor force owes its pay check to defense spending and that nearly all that group is unionized. Thus workers employed in those industries are dependent upon defense expenditures for their livelihood. Nearly half of the defense related employment in 1970 consisted of blue-collar workers, and craftsmen and other skilled workers made up over a fifth. These were significant numbers, especially since the two groups constituted smaller percentages in the overall work force (see Table 5).[14]

No one can accurately gauge the total economic and social impact at any one time of defense spending, though one estimate some years ago claimed that for every one dollar spent on national defense, another $1.00 to $1.40 of economic product is stimulated. This would double the number of persons employed due to the economic stimulus of defense spending.

TABLE 5
Defense-Generated Employment in Government and Private Industry, by Major Occupation Groups, Fiscal Year 1970 (in thousands)

| Occupational group | Distribution of total U.S. employment (percent) | Defense-generated employment (fiscal 1970) | | | | | |
| | | Total | | Government* | | Private Industry | |
		Number	Percent	Number	Percent	Number	Percent
All groups	100.0	3,687	100.0	1,098	100.0	2,589	100.0
White-collar workers	46.8	1,665	45.2	623	56.6	1,042	40.2
Professional and technical workers.	13.6	606	16.4	232	21.1	374	14.4
Manager, officials and proprietors...	10.0	288	7.8	105	9.6	184	7.1
Clerical workers...	17.2	694	18.8	281	25.5	413	16.0
Sales workers......	6.0	76	2.1	4	.4	72	2.8
Blue-collar workers	36.6	1,824	49.5	427	38.9	1,397	54.0
Craftsmen and foremen..........	13.0	749	20.3	242	22.0	507	19.6
Operatives........	18.7	903	24.5	114	10.4	789	30.5
Nonfarm laborers...	4.9	172	4.7	72	6.6	100	3.9
Service workers.....	12.4	141	3.8	48	4.4	93	3.6
Farm workers........	4.2	58	1.6	.....	.....	58	2.2

* Includes civilian employment of the Department of Defense and defense-generated State and local government employment.

NOTE: Sum of individual items may not add to totals due to rounding.

The slowdown in military expenditures (from $75.7 billion in 1969 to $70 billion in 1972, 8.4 percent and 6.5 percent of the gross national product, respectively) had the reverse effect of creating depressed areas in such widely separated geographical locations as Seattle, Los Angeles, Long Island, New York, and Boston. Nixon administration economists viewed the proposed 1975 defense budget of $85.8 billion (5.9 percent of the gross national product) as a major tool for pumping up the economy to meet an expected recession. The impact of the defense economy upon working-class economic status and social values should be investigated more thoroughly, but this relationship is important in understanding the political views of many workers and the cold war mentality of many labor leaders, especially in the AFL-CIO.[15]

However, the foreign policy outlook of labor's leaders existed even before the Vietnam War or before the postwar defense establishment of the present magnitude was created. The development can only be understood in the context of domestic American labor affairs, in the fact that the AFL emerged as an interest-group trade-union association (rather than a class-conscious labor organization), that the craft unionists sought to win recognition and power in their struggles with the corporations by adopting conservative union beliefs and objectives, and that AFL president Samuel Gompers and others considered foreign labor ideologies and movements different from their own and a threat to their successes. Because the IWW and the socialists constituted or seemed to pose a challenge to Gomper's version of trade unionism during precisely those years when the AFL achieved success and power (1890-1914), the AFL leaders had to demonstrate that their brand of unionism would prevail. That involved, among other things, the acceptance of corporate capitalism and opposition to radicals. But the trade-union leaders of the AFL were not co-opted, tricked, or lured into their allegiance to capitalism. They knew what they were doing and always sought first of all to protect the interests of their organizations. They increasingly linked such interests to those of corporate capitalism. Foreign policy was and has remained a splendid example of this development.[16]

The period of general prosperity after 1897 was an era of rapid trade-union expansion. The Spanish-American War and the Boer War contributed to the economic upturn. Skilled laborers, always the base strength of the AFL, were in great demand and manufacturers were willing to enter trade agreements with labor unions in order to secure uninterrupted, disciplined production at dependable wage prices. Moreover, the development of business trusts and other forms of combinations to control prices contributed to the growth of trade unionism. Many business men, as Clarence Bonnett observed over fifty years ago, actively used labor unions to create corporate combinations. "Negotiatory associations made trade agreements with certain unions, and by means of these generally forced the independents to come into the combination if their businesses were not ruined."[17] (There were obvious outstanding exceptions to this pattern. U.S. Steel and Standard Oil come quickly to mind.) At the same time, these developments at home and abroad and the events which produced them convinced many government, agricultural, and business leaders that commercial expansion abroad was necessary and desirable for the future vitality of the American economy. Some went further, advocating the export of ideas and institutions—and the annexation of territory; between 1898 and 1899 Hawaii, the Philippines, and other areas became colonies of the United States.

Some labor organizations (the typographical union, the mineworkers, the iron molders, and the railroad brotherhoods for example) supported annexation, believing new jobs would open up as had occurred when U.S. railroad investors moved into Mexico in the 1880s, bringing American workers and their unions with them. But Gompers and most of the AFL were opposed. Annexation could mean competition from goods produced by cheap labor in those areas and unrestricted immigration of Orientals, flooding the United States labor markets and threatening union members' jobs. This outlook reflected the earliest positions taken by unions on foreign policy questions. Most important, these positions were clearly related to the domestic repercussions of foreign affairs. At the same time, early contacts with European unionists were aimed at gaining support for the AFL position.[18]

But the AFL did not oppose American economic or political expansion, or the extension of the AFL's brand of unionism overseas. The labor leaders came to share the ideas which largely dominated American foreign policy after 1897 and did so because of their acceptance of corporation capitalism and their belief that the vital interests of the unions would be served in the process. There were, of course, disagreements over particular policies (tariff questions and the recent China issue readily come to mind), tactics (American policy toward Cuba from 1959 to the present) and matters involving union rivalries, as in the case of the AFL and the CIO before the two federations merged. Conflicts about principles and broad goals were and have been exceptional, and most American labor leaders have accepted and supported the extension of American economic and political interests throughout the globe.

For example, the unions advocated the construction of the Panama Canal, to be built by American capital and American labor. Tying it to the domestic economic interests of American workers, Gompers declared in 1903 that the canal must be "the result of American enterprise, American genius and American labor." Similarly, the AFL championed Cuban independence before the war in 1898. While a commitment to freedom was involved, the AFL also emphasized that only after independence could Cuban workers be organized, stopping the flow of cheap labor and cheap nonunion goods to United States.[19]

The annexation question produced a crisis for labor unions. There was no quarrel with Americans who wanted to expand American interests abroad, in particular to conquer the markets of the world. But there was sharp disagreement about whether it was necessary to obtain colonies or to fight a war for Cuban independence. Because of their concern about labor's economic interests and also their fears that a permanent standing army would be established which might be used against workers at home, AFL leaders voiced objections. Gompers joined the Anti-Imperialist League, campaigned vigorously against annexation, but still extolled the virtues of expansion. He maintained that the latter was possible and desirable without all the burdens and dangers of old-style colonialism.

"The nation which dominates the markets of the world will surely control its destinies," the AFL leader proclaimed. Arguing for a fair deal for workers at home as the most important means of increasing production and consumption. Gompers then advocated American supremacy in economic competition abroad: "To make of the United States a vast workshop is our manifest destiny, and our duty, and thus side by side with other nations, in industrial and commercial rivalry, we are basing the conditions of the workers upon the highest intelligence and the most exalted standard of life. No obstacle can be placed in our way to the attainment of the highest pinnacle of national glory and human progress."[20]

Gompers did hedge for a time, however, on the commerical expansion-prosperity issue and in so doing revealed labor's relatively weak power in the system and the contradictions of union acceptance of and support for American corporate activites abroad. Writing in late 1898 to F. B. Thurber, President of the United States Export Association, the AFL leader denied that overseas markets were necessary because of the lack of consumer purchasing power at home. "If you are really of that opinion," Gompers lectured Thurber, "I would suggest that you go to the East Side or the other tenement districts of New York City and of all the large cities of our country, to the industrial towns, the mining districts and see the squalor and misery there existing; see the men and women and children pouring over their work long hours every day. Go to our textile centres and see there women and children are working, while husbands are walking the streets in idleness; see the numbers of idle, hungry and ragged myriads of men walking the streets and highways and by-ways of the country. Ask the Chief of Police of New York, who recently ordered the arrest of the city's idle and poverty stricken homeless people; ask the organized charities whether the people have reached the limit of their power to consume the products of our manufactures."[21]

Gompers failed, however, to push the matter any further and accepted the necessity for national economic expansion overseas. Even had the AFL wished otherwise, moreover, by itself it was still too weak to alter the outcome. When annexation did occur, the AFL moved quickly to obtain legislation to protect labor's interests at home and also to organize unions in the newly acquired regions. Gompers equated the extension of AFL unionism to the territories with the spread of "the gospel of Americanism." Efforts were made to create AFL locals, to secure higher wages, shorter hours, better working conditions, and the right to strike—goals which were not always easy to implement or always achieved. Also involved was opposition to indigenous labor organizations and radical ideologies in conflict with AFL policies.[22]

This pattern of activities in Puerto Rico, Cuba, and to a lesser extent in the Philippines was repeated in Mexico after revolution began in that country in 1910. Cooperation was also sought from government and business to secure AFL aims. This was not always forthcoming, but World War I created the conditions for a reciprocal relationship in which AFL adherence to American foreign policy was formally instituted and solidified. The Bolshevik revolution of 1917, which AFL leaders strongly opposed, fortified the alliance. Indeed, the bitterness of AFL leaders against communism and the Soviet Union meant that the AFL increasingly became part of the more conservative wing of the foreign policy consensus. The theoretically international character of the Soviet revolution was viewed as potentially dangerous to workers to whom the Bolsheviks had made their appeal, and there was concern that the Soviet success in Russia would erode the international position of the AFL.[23]

In the meantime, AFL leaders hoped that American economic expansion into the world would provide greater opportunities for AFL-style trade unionism to flourish in other countries. The power and prestige of the AFL would then be increased, and trade-union standards would remove the threat of cheap labor competition from abroad. American business did not always cooperate in this regard, of course, but after World War II many corporate leaders came to see the advantages of this arrangement. Anticommunism emerged as the common denominator by which labor and business could cooperate overseas.[24]

That the United States government sought labor's cooperation in foreign policy, especially during wartime, is clear enough. That the unions, by and large, supported not only the objectives but also the assumptions of official American policy abroad is also true. Anticommunism provided the basis for AFL-CIO endorsement of American intervention everywhere, including military invasions of the Dominican Republic and Vietnam, to combat real and alleged communist threats. Union self-interest and militant foreign policy were thus joined.

At various times, some opposition to prevailing policies did exist among union members and leaders. But the policies and the assumptions underlying them were not altered in any important way. Not even the CIO after 1946 had much of a different outlook. It also had anticommunist agents in the foreign field beginning at least in 1946. There were more similarities than differences between AFL and CIO foreign policy, and one of the prerequisites for the merger was agreement on foreign policy. This was possible after the CIO purged the left unions from its ranks and broke from the Communist-controlled World Federation of Trade Unions (WFTU) in 1949. The most protracted dispute involved in the unification negotiations between the AFL and CIO in 1955 concerned which group would exercise dominant influence over the administration of foreign affairs in the new federation—but there was no argument about fundamentals.[2]

Similarly, it may be that the Walter Reuther/United Auto Worker (UAW) break with the AFL-CIO involved more than questions of decision making, personalities, and style, but the UAW statements on foreign policy issues after the schism contained very little that was new. The opposition to the war in Vietnam did not produce a revision of basic assumptions about foreign relations. In any event, there was a good deal of sentiment at the 1974 UAW convention for resuming relations with the AFL-CIO despite the continuity of the federation's foreign policy.[26]

It is quite true that opposition to totalitarianism has been a central and continuing feature of organized labor's announced foreign policy. The record of hostility to Spanish rule over Cuba, fascism, and Stalinist repression is clear. But defending freedom against totalitarianism has also meant defending American unionism, American capitalism, and American political power against foreign rivals. In numerous instances, particularly since World War II, this has really meant support for American corporation imperialism, intervention into the internal affairs of other countries, and efforts to overthrow leftist regimes. Acting independently or in association with the U.S. government and U.S. business firms, the AFL-CIO has on a number of occasions fomented opposition to regimes or labor organizations abroad judged unfriendly and dangerous by the American labor federation and also by the United States government. A central ingredient of the opposition has been the attempt to portray such regimes as captives of international communism regardless of their actual character. Ironically, in many instances the leftist governments which the AFL-CIO has so vigorously condemned have been replaced by right-wing authoritarian rulers who have suppressed freedom and trade unions—a development which the American labor unions have deplored but about which they can do little. Greece, Guatemala, Brazil, the Dominican Republic, Vietnam, and Chile are illustrations of this result. Confronted with the choice between a leftist regime which they fear and dislike and the possibility that it may be overthrown and succeeded by a government of the anticommunist Right over which they will have little or no control, American labor unions have in many cases chosen to take the risks involved.

The AFL-CIO has, of course, had ties with some foreign unions and governments which have included socialists, and it has supported specific socialist measures. But the history of such relationship demonstrates that those friendships and alliances have existed for the most part only where the particular foreign unions or governments have accomodated themselves to the foreign interests of the United States government and the American unions, or where the AFL-CIO felt it had no alternative to an even more undesirable situation. The growth of the Left after World War II, especially in Third World countries, sharpened the dilemma for the more conservative American labor leaders.[27]

Labor's foreign policy in the post-world War II period, however, was not just "a strange carry-over" from the 1940s. It was the outcome of union labor development at home in the late nineteenth and early twentieth centuries. The majority of organized labor inside and outside of the American Federation of Labor accepted the corporate capitalist structure which emerged after the Civil War, and trade-union leaders translated acceptance into vigorous support as the unions slowly succeeded in achieving benefits and power. "Labor believes in the capitalist system, and we are members of the capitalist society." George Meany declared in 1965. "We are dedicated to the preservation of this system which rewards the workers."

Labor leaders thus believe capitalism is essential to the survival of their unions and especially their own careers. The historically long and bitter struggle which organized labor often had to make to secure legitimacy in America contributed to the commitment of labor leaders to the system. Personal success, measured in terms of money, power, or political influence obtained within limits set by far more powerful groups in the society, cemented the loyalty of labor leaders to the American corporate political economy. The unions and their leaders have had to settle for a junior partner status in the power arrangements of society but have been willing to accept this so far in return for the benefits and recognition they have obtained and the considerable influence they have come to have in many decisions.

Antiradicalism, including anticommunism, became an established part of the rhetoric and action of American union leaders because of real or imagined threats from rivals to their power and the privileged position of their unions, or because it served to demonstrate their loyalty to capitalism and Americanism. In the process they contributed to the extraordinary hostility to radicalism in our society. Such a posture also enabled them to secure the support of business and government in their activities abroad. Two world wars, the growth of the military-industrial complex, and the vast expansion of trade-union bureaucracy reinforced these tendencies.[28]

The AFL-CIO has not always had its way in foreign affairs. Sometimes, as has been mentioned, there have been differences with official foreign policy. AFL-CIO opposition to friendlier relations between the United States and Communist China (however tarnished by fallout from Watergate and the impeachment process) is also the result of great concern about the effects of possible trade agreements between the two countries. Not only will such contacts increase Chinese power; the Chinese will be able to secure credits and technological assistance from the West and thus compete with American goods at home. As an alternative, the AFL-CIO "demands" closer ties with Japan. "Every effort should be made to have Japan expand her domestic market by increasing the purchasing power of her workers and farmers. Tokyo should be encouraged to step up her trade and investment in the developing countries of Asia." Ironically, this is precisely the policy the United States government pursued in Asia from the mid-1950s to the beginning of the Nixon administration, when the Vietnam War, the growth of Japanese economic power, and the reversal of America's international trade position forced a change.[29]

The AFL-CIO's adherence to the older official strategy is, of course, intended as an alternative to relations with China and also to maintain the federation's position in Japan, where it has supported with a good deal of investment a faction of the labor movement for many years. But the AFL-CIO also wants to divert Japanese exports away from the United States and to the Japanese domestic market and the countries of Southeast Asia. At the same time the unions were advocating these measures, they expressed dismay at the removal of American production from parent, U.S.-based companies to their affiliates abroad, including Japan where the goods presumably cost less to make. Such export of investment and production overseas, claims the AFL-CIO, has even involved the cooperation of the U.S. government. The AFL-CIO argued and "the Administration did not deny the....claim that the Thor-Delta rocket technology had been transferred to Japan and that U.S. corporations profits [sic] would benefit, while jobs, production and U.S. developed missile technology had been transferred to Japan."[30]

Nothing, of course, illustrates so well the junior partner status and dilemma of organized labor's position in foreign affairs as does the issue of giant multinational corporations. On the one hand, most of the unions have supported American capitalism and its expansion abroad in the past, while on the other hand, they have sought protection for themselves at home when jobs have been threatened by the overseas activities of the corporations. But the unions have never been able to determine or to restrict any corporation activity abroad in the past, only react to it.

So long as the domestic economy continued to expand and exports from America continued to flourish, the unions were able to accomodate themselves to this arrangement. But these conditions have vastly changed, and labor unions and their leaders charge the multinationals are not only exporting jobs, capital, and technology to low-wage areas of the world—a long-standing complaint—but are also contributing to a shrinking domestic economy and the decline of American exports. The alliance between labor and business abroad has come under severe strains as a result. Anticommunism, moreover, is no longer the binding force it once was as many American corporations see real and potential profits in better relations with communist countries.[31]

Has labor's foreign policy met the needs of the workers in this country? In a narrow sense and on a limited basis, perhaps. But in the long run and in terms of actual worker economic and psychological security, the answer is no. American economic expansion abroad has provoked war, with its price of physical casualties, higher taxes, inflation, and discriminatory economic and political controls and dislocations; it has created gigantic multinational corporations which compete with American labor rather than foreign enterprises; it has stimulated a vast armaments industry in which employment has become an unreliable dependency of war, and much of organized labor's leadership has forged questionable political alliances in Congress with precisely those legislators (e.g., Senator Henry Jackson of Washington) who have supported an enlarged defense establishment. Rigid anticommunism has distorted labor's view of the world and contributed to the decline of union democracy at home as well as to the building of tensions abroad.

Above all, the independence and integrity of the labor movement have been sacrificed to the cold war and its excesses. The AFL-CIO has participated extensively in cold war politics throughout the world—with results that are uncertain at best. Leftist unions are very strong in France, Italy, Japan, and elsewhere despite AFL-CIO efforts to dislodge them. The American labor federation withdrew from the ICFTU and is regarded with widespread distrust nearly everywhere. B. J. Widick stated flatly in late 1971 that the AFL-CIO "has less influence overseas today than at any time since World War II." All this even though 25 percent of the federations's budget is allocated for international affairs, and since 1945, there has developed a considerable union bureaucracy devoted to international activities. The end result is the most ridiculous of all conditions: an interventionist AFL-CIO isolated from most of world labor and a divided, insecure working class at home.[32]

None of this means the AFL-CIO has become a weak giant at home or abroad. It does suggest that in the 1970s, as on earlier occasions, much of organized labor is at a crossroads which could affect its foreign policy as well as its direction at home. Increasing numbers of young and minority-group workers are entering unions, which is part of the explanation for the gap which Lou Harris found in his polls between the aggregate views of rank-and-file members and the hierarchy on many issues. Women are becoming a more militant force and low-wage unionism is on the rise. Newer unions such as the American Federation of State, County, and Municipal Employees are growing at a very rapid rate while several important older unions stagnate or lose members.[33]

These developments, among others, have given hope to some that the values which these new members of the working class hold will produce alternative policies.[34] Perhaps. Certainly these workers will have to be listened to if union democracy is to have any meaning. Ironically, too, the growth of the multinational corporations has necessitated labor union attention to an international labor strategy to defend union interests, and this could lead to the disintegration of existing, narrow national loyalties of many workers. But it is important to realize that it is the whole set of assumptions about the world and American society which must eventually change. This need not involve total withdrawal from the world or conversion of American labor into a branch of the Communist International. Neither is desirable nor likely. It does mean a reordering of priorities at home, an end to antiradical crusades around the globe, a willingness to set limits on American power, and a conversion from narrow interest-group politics to a politics which is dedicated to the interests of the whole community. American labor unions possess the power base from which they can undertake these efforts. It remains to be seen whether or not the workers will use this power, or whether if they do use it, the contradictions of American labor in a corporate capitalist society can be resolved.

NOTES

1. George Meany, "No Return to Isolationism," *AFL-CIO Federationist* 79 (October 1972): 13-14.
2. Ibid.; *John Herling's Labor Letter* (Washington), April 13, 1974.
3. *New York Times,* August 11, 1971 and February 19, 1972; *Proceedings, AFL-CIO 1973 Convention,* pp. 131, 451-53, *AFL-CIO Executive Council's Report* in *Proceedings, Part II,* pp. 119-56; and *Wall Street Journal,* March 28, 1974.
4. See appropriate references from *Proceedings* in note 3 and also the Chilean reference on pp. 468-69 of the *Proceedings.*
5. U.S. Department of Commerce, Bureau of the Census, *Handbook of Basic Economic Statistics* (Washington: various years) and *Historical Statistics of the United States* (Washington: 1961), pp. 67-78, 97-98; U. S. Department of Labor, Bureau of Labor Statistics, *Directory of National Unions and Employee Associations, 1971* (Washington: 1972), pp. 68-85; and Irving Bernstein, "Forces Affecting the Growth of the American Labor Movement," in William Haber, ed., *Labor in a Changing America* (New York: 1966), pp. 121-32.
6. *Wall Street Journal,* April 8, 1974; Louis Harris, *The Anguish of Change* (New York: 1973), p. 50.

7. The following are some of the better published studies of American labor's foreign policy: Margaret Hardy, *The Influence of Organized Labor on the Foreign Policy of the United States* (Liege, Belgium: 1936); Lewis Lorwin, *The International Labor Movement* (New York: 1953); Sinclair Snow, *The Pan American Federation of Labor* (Durham: 1964); John Windmuller, *American Labor and the International Labor Movement, 1940-1953* (Ithaca, New York: 1954); and by the same author, "The Foreign Policy Conflict in American Labor," *Political Science Quarterly* 82 (June 1967): 205-34. See also the relevant sections of Joseph Goulden, *Meany* (New York: 1972). A recent "in-house" and impassioned defense of labor's foreign policy is Philip Taft, *Defending Freedom: American Labor and Foreign Affairs* (Los Angeles: 1973). Other works are cited in subsequent footnotes.

8. See for example, Windmuller, "Foreign Policy Conflict in Labor," and also "Foreign Affairs and the AFL-CIO," *Industrial and Labor Relations Review* 9 (April 1956): 419-32.

9. Hazel Erskine, "The Polls: Is War a Mistake?" *Public Opinion Quarterly* 34 (Spring 1970): 144.

10. Roper Surveys AIPO 00 725 001, 74100, and 760 were provided through the courtesy of Professor Richard Dawson, Department of Political Science, Washington University.

11. The Roper polls were obtained from Professor Dawson. The Harris poll is reprinted from Derek C. Bok and John T. Dunlop, *Labor and the American Community* (New York: 1970), p. 61. Harlan Hahn's article, "Dove Sentiments Among Blue-Collar Workers," is in *Dissent* (May-June 1970): 202-05. Hahn also cites the concentration of antiwar sentiment in referendums held on the Vietnam War in seven communites between November 1966 and November 1968: Cambridge and Lincoln, Massachusetts; Madison, Wisconsin; Dearborn, Michigan; and Beverly Hills, Mill Valley, and San Francisco, California. It would, however, be difficult to reach solid conclusions based on these examples because of the few number involved and the absence of a large cross section of labor in the working-class districts of the towns and cities.

12. Roper Surveys AIPO 0773 and 0793. Courtesy of Professor Dawson.

13. Harris, *Anguish of Change,* pp. 141-44, 150.

14. Table reproduced without change from Richard Dempsey and Douglas Schmude, "Occupational Impact of Defense Expenditures," *Monthly Labor Review* 94 (December 1971): 13. See also Richard P. Oliver, "Employment Effects of Reduced Defense Spending," ibid., pp. 3-11 and Frederick Dutton, *Changing Sources of Power: American Politics in the 1970s* (Chicago: 1971), p. 178.

15. U.S. Arms Control and Disarmament Agency, *Economic Impacts of Disarmament* (Washington: 1962); U.S. Department of Commerce, Bureau of Census, *Defense Indicators* (Washington: November 1973), pp. 4, 14; and *Wall Street Journal,* January 23, 1974.

16. For a general discussion of these matters see the following: James Weinstein, *The Corporate Ideal in the Liberal State, 1900-1918* (Boston: 1968); Stephen Scheinberg, "The Development of Corporation Labor Policy, 1900-1940," unpublished Ph.D. dissertation, University of Wisconsin, 1966; William A. Williams, *The Contours of American History* (Cleveland: 1961); and Ronald Radosh, *American Labor and United States Foreign Policy* (New York: 1969). For a somewhat different view of Gompers and socialism, see two recent studies: Stuart B. Kaufman, *Samuel Gompers and the Origins of the American*

Federation of Labor: 1848-1896 (Westport: 1973); and William M. Dick, *Labor and Socialism In America: The Gompers Era* (Port Washington: 1972). One book which traces the emergence of national union leadership in the corporate-political structure and finds continuity in the process from the post-Civil War era to the end of World War I is Warren R. Van Tine, *The Making of the Labor Bureaucrat: Union Leadership in the United States, 1870-1920* (Amherst: 1973).

17. Van Tine, *Labor Bureaucrat*, p. 74; and Clarence E. Bonnett, *Employers' Associations in the United States: A Study of Typical Associations* (New York: 1922), pp. 23-24.

18. On the post-Civil War concerns of labor unions and foreign affairs, consult the following: Richard U. Miller, "American Railroad Unions and the National Railways of Mexico: An Exercise in Nineteenth Century Proletariat Manifest Destiny," *Labor History* 15 (Spring 1974): 239-60; David M. Pletcher, *Rails, Mines, and Progress: Seven American Promoters in Mexico 1867-1911* (Ithaca: 1958); Alexander Saxton, *The Indispensable Enemy: Labor and the Anti Chinese Movement In California* (Berkeley and Los Angeles: 1971); Charlotte Erickson, *American Industry and the European Immigrant, 1860-1885* (Cambridge: 1957); William G. Whittaker, "Samuel Gompers: Anti-Imperialist," *Pacific Historical Review* 38 (November 1969): 429-45; Delber L. McKee, "Samuel Gompers, the AFL, and Imperialism, 1895-1900," *The Historian* 21 (February 1959): 187-99; John C. Appel, "American Labor and the Annexation of Hawaii: A Study in Logic and Economic Interest," *Pacific Historical Review* 23 (February 1954): 1-18; Philip Foner, *History of the Labor Movement in the United States,* vol. 2 (New York, 1955), ch. 26; and the introductory chapters of Henry W. Berger, "Union Diplomacy: American Labor's Foreign Policy in Latin America, 1932-1955," unpublished Ph.D. dissertation, University of Wisconsin, 1966.

19. Appel, "The Relationship of American Labor to U.S. Imperialism, 1895-1905," unpublished Ph.D. dissertation, University of Wisconsin, 1950, pp. 212-14, 306-7; *Proceedings, AFL Convention, 1903,* p. 205; Appel, "The Unionization of Florida Cigarmakers and the Coming of the War with Spain," *Hispanic American Historical Review* 25 (February 1956), 38-49. *Proceedings, AFL Convention, 1895,* p. 52; *1896,* 50-51, 53-54; *1897,* 73-75, 89-91; *1898,* 18-20. Samuel Gompers to Henry Demarest Lloyd, March 15, 1898 and to William McCabe, April 9, 1898, *Samuel Gompers Letterbooks,* Library of Congress, Washington, D.C. Willis Baer, *The Economic Development of the Cigar Industry In the United States* (Lancaster: 1933), pp. 106-07.

20. Gompers, "The Foreign Policy of the United States," speech before the National Conference on Foreign Policy, Saratoga, New York, August 20, 1898, in *Samuel Gompers Papers,* Box 46, Wisconsin State Historical Society, Madison, Wisconsin. Also, Gompers to F.B. Thurber, November 25, 1898, *American Federationist* 5 (December 1898): 206-07; and Gompers speech before the National Committee of the Chicago Peace Jubilee, October 18, 1898, *American Federationist* 5 (November 1898): 182; Gompers to *New York Journal,* December 30, 1899 in *American Federationist* 5 (January 1899): 223.

21. Gompers to Thurber, November 25, 1898, *American Federationist* 5 (December 1898): 205-07.

22. Appel, "American Labor and U.S. Imperialism," pp. 203-04, 242; and Lyman J. Gould, "The Foraker Act: The Roots of American Colonial

Policy," Ph.D. dissertation, University of Michigan, 1958, esp. pp. 44-45, 76, 91-95. Also, Herbert Myrick to Gompers, December 6 and 8, 1899, *Gompers Papers,* Wisconsin; and Gompers to George W. Perkins, September 7, 1899, *Gompers Letterbooks,* Washington. Opposition to indigenous labor organizations in Puerto Rico and Cuba is discussed in Berger, "Union Diplomacy," ch. 1.

23. On Mexico, see Harvey Levenstein, *Labor Organizations in the United States and Mexico* (Westport: 1971). On World War I, the following: Radosh, *Labor and U.S. Foreign Policy,* pp. 30-303; Frank L. Grubbs, *The Struggle For Labor Loyalty: Gompers, the A.F. of L. and the Pacifists* (Durham: 1968); Alexander Bing, *War-Time Strikes and Their Adjustment* (New York: 1921); Grosvenor Clarkson, *Industrial America in the World War: The Strategy Behind the Lines* (Boston: 1923), pp. 276-92; and Gordon Watkins, *Labor Problems and Labor Administration in the United States During the World War* (Urbana: 1920). On Russian policy, see Radosh, *Labor and U.S. Foreign Policy;* and D.F. Wieland, "American Labor and Russia, 1917-1925," M.A. dissertation, University of Wisconsin, 1948. Peter G. Filene, *American Views of Soviet Russia, 1917-1965* (Homewood, Illinois: 1968); Philip Foner, *The Bolshevik Revolution: Its Impact on American Radicals, Liberals and Labor* (New York: 1967); and the earlier study, Meno Lovenstein, *American Opinion and Soviet Russia* (Washington: 1941) record the divisions within American labor concerning the Russian revolution and the unflinching opposition to the revolution from AFL leaders.

24. One essay which explores American labor and foreign policy from the depression to World War II and develops in detail these issues and also the CIO's early foreign policy is Henry W. Berger, "Crisis Diplomacy, 1930-1941," in William A. Williams, *From Colony to Empire: Essays On The History of American Foreign Relations* (New York: 1972), pp. 293-336.

25. See, for instance, Windmuller, "Foreign Policy Conflict in American Labor," pp. 228-31; and Gerald R. Gordon, "The Coming of the Cold War: The American Labor Movement and the Problem of Peace, 1945-1946," *Susquehanna University Studies* (June 1968): 14-29. Also, Stanley Meisler, "Meddling in South America," *The Nation* 198 (February 10, 1964): 133-38; and two articles by Berger: "American Labor Overseas,"*The Nation* 204 (January 16, 1967): 80-84; and "Labor and State: Marriage of Convenience; What's Good for Latin America," *The Nation* 208 (January 13, 1969): 46-48.

26. Disagreement about reaffiliating with the AFL-CIO also existed, however, and no action was taken. *John Herling's Labor Letter,* March 16 and June 8, 1974. For accounts of the Reuther-Meany split, see the following: Alfred O. Hero and Emil Starr, *The Reuther-Meany Foreign Policy Dispute* (Dobbs Ferry: 1970); Frank Cormier and William J. Eaton, *Reuther* (Englewood Cliffs: 1970), pp. 405-19; and Goulden, *Meany,* pp. 263-89, 371-403. Also *John Herling's Labor Letter,* 1968-1970; and *New York Times,* June 19 and December 30, 1966; February 10, 21, and April 23, 1967; July 24, 1968; and April 11 and May 28, 1969.

27. Much of the documentation for the foregoing is based on a wide range of sources, including public and private materials collected by the author over the past decade. But see Radosh, *Labor and U.S. Foreign Policy,* pp. 304-452.

28. The quotes are from Harris, *Anguish of Change,* p. 137, and George Meany, Speech to Council on Latin America, April 2, 1965 (AFL-CIO News Release in author's possession). The argument that the sources of labor's internation-

al outlook are located in its historical acceptance of corporate capitalism does not mean that *every* subsequent issue in foreign affairs to which labor paid attention was determined only by that fact. It does mean, however, that much of organized labor's activity in foreign matters occurred within this framework, rested on shared assumptions with corporate and government officials concerning priorities and objectives of the system, or took place in an atmosphere of log-rolling in which the unions supported certain policies in return for economic benefits and political power at home and overseas.

The fact that there existed a vigorous debate inside labor's ranks over the results of the Spanish-American War should not obscure two points: (1) the broad expansionist, antiradical views of the corporate leadership prevailed and labor leaders accepted this result; (2) the support for basic foreign policy goals of the United States and of the unions themselves was not original with the AFL. The independent railroad brotherhoods and the nearly defunct Knights of Labor, many of whose members became part of the AFL well before the Spanish-American War commenced, also supported economic expansion abroad, immigration restriction, and protective measures for labor unions in other countries. Van Tine's study of union leadership which blurs the sharp distinction others have made between reform and business unionism tends to be confirmed when the views of labor leaders of the two groups concerning foreign relations issues are examined.

29. *Proceedings, AFL-CIO Convention, 1973,* p. 131.
30. *AFL-CIO Executive Council's Report* in *Proceedings,* Part II, p. 152.
31. Concern about the impact of multinational corporation activity and competition from foreign trade is found most recently in the following national trade union publications: *AFL-CIO Federationist* 76 (February 1969): 17-23; 77 (May 1970): 9-20; 78 (August 1971): 9; 79 (July 1972): 1-7. *AFL-CIO Executive Council's Report in Proceedings, AFL-CIO Convention, 1973,* pp. 147-56. *American Labor* 3 (May 1970): 47-48; 4 (December 1970 - January 1971): 18. See also "An American Trade Union View of International Trade and Investment," in U.S. Senate, Committee on Finance, *Multinational Corporations: A Compendium of Papers,* 93rd Cong., 1st Sess., February 21, 1973, pp. 59-84; Testimony of Leonard Woodcock, President, United Auto Workers, and Andrew Biemiller, Director of Legislation, AFL, before the Subcommittee on International Trade, U.S. Senate, Committee on Finance, *Multinational Corporations,* 93rd Cong., 1st Sess. February 28 and March 6, 1973, pp. 275-367; Charles Levinson, *International Trade Unionism* (London: 1972), pp. 38-141; Duane Kujawa, ed. *American Labor and the Multinational Corporation* (New York, 1973).
32. B.J. Widick, "1971: Labor's Rough Year," *The Nation* 213 (September 6, 1971): 171.
33. Jack Barbash, "Unionism Among Low-Wage Workers," excerpted in *John Herling's Labor Letter,* January 5, 1974; Stephen C. Schlesinger, "Black Caucus in the Unions," *The Nation* 218 (February 2, 1974): 142-44; and Ben J. Wattenberg and Richard M. Scammon, "Black Progress and Liberal Rhetoric," *Commentary* 55 (April 1973): 36-38. For an example of continuing difficulties of blacks in labor unions and places of employment, see "Uphill Fight: Bringing Racial Equality to Nation's Steel Mills is Long and Bitter Task," *Wall Street Journal,* August 8, 1973.
34. For example, Brendan and Patricia Sexton, "Labor's Decade—Maybe," *Dissent* (August 1971): 365-74.

12

Job Unionism versus
Political Unionism
in Four Countries[1]

William H. Form

INDUSTRIAL DEVELOPMENT AND UNION GOALS

Historically, the major struggle within unions has concerned whether to bargain with management to improve wages, hours, and working conditions or to attack the institutional sources of worker subordination through political action. American unions have usually opted for "bread and butter" bargaining while unions in the rest of the world have typically chosen the political approach. Union officials and workers do not always agree on which issue to emphasize.

The failure of union leaders to activate workers politically has been the despair of liberals and radicals since Marx's time. Many reasons have been given for workers' refusal to follow their officers' politics: dominance of bourgeois institutions, false class consciousness, authoritarian personalities, repressive legislation. In a study of the automobile industry in four countries at different levels of industrialization, found that workers tend to reject political unionism for job-conscious unionism regardless of the national level of industrialization or the emphasis which unions place on political action and ideology. This finding suggests that certain common factors must be present throughout the automobile industries in these countries.

The "industrial man" hypothesis holds that workers exposed to similar industrial conditions generally respond in the same way whatever the broader cultural milieu. The familiar Marxist proposition concerning the homogenizing effects of technology on worker behavior may well extend to union behavior. Other theories specifically include the union in their discussion of the logic of industrialism. They claim that whatever the cultural milieu, a certain "logic," or predictable organizational consequences, flows from the introduction of industry: unions, labor laws, labor courts, strikes, and so on. Kerr and Siegel have shown that unions in the same industry in different countries (mining and shipping) behave similarly because they respond to similar organizational and technological features. But they remain silent on whether union officers and workers agree about the priority of standard union goals: economic bargaining, political action, improving working conditions, and promoting social solidarity.

Our position is that disagreement between officers and workers on the priorities of union functions is a normal consequence of the growth of industrialism and unionism. Unions inevitably arise with the growth of mechanical industry because of the emergence of two broad occupational groups which vary in power and goals: managers who plan and control production and workers who produce and obey. Moreover, the very organization of production throws workers together socially and organizes them informally, thus providing preconditions for formal unions. Without their union, workers are organizationally isolated in an organizational society. The union is the only organization exclusively dedicated to serving their interests in the plant and giving them recognition and influence in the wider society. Consequently, once unions arise, workers are loyal to them almost irrespective of their policies or organizational effectiveness.

In order to survive in a market economy, unions must try to control the forces which affect their labor markets; they must cooperate with other unions and political parties to protect and further their interests. As in most organizations, the higher the officers are in the union hierarchy, the more they focus on national political problems and the less they know about local plant concerns. To be effective nationally, officers need worker support; officers therefore pressure workers to contribute money to the party and to vote for it. Their perennial task is to convince workers that union influence in national politics will pay off in local benefits.

Why is it so hard for officers to persuade workers to go along? First, since workers spend most of their waking hours on the job, they are most concerned with pay and the conditions of work. Second, politics is an organizational game and workers live in an organizational desert. Furthermore, workers are disadvantaged in learning how the political system works and how it can be changed; yet they must exert more effort to extract benefits from it. In conflict situations, the upper strata have the advantages; they need only to fight defensive battles to maintain the status quo. Higher strata are more organizationally involved than lower strata and more adept at managing organizations to their own advantage. They also know how to preserve their advantage in the political marketplace. Union officers want workers to be sophisticated about the political process even though workers are isolated from organizations and politics. Understandably, workers see little relationship between union functions at the plant level and the political concerns of their officials. Workers may approve of certain parties and vote for them, but they do not understand why the union should spend its organizational resources in a game whose benefits are uncertain at best.

Varying circumstances influence which union goals workers emphasize, including their newness to industry, the technological pressures they experience, and their place in the skill hierarchy. Thus when industry is first introduced and workers move from subsistence to cash markets, they want economic security and protection from arbitrary management rule. Since unions are inexperienced at this stage, workers recognize the importance of emphasizing social solidarity. With continuing industrialization, growing union strength, and conflict, wage increases become almost routine, but other pressures build up. As technology improves, as work operations are rationalized and as production quotas are raised, workers become more concerned about working conditions.

Workers also respond differently to union goals according to their place in the skill hierarchy. Poorly educated, economically insecure, unsophisticated in ways of organizations, unskilled workers avoid conflicts. Their major concern is a stable income. They are typically apathetic toward unions and politics, easily pressured and hold political beliefs which are both radical and conservative. Urban-born semiskilled workers, often better educated and blocked in upward mobility, tend to be the most militant unionists and are most inclined to radical political action. In contrast, skilled workers have the most job freedom and greatest power to influence the conditions which affect their welfare. Often recruited from a privileged background, skilled workers constitute an income, status, and power elite among manual workers. They often control the local union and use it to preserve their advantageous niche. Since they can usually attain their ends through peaceful bargaining, they avoid militant tactics. They are most active in union affairs, most involved in local flow of communication and most influential in exerting a conservative influence on union politics.[2] In short, union officials who want workers to recognize the importance of political objectives face two important obstacles: the workers' persistent concerns with local plant issues and counterpropaganda on political action from the skilled workers.

SAMPLE DESIGN

A difficult problem in cross-national research is to select sites which permit the control of important variables. In this study, automobile manufacturing was held constant and level of industrialization of the country and type of labor union were varied. The United States represented a mature industrial society; Italy, a society with an old but rapidly expanding manufacturing sector; Argentina, a society undergoing more recent industrial growth; and India, a society with a small industrial base. The plants selected had been in operation for at least ten years and were run by indigenous managers. Oldsmobile (OLDS) in the U.S. had the most automated machinery; Fiat in Turin, Italy had modern equipment but it was not as automated as OLDS; Industrias Kaiser Argentina (IKA) had less modern equipment than FIAT: and Premier Automobiles Limited (PAL) had relatively primitive equipment. FIAT, IKA, and PAL were the largest producers of automobiles in their countries, and OLDS was the third largest. The companies therefore represented their industries, but they may not represent industrial workers generally.

The samples were selected to represent the skill composition of the manufacturing divisions of the plants.[3] Workers were randomly selected in departments classified by skill composition. Most skilled workers were in the experimental and maintenance departments, the semiskilled in parts manufacturing, and the unskilled were in assembly (Table 1). All workers except those at PAL were interviewed at home.

LABOR UNION STRUCTURES AND IDEOLOGIES

The labor unions varied in structure, autonomy, and political ideology (see Table 2). The United Automobile Workers of America (UAW) is an industrial-type union. Strong and aggressive, it has been reasonably successful in wresting economic concessions from management. Its leadership is politically liberal and it has consistently supported the Democratic

TABLE 1
Occupational Composition of Workers in Four Automobile Plants
(percent)

OCCUPATIONAL LEVEL	U.S.A. OLDS (Lansing)	ITALY FIAT (Turin)	ARGENTINA IKA (Córdoba)	INDIA PAL (Bombay)
Skilled craftsmen	27	18	22	25
Semiskilled machine tenders, etc.	49	51	35	39
Unskilled assemblers	24	31	43	36
Total	100	100	100	100
N	(306)	(306)	(315)	(262)

party. Factions have been few and unimportant, but the turnover of local officers has been high. Bargaining is certralized in the International, but locals monitor the application of the contract, handle grievances, and make policy suggestions to the International.

TABLE 2
Characteristics of Labor Unions in Four Automobile Plants

CHARACTERISTICS	OLDS U.S.A.	FIAT ITALY	IKA ARGENTINA	PAL INDIA
Name of union	UAW	CGIL, CISL, UIL, SIDA	SMATA	EMS, INTUC
Economic bargaining	National	National and local	Local	Local
Grievance handling	Rationalized	Semi-rationalized	Rationalized	Personalistic
Dues structure	Check-off	Voluntary	Check-off	Normative
Power vis-a-vis management	High	Moderate	Moderate	Low
Wage structure rationality	High	Medium	Medium	Low
Political ideology of officials	Liberal	Conservative to radical	Laboristic	Socialistic
Ideological insistence	Low	Very high	Moderate	High
Party linkages	Moderate	Strong	Moderate	Weak
Factions	Weak	Strong	Moderate	Weak
Workers in manufacturing departments	12,000	33,000	11,000	8,200

Three major labor confederations compete in Italy and each is associated with a political party. All three unions may be represented in a factory's Commissione Interna according to the percentage of votes each received in the local election. As a body, the Commissione modifies the national contract, interprets it, settles local grievances, and makes suggestions for the future contracts.

The Confederazione Generale Italiana del Lavora (CGIL), dominated by communists and left-wing socialists, was the largest union in FIAT. The Sindicato Italiano dell'Automobile (SIDA), second largest, was exclusively a FIAT union and unattached to any political party; other unions accused it of being supported by the company. The Unione Italiana del Lavoro (UIL), third largest, was allied with moderate socialist parties. Finally, the Confederazione Italiana Sindicati Lavoratori (CISL) was Catholic, traditionally loyal to the Christian Democratic Party. In the last plant election, CGIL polled 30 percent of the vote; SIDA 28 percent; UIL 23 percent, and CISL 16 percent. The remaining 3 percent was for CISNAL, a fascist union. From radical to conservative, the unions were: CGIL (Communist), UIL (Social Democratic), CISL (Catholic), and SIDA (Independent). The formal political ideology of UIL was more radical than CISL, but CISL was a more militant union.

Only 15 percent of FIAT's workers were dues-paying union members, but 90 percent voted for slates to the Commissione Interna. FIAT management would not meet with the representative of CGIL and dealt with each union individually, thus weakening the Commissione as a collective body. All unions were highly centralized. Membership meetings were rare and attendance at them was very low. All the unions were moderately well-financed; each supported spacious quarters and full-time officers, and each published newspapers which stated the union's position on plant issues and the party's positions on local and national questions.

The Argentine union was the Sindicato de Mecánicos Automotores y Trabajodores Afines (SMATA), an industrial-type union with headquarters in Buenos Aires. About 85 percent of the workers were members, and almost all of them voted in elections. Although the national officers were heavily involved in Peronist politics, local officials handled grievances, economic bargaining, and services. However, local Peronists successfully pressed the union to support the antigovernment, antibusiness, prolabor ideology of its national leaders and to get the union involved in local politics. The small Socialist-Communist faction defined local officials as promanagement, but the majority of workers supported the faction then in power.

The Bombay plant had two unions: The Ghandian moderate Indian National Trade Union Congress (INTUC) and the socialist Engineering Mazdoor Sabha (EMS). Although INTUC originally held power, it was superseded by EMS after a long strike of 110 days. EMS proclaims the necessity of building class-consciousness among the workers through strikes and passive resistance with the aim of eventually seizing control of the government by peaceful democratic means. The union probably represented 75 percent of the workers, INTUC 10 percent, and 15 percent were not members. Like most India unions, EMS was highly centralized and dominated by officers who seemed to have permanent tenure. They were involved in national politics and appeared to be uninformed about problems in the plant. Higher officials "nominated" the local officers who collected dues and reported on local events. Regional officers of EMS would occasionally hold open air meetings at the factory and simply announce their decisions. Bargaining usually followed government standing orders and grievances were informally processed. About a third of the workers complained about undemocratic procedures in the union, but there were no organized factions (see Table 2).

We interviewed four officials of each union except for FIAT where we interviewed three officials in each of four unions. A top regional official was interviewed in each union and the remainder were top locally elected or appointed officials. In addition to providing background information on the unions, officials were asked to rank the importance of four union goals: economic bargaining, improving working conditions, political action to change the social and economic system of the country, and building social solidarity among workers. Almost unanimously, officers responded that all functions were equally important, but only five of the twenty-four, when pressed, ranked economic bargaining as more important than other goals, and these were all local officials. When asked to rank the economic and political functions of the unions, seventeen insisted that they were equal. Except for SIDA officials in FIAT, all officials believed that unions should engage in political action; only UAW officials did not endorse the statement that a primary goal of the union was to change the political and social system of the country. FIAT unions placed most emphasis on political action, followed by PAL, IKA and OLDS.

UNION INTEREST, EVALUATION, AND PARTICIPATION

Because of their organizational isolation, we expected that workers would approve of their unions and respond to them similarly regardless of the union's political stance. Table 3 shows that about nine-tenths of the workers judged unions to be necessary, seven-tenths evaluated them favorably, somewhat fewer evaluated the performance of their locals highly, and less than one-third were highly interested in unions. Phenomenal equivalents for participation were poor because membership, voting, and attendance were structured differently in each factory. Voting was quasi compulsory in FIAT, normative at IKA, optional at OLDS, and almost nonexistent in PAL (see Table 2). However, attendance at meetings was optional and low everywhere, but it was higher in the smaller plants, IKA and PAL. These findings on union involvement confirmed earlier studies: workers everywhere considered unions to be institutionally legitimate; they evaluated unions highly, but interest and participation in them were low. The association between degree of political emphasis on the part of officials and union involvement on the part of members was negligible except in FIAT where it was inverse.

TABLE 3
Automobile Workers' Evaluation and Participation in Unions (percent)

EVALUATION–PARTICIPATION	OLDS	FIAT	IKA	PAL
Evaluation of unions				
Unions necessary	95	86	92	91
Favorable toward unions in general	83	81	69	77
High evaluation of local union's performance	45	25	66	50
High interest in unions	15	11	12	33
Participation in unions				
Membership	100	12	91	88
Attended half or more of the meetings	7	5	32	37
Voted in last election	63	94	74	*
Identified one or more union officers	51	39	94	95
Participated in union activities	22**	5	4	***
N	(306)	(306)	(315)	(262)

* Not available, elections rarely held.

** Mostly in sports and recreation.

*** No other union activities existed.

UNION FUNCTIONS

We found that workers everywhere agreed on major union functions and eschewed political unionism. We asked workers about their union beliefs in four contexts: first, to identify the most important union function; second, to rank four stated functions (secure higher wages, obtain better working conditions, promote social solidarity, and change the political and social system of the country); third, to name the most important problems the union should face locally; and last, to rank local problems from a list provided by their officials.

In the open questions, workers failed to mention the political function of the union, and when they were forced to consider it, they ranked it least important. Only 3 workers of the 1,189 interviewed indicated in the two open response questions that the union should be concerned with political questions.[4] This failure to emphasize political unionism was not due to the absence of political radicals in the samples.

When forced to rank the political function of the union, the vast majority of workers ranked it least important (see Table 4). Less than a tenth of the workers in three plants ranked it most important, and six-tenths or more ranked it as least important. Job unionism (raising wages and improving working conditions) was the dominant response everywhere except for PAL. Workers in OLDS, who were exposed to the most complex technology, ranked the improvement of working conditions most important, while more workers in plants with less complex technologies (FIAT and IKA) ranked higher wages as most important. Finally, workers in IKA and PAL, whose unions were the newest and most insecure, placed greater emphasis on union efforts to increase social solidarity.

TABLE 4
Most Important and Least Important Functions of the Union (percent)

FUNCTIONS	OLDS Importance Most	OLDS Importance Least	FIAT Importance Most	FIAT Importance Least	IKA Importance Most	IKA Importance Least	PAL Importance Most	PAL Importance Least
Secure higher wages	7	12	46	11	37	11	25	15
Obtain better working conditions	75	0	31	5	25	8	23	14
Promote social unity of the workers	15	5	17	17	32	10	36	11
Change political and social system*	2	83	6	68	6	72	16	60
Totals	99	100	100	101	100	101	100	100

*If first and second in importance are combined, the results were: OLDS, 4 percent; FIAT, 14 percent; IKA 15 percent; and PAL, 29 percent.

POLITICAL UNIONISM AND POLITICAL IDEOLOGY

We expected workers who emphasized political unionism to be most radical politically and the most militant unionists. To be sure, militancy is not always associated with radicalism; in the United States, some conservative unions are very militant and in Europe some of the most radical unions are quite placid.

To tap feelings about union militancy, workers were asked if, in order to improve the economic and social conditions of the workingman, unions should fight militantly, work with determination, negotiate freely with management, or cooperate with management's suggestions. PAL workers were most militant (53 percent), followed by IKA (39 percent), OLDS (29 percent), and FIAT (17 percent). This order is the same as that for preference for political unionism, except that FIAT workers were least militant. The correlation between union militancy and political unionism was inverse for OLDS, curvilinear for FIAT, and absent for IKA and PAL.

Finally, we constructed a conservative-radical index of political ideology for each country. The nine items for OLDS and the five items for PAL focused on the desirability of decreasing the power of business in government in favor of the working class. For FIAT, the most feasible indicator was the union and party with which the workers identified most; from left to right: communist, social democratic, Catholic, and independent.[5] Workers who were hostile or apathetic toward unions and parties were classified as conservative. In Argentina, the union movement's allegiance to Peronism constituted a threat to the conservative government then in power. For IKA, a seven-item index of support for the union movement and its national politics constituted the measure of radicalism. These indices reflect a wider range of political ideology than the political unionism indicator, which tapped only the radical extreme.

A direct comparison of the percentage of radicals, liberals, and conservatives in each country is risky because the categories are not equivalent and because the cutting points separating the categories are arbitrary. However, the two categories at each extreme can be combined and profitably compared across nations. Accordingly, FIAT workers were the most radical, followed by PAL, IKA, and OLDS (see Table 5).

When indicators of political unionism and general political ideology are compared, Table 6 shows a strong association for FIAT and IKA, a weak association for OLDS, and a random association for PAL. The relatively strong relationship between the two indicators for FIAT and IKA partly reflects the items on unions in their indices of political ideology. However, since the coefficients of contingency are all below 0.50, one may conclude that the political views of workers do not directly reflect their views on political unionism. Thus, although only 6 percent of the Italian workers endorsed political unionism (see Table 4), 23 percent were identified with the left-wing union (CGIL) most strongly dedicated to this principle. Similarly, only a bare majority of political conservatives evaluated the Commissione Interna positively even though it was dominated by their unions (SIDA and UIL).

TABLE 5
Conservative-Radical Political Ideology of Automobile Workers (percent)

POLITICAL IDEOLOGY	OLDS	FIAT	IKA	PAL
Conservative	25	13	19	29
Neutral	48	20	48	26
Liberal	27	44	18	23
Radical	--	23	15	22
Total	100	100	100	100
N	(306)	(306)	(315)	(262)

The conservative category for FIAT refers to those who were apathetic or hostile toward unions and parties and the neutral category contains those who were politically conservative. For PAL, the conservative and neutral categories should read very conservative and conservative respectively.

TABLE 6
Political Ideology of Workers Who Believe in Political Unionism
(percent)

	Political Unionism		
	(first and second choice)		
POLITICAL IDEOLOGY	OLDS	FIAT	IKA	PAL
---	---	---	---	---
Conservative	--	6	2	30
Neutral	5	9	7	31
Liberal	4	11	14	25
Radical	--	29	57	31
Total	3	14	15	29
N	(10)	(40)	(47)	(75)
p of x^2	20/10	$<.01$	$<.001$	.50
Coefficient of Contingency (uncorrected)	.113	.233	.455	--

Combined first and second rank in the question dealing with the functions of the union (See Table 4).

In OLDS, the politically liberal UAW supported the Democratic party and urged its workers to do the same. Yet only half of the workers classified themselves as Democrats, half thought the union had too much political influence, and 80 percent thought the union should not spend workers' dues for political action. In IKA, almost one-quarter of the workers volunteered the opinion that their union leaders were too politically involved, but undoubtedly a larger proportion felt the same way. About one-quarter of the Indian workers of all ideologies felt that, despite the professed socialist ideology of the union, union leaders were indifferent to their interests and were colluding with management to retain power.

Clearly, workers and officials disagreed on politics, and union officials had failed to make workers conscious of the political world. Up to 30 percent of the workers in each country were not able to mention a single national problem, and the overwhelming majority were unable to specify what stance the union might take on any national problem.

SKILL LEVEL AND UNION FUNCTIONS

Workers were asked what they considered the most important union function and then were required to rank four stated functions. We expected skilled workers to be defensive and emphasize economic returns and fringe benefits, semiskilled workers to emphasize improvement of working conditions, and unskilled to seek immediate economic gains. No findings on the free response questions were statistically significant for the four nations, but two trends appeared. First, skilled workers, more than others, emphasized "defending the interests of the worker." Second, in all four nations, unskilled workers, more than others, empasized economic bargaining. Although similar trends appeared in response to the request to rank the four union functions, clear differences appeared only for FIAT and IKA.

We expected that semiskilled workers would be most sympathetic to political unionism, the skilled most opposed, and the unskilled most apathetic. In addition, we expected assembly-line workers and operators of automatic machines to prefer political unionism more than those whose jobs were varied. To our surprise, the expected relationship between the worker's skill level and his priority of union functions was only weakly supported, and no relationship was found between skill or job routines and support for political unionism.

SKILL LEVEL AND PLANT POLITICAL CLIMATE

Why do union officers who endorse political unionism fail to raise the political consciousness of workers? To answer this question we had to find out about political communication in the plant and social participation in the union and the wider community. Workers were asked whether they engaged in political and economic discussions, whom they talked to, whose opinions they valued, and who solicited their opinions and their involvement in union, community, and national affairs.

We assumed that skilled workers because of advantages in background, training, and current status, exercise more influence in political discussions which take place in the plant and tend to control local union affairs. Also, more skilled workers understand the relationship between economic and political events, engage in discussion of these events, discuss issues with workmates rather than kin and friends, hold their beliefs less tenaciously, and encourage others to express their views. Finally, since skilled workers participate more in union and other local organizations, they exercise more influence. This influence is often self-serving and conservative.

The data for OLDS strongly support our assumptions. Skilled workers exhibited middle-class norms; more of them identified with the middle class, had higher rates of union participation, community participation, church attendance, and social interaction inside and outside the plant. They were the most active politically and the least supportive of the union's political stand and activities. Even conservatives with lesser skills were more active politically and more involved in economic discussions than political liberals of similar skills. Moreover, the highest participators in union activities were politically more active and more conservative than the low participators regardless of skill. Finally, those with high educational achievement tended to be more conservative but more active in union affairs than the lesser educated.

The pattern for FIAT was not as clear as that for OLDS. More skilled workers engaged in political and economic discussions with their workmates rather than kin and friends. They were more sympathetic toward the union and more heavily involved in community and national affairs, but they were less militant in their unionism. However, more of the liberal and conservative workers were both sympathetic toward unions and more militant than either the radical or the politically apathetic workers. Compared to the radicals, the conservatives were more concerned about the internal problems of unions, and they wanted unions to pursue economic objectives exclusively. Thus, while the theory proposed is not strongly supported, it seems to hold for workers sympathetic to the conservative unions in power (SIDA and UIL).

The IKA pattern was the clearest of all. Unlike OLDS, the skilled workers were the most radical, but like the OLDS, more of the skilled discussed both economic and political events with their workmates rather than friends and relatives, and more people solicited their opinions. The skilled also had lower ideological tenacity scores, higher rates of union, community, and national participation, and higher rates of interaction with coworkers both inside and outside the plant. As expected, the skilled had higher levels of education, higher family incomes, and surprisingly for radicals, higher identification with the middle than the working class. Yet their anomie scores were similar to those of less skills.

In both IKA and OLDS, skilled workers controlled the work and union situation. The different ideological posture of the skilled in IKA[6] may be understood in terms of the meaning of radicalism in Argentine politics. Support for unionism was radical activity because the unions were associated with the then outlawed Peronist movement. Militant unionism represented a "radical" movement of the working class to consolidate its power in the nation, and the skilled were in the vanguard. Unlike radical movements elsewhere, the aim did not appear to be the overthrow of the property system, but establishing the legitimacy of unions within the political system. As aristocrats of labor, skilled workers identified with the middle class and sought to control the union movement for their own advantage. The most militant unionists in IKA were not only more interested in economic rather than political issues, they were also more critical of the union's internal political problems. American skilled workers who fought to establish unions in the late nineteenth and early twentieth century were considered radicals. After they became legitimately established, they became supporters of the status quo.

The pattern concerning ideological discussion in PAL was not clear. Somewhat more skilled than less skilled workers tended to participate in discussions and to have higher rates of social participation and social interaction. Also, more of the skilled tended to identify with the upper middle class, while the semiskilled identified with the middle class, and the unskilled with the lower. Skilled and highly educated workers were concentrated among the conservatives, but many semiskilled and some unskilled workers, who had the longest tenure and the highest incomes, were very conservative (see Table 5). A large number of less skilled workers were employees of the plant when it was exclusively an assembly-line operation. Although poorly educated and from the lower castes, by virtue of their long tenure, they had become highly paid workers. The newer employees tended to be young, highly educated, and from higher castes; they became semiskilled machine operators and exhibited radical political beliefs.

The older, moderately educated skilled workers who had long tenure conformed to the expected pattern: more of them participated in discussions, talked to their workmates rather than friends and kin, had their opinions solicited more often, valued the opinions of workmates more highly than those of friends and kin, held their political beliefs less tenaciously, participated more heavily in community affairs, and identified with the upper middle class. Most important, they were political conservatives but politically most active. The very conservative workers had opposite characteristics. The highly educated semiskilled radicals, on the other hand, participated little in the work group and union, but their participation in extra-plant activities was relatively high. Given their high education, higher caste background, downward mobility, blocked mobility in the plant, and upper-middle-class identification, it is not surprising that they exhibited the highest anomie scores. Their radicalism seemed to reflect their pessimism rather than their political commitments.

DISCUSSION

In general, workers everywhere, regardless of union ideology, see unions as legitimate and become similarly involved in them. Political unionism is emphasized by union officers, but not by the workers. Whatever the political views of either officers or workers, the vast majority of workers feel that unions should pursue improvements in wages and working conditions and, secondarily, social solidarity. The more complex the technology of the plant, the more workers focus on working conditions; the less complex, the more they stress wages and social solidarity. In the eyes of the workers, union goals and political ideology seem unrelated.

Contrary to our expectations, skill level and priority given to union functions are weakly related: the unskilled emphasize immediate wage increases the most; the semiskilled, working conditions; and the skilled, long-term economic and other advantages. Skill level and support for political unionism are unrelated. The historical grip of skilled workers on the union is indicated everywhere. In all plants, skilled workers occupy the most favored positions and are more involved in plant, union, and local social systems. They also participate most heavily in the plant communication system and tend to exert a conservative political influence in it.

Emphasis on job-conscious unionism by labor in the United States and a few other countries is allegedly the exception rather than the rule. Elsewhere, unions and parties have been said to cooperate to transform society for the benefit of the working class. Our research suggests that regardless of the ideologies of their unions or their own personal politics, workers everywhere emphasize principles of job-conscious unionism. Periodically, scholars assert that American workers are finally becoming politicized and radicalized, but our data confirm the historic pattern of job-consciousness. No scholar, to my knowledge, has denied the ideological character of Italian labor unions. Yet the data demonstrate that the great majority of FIAT workers, irrespective of their political positions, reject political unionism. On the contrary, more active participants in union affairs display more attributes of middle-class job-conscious unionists. Radicals as well as conservatives are critical of the political conflict which made the Commissione Interna an ineffective organization. Even where radicals control the local union, as in Argentina, their main objective is to gain advantages in the system and not to overturn it. Identifying with the middle class and bent on upward mobility, radicals want to establish the legitimacy of the union in order to gain economic security and economic mobility.

One may argue that unions in the United States, Italy, and Argentina are led by middle-class elites, hence their job-conscious orientation. But this claim has less credibility in India. A relatively higher proportion of Indian workers had embraced political unionism and radical politics, but these beliefs seem to have no bearing on plant or national politics. Workers evaluate the union in terms of what it is doing for them; those sheltered by it are favorable, those who are not are opposed. Those most alienated from the union are the middle-class well-educated radicals whose primary concern is to get the union to behave universalistically in the plant.

The persistent cleavage between officials and workers over political unionism is probably exacerbated in many places by the activities of skilled workers who are active in both the union and in politics. Officers may not be able to make workers politically militant until the silent sabotage of the working-class elite is overcome.

NOTES

1. I am indebted to the following for research support: Social Science Research Council, The National Science Foundation, The American Fulbright Commission, Institute of Labor and Industrial Relations at the University of Illinois (Urbana-Champaign). I am indebted to the field directors of this research: Steven E. Deutsch in the United States, Paolo Ammassari in Italy, Richard P. Gale in Argentina, and Baldev R. Sharma in India. I am grateful to Joan Huber and John Pease for valuable suggestions to improve this paper. A similar version of this paper appeared in *Industrial Relations,* May 1973.
2. The research on the relationship between skill level and politics is in such disarray that evidence can be found to support almost any position.
3. Advanced technology reduces the need for skilled labor and increases demand for semiskilled workers. An additional sample of skilled workers was drawn to provide sufficient numbers for statistical analysis for OLDS and IKA. The slightly augmented analytic samples were used throughout this paper.
4. The most recurrent response in all plants was "defend the interests of the workers" and the second, "economic bargaining." The first response has both an economic and protective connotation. The economic component in both questions make it the primary concern of the workers.
5. The researchers were persuaded by local consultants not to ask workers what union they preferred. This advice was later abandoned with the result that information on union identification was obtained for only 52 percent of the

workers. For the others, the entire interview was examined for evidence of political identification, and decisions were made for each individual.

6. Skill level, education, and union participation were all highly and positively related, so that the findings for skill level generally apply for the other variables.

13

Divisions In The Working Class: The Political Implications of Industrialization in Puerto Rico

Helen Icken Safa

The rapid urbanization and industrialization of Puerto Rico in the last twenty years has brought about profound changes in the class structure of Puerto Rican society. It is no longer possible to describe Puerto Rico adequately in terms of the rural subcultures described by Julian Steward and his associates in *The People of Puerto Rico* in 1956. From 1940 to 1968, for example, the population of the San Juan metropolitan area increased 135 percent[1] to a population of 797,000 people, well over one-fourth the total for the entire island.

The bulk of this urban increase came from impoverished rural migrants seeking jobs in the city or, as the Puerto Ricans call them, *buscando ambiente*. While the San Juan metropolitan area was booming, agriculture stagnated, plagued not only by natural disasters, such as the San Felipe hurricane of 1939 which virtually destroyed the coffee industry, but by sagging prices, competition from U.S. imports, and lack of manpower and government support. Workers refused to labor in the fields cutting cane for a subsistence wage[2] (which today still stands at about 80 cents an hour) when they could find more remunerative work in the city. When Operation Bootstrap was initiated in 1947, the government poured most of its resources into industrialization and tourism, building new plants and hotels, training workers, and advertising in the U.S. media Puerto Rico's attractions as a tourist resort and its potential for investors. To lure private capital from the United States, the government granted a ten-year tax exemption from income, property, and excise taxes to all new industries.[3] After 1952, industry became the dominant mode of economic activity on the island, with manufacturing generating $999 million of net income in 1971.[4]

The result was a constant decline in agricultural employment, from 229,000 in 1940 to 74,000 in 1970.[5] In comparison, employment in manufacturing, construction, trade, services, and government jobs has shown a steady increase, with the largest number now employed in manufacturing (141,000), trade (138,000), and services (123,000). We must then begin to define the urban subcultures of Puerto Rico and their relationship to the national class structure.

EMERGENCE OF A PRIVILEGED WORKING CLASS

This essay is an attempt to distinguish between two broad categories of the urban working class in Puerto Rican society:[6] the stably employed, relatively well-paid, skilled blue-collar and lower-level white-collar employees found largely in manufacturing, trade, and the government bureaucracy, and the unemployed and underemployed mass of urban poor who find low-paid jobs largely in services or construction and who often depend on public welfare for all or a substantial part of their income. This division largely results from the fact that in Puerto Rico, as in most developing countries, the rate of urbanization has far outpaced the growth in industrial employment, so that industry and other nonfarm sectors cannot absorb the ever-increasing urban labor force. This trend is accentuated by the highly technological nature of recent heavy industrialization with its emphasis on capital-intensive rather than labor-intensive techniques.[7] The best example of this in Puerto Rico today is the petrochemical industry, which operates sixty petroleum refineries employing over 6,000 people and a huge petrochemical plant with its own port facilities which has already polluted most of the southern coast of the island.[8] As early as 1963-64, the average wage in the petroleum refining sector was $2.23 compared to $1.16 in manufacturing.[9] The employees of the petrochemical industry are clearly a labor aristocracy, though the number of employees in this type of capital-intensive heavy industry is much lower than in more labor-intensive industries.

This trend toward capital-intensive industrialization has been observed in industrializing Latin American countries such as Argentina, Brazil, Chile, Venezuela, and Mexico. Though the same phenomenon is occurring in developed industrialized countries such as the United States and Western Europe, Latin America (as well as other areas of the Third World) appears to be bypassing the early period of industrialization in these developed countries, which was characterized by a labor-intensive technology and the use of large numbers of unskilled workers. At the same time, Latin America has not produced sufficient alternative sources of employment in the services sector of the urban economy to absorb the excess urban labor force. As Glaucio Soares, the Brazilian sociologist, notes:

> The developing countries are not marching straight into the middle-class service society [such as we have in the U.S.]. Rather, their class structure indicates that they are becoming polarized societies with a growing middle class...and a growing unemployment sector in the working class.[10]

Soares points out that this development leads to a different type of class conflict than that predicted by Marx. The opposition is not between owners of the means of production and the proletariat, but between the growing middle class and the unemployed and underemployed sectors of the working class. Soares sees the steadily employed working class as a cushioning element between these two sectors, rather than the middle class as a cushioning element between the upper and working class.[11] We shall discuss the significance of the stably employed working class in terms of Marx's notion of class conflict later in this chapter.

At this point we would like to describe the emergence of a stably employed working class in Puerto Rican urban society and their growing differentiation from the mass of urban unemployed and underemployed.[12] As early as 1959, when we conducted an ethnographic study of a shantytown in the San Juan metropolitan area, there were clear occupational differences between adult males which coincided with differences in salary, education, and life-style. Skilled artisans were clearly at the top of the hierarchy, with the highest educational and salary levels, with service workers such as porters, waiters, and hotel employees at the bottom. Factory workers and dockworkers fell somewhere in between, and their salary and educational levels varied extensively. Only half of the employed labor force in the shantytown belonged to unions, with the lowest percentage among service workers, reflecting the weak and fragmentary nature of the labor union movement in Puerto Rico as a whole. Since unions are heavily involved in politics, workers tend to look to the government rather than the union to solve their labor problems.[13] This paternalistic dependency upon the government has until recently greatly inhibited the growth of an independent labor movement.

Occupational and salary differences among workers in the shantytown also inhibited the growth of class consciousness. A man's occupation and salary were important determinants of his family's potential for social mobility. The stably employed had the nicest houses and furnishings, the best diets, and the highest aspirations for their children. For example, Don Francisco, a self-employed mason, moved from the shantytown to a large though modest home in a private *urbanizacion* or subdivision. He put eight children through high school, and one has just completed college and is now studying medicine in Spain. Don Francisco, a devout Seventh Day Adventist, believes that life is a never-ending ladder of social mobility, ordained by God, which individuals ascend step by step with His help. He observes:

> Lean on a good tree and good shade will cover you. That means if I stick by someone worse off than I, in what conditions shall I put myself? In the same conditions as he, right? But if I try to improve, I don't try to look back....Thus we should all be looking up. He who wants to remain below, it's because he likes it....Rising and falling, rising and falling, from that no one can mislead us, because that is the word of God.[14]

Despite the emphasis on social mobility among some shantytown families, there was a strong egalitarian ethic, which Jayawardena, in a provocative article on ideology and conflict in lower-class communities, claims is quite characteristic of subgroups that are "denied social equality by the wider society or its dominant class."[15] This egalitarian ethic stresses individual *personal* or human worth (comparable to the Latin American/ Catholic concept of *dignidad*) rather than the more American and Protestant concept of *social* equality or equality of opportunity. Such subordinate groups, Jayawardena notes, lack any formal organization, permanent leadership, or sharp differentiation of roles.[16] This was certainly true of the shantytown, as I have described extensively elsewhere.[17] However, collective action was manifested in the widespread pattern of mutual aid, in the work of *barrio* committees, and in the overall growth and improvement of the shantytown which was due largely to community efforts.

However, as Jayawardena observes, the egalitarian ethic is confined to the local community or subgroup and is constantly challenged by the individualism prevalent in the larger society, giving rise to personal quarrels and other forms of conflict as a means of maintaining group cohesion.[18] In the Puerto Rican shantytown, the bases for social cohesion which sustained the egalitarian ethic were eliminated by the eradication of the shantytown and the relocation of the families to various parts of the San Juan metropolitan area. The result was reinforcement of the individualism prevalent in the larger society and greater emphasis on status striving and social mobility.

The stably employed moved into *urbanizaciones,* private subdivisions newly built on the outskirts of the San Juan metropolitan area. They now own their own home complete with modern furnishings and appliances, including a color television and usually a car. There is strong emphasis on competition and conspicuous consumption, which often forces the family into debt in order to "keep up with the Joneses." Lidia, Don Francisco's daughter who just finished college and who lives in an *urbanizacion* with her family, observed:

> Everyone wants to live better than his neighbor, everyone wants to have things in his house, which show that he has a higher income than his neighbor....For example, there are individuals...that change their living room set every year for a better one, a more expensive one, to show the neighbor that they can. There are others who change their car every year and try to make it a better and prettier car with more new gadgets....But the debts are eating them up as we say currently.

This emphasis on status and conspicuous consumption contrasts sharply with the sharing and mutual aid found earlier in the shantytown, where, as Lidia notes, "we were all equal so we treated each other as equal." As we noted previously, they were not all equal, but it would appear that the fact of common residence in a shantytown to some extent overrode the socioeconomic differences among them. The increasing residential segregation by socioeconomic status in Puerto Rico during the past decade reinforces the growing divisions in the urban labor force.[19]

The unemployed and underemployed urban poor are increasingly shuttled into public housing, as the shantytowns are cleared to make room for new highways, apartment and office buildings, and other lucrative urban real estate. In comparison to the shantytown, the population of the public housing project studied in 1959 in the San Juan metropolitan area showed a higher percentage of fatherless families, unemployed, and families on welfare. [20] They move to public housing because they cannot afford private housing (outside of a shantytown) and for the same reason, they tend to remain in public housing indefinitely, becoming a permanent housing population. They are totally dependent on housing management, not only for the repair and maintenance of the apartment, but also for social control and leadership in local community activities, areas in which shantytown residents exerted considerable influence. As one project resident complained: *"Aquí todo es público y uno no puede mandar en nada."* ("Here everything is public and one has no authority in anything.") Public housing tenants are a totally dependent population.

The egalitarian ethic characteristic of the shantytown is not carried over to public housing because of its lack of local community autonomy. The dependence of public housing tenants on management prevents the growth of any form of collective action or sentiment, and results in a totally atomized community. In contrast to the cohesion of the shantytown, public housing tenants tend to keep to themselves and to be suspicious and cautious of their neighbors. Raquel, the female head of one of the former shantytown families, now living in public housing, notes:

> If they come by here and ask me for something and I have it, I give it to them. But from outside [e.g. on the balcony or at the door]. I never ask them to enter nor do I stop to converse with anyone so that there are no problems. That's what brings problems, entering houses and looking for gossip, talking about everybody, that brings problems.

Jayawardena notes that the egalitarian ethic is unlikely to develop in closed communities (like the East European *shtetl)* because their autonomy makes them relatively resistant to outside societal pressures and values.[21] However, at the opposite extreme, totally dependent communities like public housing are also unlikely to develop an egalitarian ethic because they are so controlled by the norms and institutions of the larger society. This qualification would appear to extend to such "total institutions" as mental hospitals, prisons, and even some ghetto neighborhoods, which are subject to tight societal controls.

Public housing tenants depend upon the government not only for housing, but for food, health care and other necessities as well. Rents in public housing are pro-rated according to income and size of family, but many tenants are totally subsidized and pay little or no rent, especially if they have no employed adult male in the household. Thus Raquel pays $18 a month for her five-bedroom apartment in a new project, since her husband, before his death some years ago, was a chronic alcoholic and never supported the family. She used to supplement her husband's sporadic employment with the sale of *cañita* or bootleg rum in order to support her family of eight children. Now she received $150 a month in social security payments, a higher stable income than she has ever enjoyed.

Social security payments are considerably higher than public welfare, which is still very low by U.S. standards.[22] In 1959, for example, Carmen, a young widow with five small children, received $50 a month in public welfare. She worked three days a week as a laundress and eventually took up with an older man who helped support her and her family. Now she has broken up with this man and lives alone with her children in a three-bedroom apartment in public housing, for which she pays $10 a month. She manages very well on the $82 a month she receives in public assistance plus the $15 a week her older daughter gives her from her job at the project nursery school. In her own words, *"Estoy viviendo más desahogada que en aquél tiempo."* ("I am living less suffocated than at that time.")

Though payments in public welfare have increased and are supplemented by food stamp programs (*el mantengo*), public health care, public education, and, of course, public housing, they are still insufficient to meet the growing number of unemployed and underemployed urban poor. In response to this growing need, between 1970 and 1971, federal grants to the Puerto Rican government for the Department of Social Services increased from $28 million to $44.1 million, while the federal grant for the Unemployment Trust Insurance Fund increased from $29.4 million to $42.8 million.[23] Thus the Puerto Rican government, subsidized by the federal government, increasingly supports the surplus labor supply forced out of the labor market by a capital-intensive industrialization.

Although per capita income in Puerto Rico continues to increase and the percentage of families with incomes under $2,000 decreased from 78 percent in 1953 to 39 percent in 1969, the number of families below the poverty line actually increased from 212,000 in 1963 to 229,000 in 1969.[24] This appears due largely to continued population increase and to a slowdown since the 1960s in migration to the mainland, which still absorbs a large segment of Puerto Rico's poor. It may also reflect a leveling of employment in the manufacturing sector, which actually registered a decline in employment since 1969.[25] The distribution of income has also shown no improvement, since in the decade from 1953-63, the top 20 percent increased their earnings from 50.5 percent to 51.5 percent, while the earnings of the bottom 20 percent dropped from 5 percent to 4 percent.[26] Growth in industrial and nonfarm sectors has resulted in a large increase of middle-income families, including both stably employed blue-collar workers and white-collar clerical workers and professionals. [27] The percentage of total income earned by this "intermediary group" increased from 46.8 percent in 1953 to 49.5 percent in 1963.[28]

POLITICAL IMPLICATIONS

This growing division in the working class has increasing political significance. One might expect the unemployed and underemployed poor to favor a radical change in the economic and political policy of the Puerto Rican government, since they would stand to gain the most from a redistribution of wealth and power. However, even in 1959, there was a higher percentage of *Estadistas* or statehood supporters in public housing than in the shantytown. The *Estadistas* have traditionally been identified with the wealthy elite of Puerto Rican society, with the president of the party and candidate for governor being first a large landowner and sugarcane producer, and then Luis Ferré, his brother-in-law, a millionaire industrialist (a change which in itself reflects the changing nature of the Puerto Rican elite). They obviously desire full incorporation of Puerto Rico into the United States because of the benefits it will bring to them in terms of increased capital, credit, and market facilities.

In 1968, Ferré was elected governor under a new political party, the New Progressive Party (PNP), which had split off from the old *Estadista* party.[29] His strongest support came from the urban areas, both in the high- and low-income sectors.[30] Both divisions of the working class voted for Ferré (the privileged sector in greater numbers), though for different reasons. It would seem that the unemployed and underemployed poor were discontent with the services provided by the Popular party after twenty-eight years in power and felt that the PNP could extent the benefits of a paternalistic government through closer ties to the United Sta- tes.[31] They are aware that much of the source of funds for social welfare programs in Puerto Rico comes from the federal government, and they wished to increase these benefits rather than end them.

For the privileged working class, on the other hand, a vote for the PNP represented more industrialization, more employment, and higher wages. They looked to Ferré, himself an industrialist, to further the industrial progress of Puerto Rico, though industrialization had started and was largely promoted by the Populares. It would seem that Ferré deliberately cultivated this constituency when he came into power. Under Ferré, the government bureaucracy, an important element of the privileged working class, expanded considerably, making the government the third most important employer in the economy. One of his most popular measures was the institution of a Christmas bonus to all government employees as well as steady employees of private enterprise, again benefiting the privileged working class.

Thus both divisions of the working class have looked to the government to protect their interests. The privileged working class seeks to pressure the government into increasing job opportunities, wages and other fringe benefits, while the lumpenproletariat are bought off by extending social welfare programs. Ultimately both of these sources of control are heavily dependent on assistance from the United States, since Puerto Rican industries are largely American-owned and the federal government sets guidelines for minimum wages, tariffs, shipping, and other aspects of the industrialization program as well as being the major contributor to social welfare programs.

This dependency of the Puerto Rican working class on continued capital investment and federal aid from the United States hinders the growth of a nationalistic class consciousness among this subordinate group. Both feel that their survival and continued progress depend on continuing association with the United States; thus they share a common interest in preserving the present colonial status of Puerto Rico. They desire neither independence for Puerto Rico nor direct political power for themselves. They merely seek a government which is responsive to their needs, and they view the new sources of employment created by industrialization as beneficial to them. In this regard, it is interesting to note that the vote for the Puerto Rican Independence party fell sharply after 1952, just when industrialization was taking over the economy,[32] though working-class support for independence has increased recently. Though many of the Puerto Rican rural proletariat opposed the exploitation of American sugarcane corporations on the island, much of the urban proletariat, at least until recently, failed to perceive a similar threat by the more "benevolent" American industrialist.

ECONOMIC DEVELOPMENT AND
PROLETARIAN CONSCIOUSNESS

Economic growth in the form of industrialization and urbanization can retard the growth of proletarian class consciousness, at least temporarily. As previously shown,[33] expanded employment and educational opportunities create the myth of an "open society" in which it is assumed there are limitless opportunities for social mobility to all those who are willing to work hard and save, get an education, and so on. In short, the egalitarian ethic, a product of strong barriers to social mobility, is replaced by the notion of social equality in which inequality is justified on the basis of "equality of opportunity."[34]

Certainly economic development introduces a much greater variety of occupations and life-styles, even among the working class. Liberal social scientists have tended to view this expanded social mobility as a sign of the breakdown of old class distinctions and the "convergence" of classes, and to use this as a basis for repudiation of Marx's notion of class conflict. However, these social scientists ignore the fact that, as in Puerto Rico, the gap between the rich and the poor is greater than ever, and that with capital-intensive industrialization, wealth is increasingly concentrated in the hands of foreign-owned capital (not even counted in national income statistics) while the number of unskilled unemployed also increases.

Meszdros, a Marxist follower of Lukacs, totally repudiates the claims of the "convergence" theory:

> ...All the available comprehensive sets of empirical data point to increasing polarization, growing inequality, and the concentration of the means of production in fewer and fewer hands, on a global scale—i.e...they demonstrate the exact *opposite* of the claimed equalization, convergence and structural integration of the classes.[35]

It is quite possible that the growing concentration of wealth and increasing inequality will force a realignment of classes, which appears to be growing recently in Puerto Rico with large-scale unemployment and the failure of Operation Bootstrap. The key lies in the political and social consciousness of the emerging privileged working class. The privileged working class and the large mass of urban unemployed and underemployed are hardly antagonistic. Until now the urban poor have looked up to the privileged working class as an example of what they themselves might achieve with hard work and more education. The stably employed are living proof, for themselves and those less fortunate, of the benefits to workers of industrialization and economic development.

If the job market in industry slackens, as it seems to be doing, particularly with the trend toward capital-intensive industrialization, and increasing numbers of the urban poor are left without steady employment,[36] the welfare rolls may not be able to continue to absorb this growing surplus labor force, even with massive federal aid. In the mid-1970s, reportedly three-fourths of the population received food stamps. They cannot even be called a reserve anymore, in the Marxist sense, since they may never be called upon to work. They simply become redundant. If the privileged working class is called upon to help shoulder the burden of the unemployed urban poor through taxes, as they are in the United States, they may turn antagonistic to this less fortunate group, as the blue-collar workers have turned against the welfare poor in the United States. Indeed, the heavy tax burden placed upon the American working class, ostensibly to meet the needs of the "undeserving poor" (usually identified as black, Puerto Rican, or otherwise ethnically differentiated) has proven one of the most potent divide-and-rule strategies yet devised by modern industrial capitalism to hinder the growth of proletarian consciousness.

It is also possible that, because of the greater cultural and ethnic homogeneity among the Puerto Rican working class and the recent emergence of the privileged working class, such antagonisms will not develop. Instead, this class may become increasingly aware of the exploitation of all workers under a capitalist system, particularly as the percentage of workers in their privileged position continues to dwindle. There is already some evidence for this in our data, as parents complain of their children's inability to find decent jobs, though they have gone to great sacrifice to send them through high school and to raise them in "good" neighborhoods. [37] In other words, the myth of the open society is already beginning to be questioned. The adults feel they have made substantial gains, starting (as most of them have) as poor agricultural laborers. But they do not perceive the same opportunities for their children, because the requirements for admission into the privileged working class continue to rise.

Moreover, as Meszdros (and others) have noted, "the development of class consciousness does not imply its constitution as a 'homogeneous *psychological bond*'....but the elaboration of strategically viable *programmes of action* embracing a multiplicity of specific social groups in whatever variety of organizational forms may be required."[38] That is, for class consciousness does not imply its constitution as a 'homogeneous action programs which aim to make major structural changes in the society and to end worker exploitation.

The first level of development of proletarian consciousness, (what Lenin called "trade union consciousness") is likely to be aimed at immediate, localized demands, while the higher level, or "socialist consciousness" aims at the total transformation of the society.[39] In a sense, the shantytown had already developed the first level of proletarian consciousness, though on a territorial rather than on an occupational basis. The shantytown had the advantage of uniting the urban poor in a common struggle, despite the occupational and status differences between them, thus not excluding the unemployed and underemployed poor who are unlikely to be encompassed in any trade-union strategy. However, the unity of the shantytown never extended beyond the boundaries of the local community and was shattered by the process of relocation, which dispersed residents into public housing projects and private *urbanizaciones.* Urban renewal, by further fragmenting the working class, has been a serious obstacle to proletarian consciousness in Puerto Rico.

It may be argued that revolutionary "socialist consciousness" is most likely to develop in advanced capitalist countries such as the United States and Great Britain, where trade unionism is stronger and has a longer history. However, Bottomore and others have recently questioned this view, noting that "on the contrary, it may be claimed with great plausibility that a revolutionary consciousness has established itself most strongly in those capitalist countries which were relatively backward and had a low *per capita* income."[40] Unlike even capitalist West European countries, workers in the United States have never had a political party to represent their interests exclusively. Thus the trade-union movement in the United States has never gone beyond the first level of proletarian consciousness.

It would seem that socialist consciousness aiming at total structural transformation can only be achieved through the politicalization of the working class. As in the United States, workers in Puerto Rico also lack clear political representation,[41] though the Popular party claimed to represent the interests of the rural *jíbaro* and its basic support still lies in the rural areas.[42] The independence movement has never had a strong mass base among workers or peasants, as even its leaders are willing to acknowledge.[43] This is due partly to the benefits gained by workers from the continuation of colonialism (as explained previously) and partly to the fact that the independence movement aimed primarily at nationalism rather than class consciousness, and therefore found its strongest adherents among middle-class intellectuals. Only recently has the independence movement, under both the Puerto Rican Socialist party and the Puerto Rican Independence party, adopted an openly socialist platform aimed at meeting the needs of the working class.

In short, the key to which way the privileged working class will turn appears to lie in the politicalization of this crucial new class in Puerto Rican society. If they are incorporated into reformist elements, as they were under the New Deal in the United States, then they are likely to side with the bourgeoisie against the mass of unemployed and underemployed urban poor, as Soares predicts. However, if they are radicalized by progressive movements and made aware of the growing exploitation of all workers under a colonial, capitalist system, then a truly revolutionary socialist consciousness may develop.

NOTES

1. Informe Economico al Gobernador, *Estado Libre Asociado de Puerto Rico* (1970), Table 2, Appendix A.
2. According to the 1970 census, the annual median earnings of male farm laborers in 1969 were $913 compared to $2,003 for nonfarm laborers and

were even higher for skilled workers. (U.S. Census on Puerto Rico: Table 51, General Social and Economic Characteristics).

3. Henry Wells, *The Modernization of Puerto Rico* (Cambridge, Mass.: Harvard University Press, 1969), pp. 150-51.

4. Informe Economico al Gobernador, *Oficina del Gobernador, Junta de Plantificacion* (1971), Table 8.

5. Ibid., Table 17. The decline in agricultural employment can also be noted in advanced industrial societies like the United States, but in Puerto Rico it would seem that the rate of decline has been even more precipitous.

6. These categories are by no means sharply defined or tightly bounded, particularly in developing countries like Puerto Rico, where workers may shift back and forth several times in one lifetime. This fact contributes to the lack of antagonism between these two broad groups among the Puerto Rican urban poor.

7. Puerto Rico Planning Board, Bureau of Social Planning, *La Problematica de la Pobreza en Puerto Rico* (1971), p. 26.

8. "Industrialization Comes to the Caribbean with more Pollution than Jobs," *New York Times,* January 28, 1973.

9. Wells, p. 154.

10. Glaucio A. D. Soares, "The New Industrialization and the Brazilian Political System," in *Latin America: Reform or Revolution?,* ed. James Petras and Maurice Zeitlin (New York: Fawcett, 1968), pp. 195-96.

11. Ibid.

12. The data given here were collected by the author in two separate studies in Puerto Rico at two different time periods. The first study in 1959 was based on participant observation and a survey of 100 families each in a representative shantytown and public housing project chosen at random in the San Juan metropolitan area. The second study, ten years later in 1969, consisted of intensive case histories of relocated shantytown families to assess the changes which had taken place in their lives over the decade as a result of the move and the overall development of Puerto Rico. A full description of these studies appears in my book *The Urban Poor of Puerto Rico: A Study in Development and Inequality* (Holt, Rinehart & Winston, 1974).

13. The tendency of organized labor in Latin America to develop paternalistic relationships with the government has also been noted by Landsberger, "The Labor Elite: Is It Revolutionary?" in *Elites in Latin America,* ed., S. M. Lipset and A. Solare (London: Oxford University Press, 1967) who attributes it partly to the numerical and economic weakness of the labor movement and to government rather than company control of labor conditions. Quijano notes that these paternalistic relationships are an important factor retarding class consciousness among Peruvian workers. Anibal Quijano, "Tendencies in Peruvian Development and Class Structure," in *Latin America: Reform or Revolution?* ed. J. Petras and M. Zeitlin (New York: Fawcett, 1969).

14. All of the direct quotes from Puerto Rican informants have been translated by the author.

15. Chandra Jayawardena, "Ideology and Conflict in Lower Class Communities," *Comparatives Studies in Society and History* 4(1968).

16. Ibid., p. 418.

17. Helen Icken Safa, "The Social Isolation of the Urban Poor," in *Among the People,* ed. Irwin Deutsches and E. Thompson (New York: Basic Books, 1968).

18. Jayawardena, p. 438.

19. Eduardo Seda Bonilla, "La Condicion Urbana: San Juan, Puerto Rico," *Caribbean Studies* 11 (171): 14-15.

20. Helen Icken Safa, "The Female-Headed Household in Public Housing: A Case Study in Puerto Rico." *Human Organization* 24 (1965): 135-39.

21. Jayawardena, p. 430.

22. The average case payment for families receiving public welfare only increased from $11.55 in 1960 to $16.88 in 1968. (Puerto Rico Planning Board, Bureau of Social Planning, *La problematica de la pobreza en Puerto Rico,* 1971, p. 36).

23. Informe Económico al Gobernador, 1971.

24. Celia F. Cintrón and Barry Levine, "¿Quienes son los pobres en Puerto Rico?" in *Problemas de Desigualdad Social en Puerto Rico,* eds. Rafael L. Ramirez, Barry B. Levine, and Carlos Buitrago Ortiz (San Juan: Edciones Libreria Internacional, 1972), p. 24.

25. Informe Economico al Gobernador, 1971, Table 26.

26. Cintrón and Levine, pp. 26-27.

27. Cf. Fuat M. Andic, "Distribution of Family Incomes in Puerto Rico," *Caribbean Monograph Series No. 1* (San Juan: Institute of Caribbean Studies, University of Puerto Rico), 1964.

28. Puerto Rico Planning Board, Bureau of Social Planning, *La Problematica de la Pobreza en Puerto Rico,* 1971.

29. The current governor of Puerto Rico, Romero Barcelo, is also a leader of the New Progressive party.

30. Marcia Quintero, *Elecciones de 1968 en Puerto Rico* (San Juan: CEREP, 1972), p. 39.

31. Cf. Rafael L. Ramirez, "Marginalidad, dependencia y participacion politica an el arrabal," in *Problemas de Desigualdad Social en Puerto Rico,* eds. Rafael L. Ramirez, Barry B. Levine, and Carlos Buitrago Ortiz (San Juan: Edciones Libreria Internacional, 1972), pp. 114-16.

32. Wells, p. 277.

33. Helen Icken Safa, *The Urban Poor of Puerto Rico: A Study in Development and Inequality* (New York: Holt Rinehart & Winston, 1974).

34. Cf. Jayawardena, p. 414.

35. Istvan Meszaros, "Contingent and Necessary Class Consciousness," in *Aspects of History and Class Consciousness,* ed. Istvan Maszaros (London: Routledge & Kegan Paul, 1971), p. 97.

36. In 1963, the total unemployment rate in Puerto Rico was 27.6 percent, most of it concentrated in the rural area and in the lower-income brackets (Puerto Rico Planning Board, p. 41).

37. In 1964, the unemployment rate among youth from 16-19 was 34 percent. (Puerto Rico Planning Board, p. 30).

38. Meszaros, p. 120.

39. Cf. E. J. Hobsbawn, "Class Consciousness in History," in *Aspects of History and Class Consciousness,* ed. Istvan Meszaros (London: Routledge & Kegan Paul, 1971), p. 15.

40. Tom Bottomore, "Class Structure and Social Consciousness," in *Aspects of History and Class Consciousness,* ed. Istvan Meszaros (London: Routledge & Kegan Paul, 1971), p. 58.

41. According to A. L. Quintero, "El desarrollo de las clases sociales y los

conflictos politicas en Puerto Rico," in *Problemas de Desigualdad Social en Puerto Rico,* ed. Rafael L. Ramirez, Barry Levine, and Carlos Buitrago Ortiz, (San Juan: Ediciones Libreria Internacional), the only Puerto Rican political party with mass worker support was the Socialist party, which drew its constituency largely from the strongly unionized landless agricultural laborers. However, with the collapse of the sugarcane industry, this politicized labor force lost much of its strength and was largely absorbed into the ranks of the Popular party.

42. Marcia Quintero, p. 16.
43. For example, M. Maldonado-Denis, *Puerto Rico: A Socio-Historic Interpretation* (New York: Vintage Books, 1972), p. 180.

14

The Concept of
Working-Class
Embourgeoisement

Elizabeth Jelin

The concept of embourgeoisement is well established in current socio-logical language. It is employed to interpret and explain such diverse events as a confrontation between the former socialist government of Chile and the mine workers; changes in the Italian government; the position of the AFL-CIO in United States elections; and even the individual behavior of our next-door neighbor getting a new car. It has become a pet word, applied to a variety of dimensions and levels of organization of social reality

How did the term embourgeoisement gain such popularity and wide-spread use in sociological discussions and writings? Is it possible to find a single conceptual framework underlying this variety of usages? This is not the place to go into a historical or etymological search of the origins of the term. For this paper, it is important to point out that it gained popularity and widespread use in Western European social science during the 1950s. The postwar revival of sociological analysis in several European countries started with a number of studies in industrial sociology, mostly centered on the working class. The interest in the subject was clear: their authors were disappointed at the conservative political turn in Western Europe, thought the working class was to a large extent responsible for this political climate, and started looking for interpretations and explanations of its behavior. The "eclipse of the working class" became a leitmotif of post-World War II European sociology.[1]

Interpretations of this embourgeoisement of the working class were based on two types of empirical evidence. First, many of the attitude surveys carried out after the war presented the image of an "integrated" worker who does not contest the existing political system; who defines his interests in terms of reformist short-term gains rather than of a revolutionary alternative model of social organization; and who is willing to fight for his grievances only within established economic and political frameworks. Second, the standard of living of the working class in advanced capitalist countries has improved considerably over the last few decades, and the image of an affluent society with affluent workers is gaining acceptance.

The hypothesis of embourgeoisement of the working class links these two trends. It claims that improvements in the standard of living are due to increasing industrialization and mass production, i.e., the emergence of an affluent worker diminishes the gap between the working and the middle classes. This is accomplished through an increasing adoption by the working class of patterns of behavior and styles of life previously held by the middle class. Among other changes, this new style means the loss of revolutionary spirit and its replacement by an emphasis on personal or family consumption. It also implies a diminishing interest in politics, or at least a loss of the ideological content of politics: not that the worker becomes completely disinterested in politics, rather there is a change in his approach to it. Political activity is now based on the defense of competing interests, and not on competing ideologies offering alternative models of social organization.

The foregoing is a simplified formulation of the core meaning shared by the various authors who present, discuss, study, and criticize the notion of embourgeoisement of the working class. Beyond this common core, differences between analysts are large. There are differences in the dimensions various authors stress, the indicators they use to establish "facts," and even more important, the interpretation they give to the same indicator or fact. While some define embourgeoisement as an emphasis on private consumption,[2] others claim that we can talk about embourgeoisement only when this consumption is conspicuous and is conceived by the worker in terms of a search for status.[3] While some take the findings of surveys of political attitudes as an indicator of ideological and political embourgeoisement,[4] others reinterpret these findings within the context of a lack of change over time in the proportion of the population voting for leftist alternatives in national elections, and build into this reinterpretation their argument about the lack of embourgeoisement.

The purpose of this paper is to clarify the various meanings and contents of the hypothesis of embourgeoisement, critically explore the limitations of the approach usually taken when presenting and discussing the hypothesis, and offer some alternative interpretations. Changes in the working class have a central role in the explanation of trends in advanced industrial societies. Therefore, the hypothesis of embourgeoisement is not an isolated interpretation, but part of wider conceptions according to which capitalist industrial societies are becoming either middle-class,[6] service-class,[7] or middle-mass rather than class societies.[8]

Our discussion will center upon embourgeoisement of the working class. Wider macrosocial trends will be introduced only when necessary for understanding the line of thought presented.

MYTH AND REALITY IN THE HYPOTHESIS OF EMBOURGEOISEMENT

The hypothesis of embourgeoisement is based on an interpretation of a series of changes in the productive organization and distribution process which took place during the last decades in advanced capitalist societies. An important dimension of change is the technical and organizational conditions of work. New processes of production, new industrial technology, and new conceptions of social organization of the plant brought about important changes in working-class composition, in types of prevalent tasks and in everyday organization of work routines.[9] Technological change predominantly takes place through the establishment of new industrial activities that introduce new technology and new organizational forms. Older activities or sectors tend to continue their operation according to the old organizational molds and technology.[10] At any given moment, a cross section of industrial organization will show great heterogeneity, explained by overlapping and coexisting technological and organizational cohorts. New industries recruit young and new workers, who are often seen by social scientists as in the forefront of the working class, enjoying working conditions that are a preview of the future of the working class.[11] Only in part are these working conditions determined by technological development; also crucial are changes in entrepreneurial ideologies and benefits previously obtained by the working class as a result of organized labor movements.[12]

The bulk of changes in working-class conditions are intercohort changes, taking place through shifts in the distribution of occupations and tasks between successive cohorts.[13] Manual labor is now cleaner, lighter, involving more responsibility and less mechanical repetition of movements. What this means is not that all or most manual jobs have changed gradually in these directions. Rather, what took place is a redistribution of the manual labor force, so that higher proportions of it (predominantly in the newer industrial sectors) have cleaner jobs requiring more responsibility and less physical effort. In the industrial sectors with older technology, the internal division of labor and work organization change slowly. In consequence, at any given moment in time there is considerable heterogeneity in the working conditions of the working class.

Through historical and comparative studies of workers in different technological and organizational contexts, precise inferences can be drawn regarding the direction and rate of change in working conditions. There is no doubt that there have been changes in the nature of work and working conditions. What we do not have is, first, clear and explicit criteria to specify the changes in working conditions that are relevant for changes in working-class orientations and attitudes; and second, an idea of the magnitude of the variations and changes discussed, that is, knowing how many workers are under what working conditions at different moments in history. To take an obvious example, the assembly line has often been considered the prototypic technological feature of the first half of the twentieth century, creating the most alienating and difficult conditions for the workers involved. However, we do not know the number of workers in assembly lines in any industrial country or industrial sector within a country; we do not know the relative weight of assembly-line jobs in the labor force; and even less do we have clues to determine historical trends in employment in assembly-line jobs, or for that matter in any other technological condition.

A second important dimension for change in the working class is the increase in income levels. Although the debate about whether or not there is income and wealth redistribution in advanced capitalist countries is still open,[14] there is no doubt that in absolute terms (controlling only changes in cost of living) workers have nowadays higher income levels than what they had before World War II. Although the increase probably affects most of the working class, workers in the newer industrial sectors benefit most. Higher income levels mean that workers have access to a series of consumption goods that were not within their reach thirty years ago.[15] Today few if any workers in advanced capitalist countries have to be concerned with obtaining the bare minimum for their subsistence. Consumption patterns are different, "needs" are defined at a higher level. An important feature of this increase in income and consumption levels in capitalist countries (and to what extent are socialist countries moving in the same direction?) is that the consumer goods the working class can now afford are for private or family use: houses (rather than apartments); electric appliances which allow for a high degree of independence from the outside world (i.e., refrigerators allowing weekly shopping trips to the supermarket rather than daily shopping in neighborhood stores); the television set as the center of private leisure time nonactivity; and of course, the car as the king in the process of privatization of transportation.

The trends in capitalist industrial societies mentioned above, namely changes in working conditions, income, and consumption levels, are well established and thus can be accepted as facts. Difficulties arise when interpreting the consequences to be derived from them. The hypothesis of embourgeoisement offers one possible interpretation of the consequences of these basic trends.

The defenders of the hypothesis of embourgeoisement claim that the new automated technological conditions confront workers with a new situation offering them a different basis for work-derived satisfaction, although not implying a return to "pride in craftsmanship." The new working conditions, more mental than manual, not too routinized and repetitive, involving dealing with symbols (i.e., reading panels) rather than with tools, based on delegation of responsibility, do not differ greatly from professionals' and technicians' work. Furthermore, they allow considerable physical mobility and some freedom to organize individual work schedules. Presumably, these new conditions would promote a greater integration of the worker in his immediate work team, a team that is highly heterogeneous in terms of stratification—it includes hierarchically different positions interacting on an equalitarian basis. They would also promote a clear perception of the importance of one's task in the process of production, thus giving more meaning to one's job and bringing about a decline in alienation.[16] In broader terms, the manual-nonmanual distinction would become increasingly blurred; the traditional proletariat would gradually disappear and be replaced by workers whose tasks are not based on physical strength but on knowledge and responsibility, workers who enter into cooperative social relations with the rest of the personnel rather than subordinates being continually supervised and controlled. In summary, workers would become increasingly similar to technicians and other higher personnel, would gradually adopt the patterns of organization men with a high degree of identification with the enterprise, and increasingly establish occupational career commitments within it.[17]

These new workers have high salaries which allow for an increase in their consumption level and a change in their life-style. Presumably, this would produce a shift in the motivation for consumption: increasingly, decisions would be based on status considerations, a typical feature of the middle class. To take only one life-style dimension, mobility to the suburbs is growing among workers. Traditional working-class neighborhoods, where workers grew up and lived all their lives, providing a basis for class identity and solidarity, are by now only memories of the past. The worker lives in a new suburb, where no deep ties are established. His life is centered around his nuclear family, around his private life—again, a typical middle-class characteristic. The hypothesis continues: if there is a process of embourgeoisement in material living conditions, working conditions, income, consumption, life-style, and leisure time activities, then all these will necessarily affect political ideologies and the types of action the working class is willing to engage in. Since workers are taking on middle-class life-styles, why shouldn't they also adopt the ideology and style of participation of the middle class? In the political dimension, embourgeoisement would imply the disappearance of working-class consciousness, of revolutionary ideologies (and eventually of ideologies generally), and a decay of collective organizations for protest, be it through political parties or labor unions. Emphasis on individual social mobility, on education as the main channel for one's children future mobility, on private achievements in general, would replace protest and grievance organizations and participation in common collective activities as a means to solve vital aspirations and expectations. If problems, needs, desires, and aspirations are stated in individual and private terms, the channels for their solution will also be conceived as individual and private.[18]

WORKING-CLASS REALITIES

The interpretation of trends in industrial societies that would support the hypothesis of embouregoisement makes a biased selection of facts. A critique of the hypothesis can be made by showing that in advanced capitalist societies, besides the facts and trends emphasized by the hypothesis of embourseoisement, there are others that run counter to it and counterbalance the embourgeoisement effects.

Regarding working conditions, there are interpretations contradicting that of the presumably liberating effects of modern technology and automation. Effects of the new technology vary according to different types of industry, different industrial plants, and even different occupations within the same plant. In many cases, instead of liberating effects, automation may produce greater isolation of the workers, involving diminishing chances of informal group formation and equalitarian contacts; it may require continuous attention and imply monotonous and

passive work. Instead of an increasingly clear conception of the importance of one's position in the process of production, workers may now feel
that rather than being the real producers with the help of machines, the
real producers are now machines and not men.[19] Furthermore, work
schedules either do not change or worsen: automated production is
continuous production, and this means work shifts, weekend work, and so
on. These continuous shifts in work schedules create new sources of
tension and disorganization, both of the workers' own physical and social
routines, and of their family relations. Thus, no closing of the gap between
middle- and working-class employment conditions is clearly present.

The results of several attitudinal surveys among modern industrial
workers indicate that an instrumental attitude toward work is more
common than a strong commitment to the enterprise and/or the adoption
of attitudes typical of organization men. In this context, instrumentalism
means taking work only as a means, in order to obtain the money
necessary to satisfy material needs and aspirations outside the work
context. It implies a "calculating" commitment to the job or enterprise,
made on the basis of the comparative advantages of the present position in
relation to other alternatives.[20] Thus positive answers to questions about
job satisfaction, justified on the basis of satisfaction with working conditions rather than with income, may simply reflect a negative selection: "I
like my job...especially when I think of the others I could have and which
are worse (such as an assembly-line position)."[21] This instrumental attitude
is described by Gorz as follows: "In summary, the worker, even the highly
paid one, tries to sell his skin at the highest possible price, since he cannot
avoid having to sell his skin."[22]

There is no question about an increase in absolute income. What is not
so clear is whether the income gap between blue- and white-collar workers
is diminishing. The overlap of income distribution of both groups is
considerable, but this is not necessarily an indication of homogeneity.
Blue-collar and white-collar workers differ in their economic cycles: blue-
collar workers earning high incomes are usually older ones at the peak of
their work careers, while white-collar workers earning low incomes are
relatively young and at the beginning of their careers. They differ also in
job stability; sex (male blue-collar and female white-collar workers
predominate); income from other sources beyond personal work; and the
number of work hours: the reduction of blue-collar workers' work week is
to some extent only nominal, and high levels of income result from many
hours of overtime. When the effects of these and similar variables are
accounted for, the income differential between blue-collar and white-collar
workers is very large. Furthermore, given the lack of research based on
time series of income data by occupational categories, no clear conclusions

can be drawn regarding whether income homogeneity between blue- and white-collar workers is growing or not.

The emphasis can also be shifted in the discussion of consumption standards: most consumption goods bought by the working class, beyond their possible meaning in terms of status-oriented consumption, have a clear use-value.[23] Shifting the discussion away from the individual motivational level, increasing levels of consumption are conditioned by the needs of the economic system of production to increase demand for industrial goods and services. These needs influence private decisions through advertising inciting an increase and diversification of consumption; and by restricting the alternative supply of goods and services satisfying basic demands. The inefficiency and growing decay of public transportation systems in many cities of advanced capitalist societies (especially the United States) is well known. What alternative does the worker have, provided he can afford it, than to use a private car? The same takes place with other consumption goods and services. The distinction between what is "necessary" and what is "superfluous and ostentatious" can be made only insofar as a choice between alternative life-styles is offered. This is not the case in advanced capitalist societies, where "only one style of life is offered, with greater flexibility or rigidity according to countries, and this style of life is determined by the production structure and the technology employed in it."[24]

Looking at indicators of participation, this "other reading of reality" casts some doubts about the presumed diminishing collective participation in grievances. With ups and downs and variations from one country to another, labor unions have persisted as the massive organized movement of the working class. Rather than evidence in favor of the hypothesis of increasing privatization implicit in the embourgeoisement argument, there is some evidence in favor of the proletarianization of the middle class. Many clerical employees and other white-collar workers such as teachers, university professors, and some in the liberal professions are increasingly adopting the style of organization typical of the industrial proletariat. White-collar unionization is growing, even in countries where individualistic ideologies prevail, such as the United States. This is taking place in spite of what any sociologist analyzing attitudes and orientations with an emphasis on status concerns would have predicted, namely, that so as not to be mistaken for the working class, and to maintain social distance from it, white-collar workers would tend to be very individualistic in the means used to attain their private goals, and refuse collective action. Teachers, public servants, and several other white-collar categories are increasingly accepting labor unions, not merely as formal organizations, but also as a forum for striking, the most typical protest action of the industrial working class. These indications of proletarianization of white-collar workers, however, should be interpreted with caution not as clear-cut facts but as emerging trends. Unionization often affects relatively small proportions of employees, and their organizations resemble more professional associations than labor unions.[25]

In advanced capitalist societies, labor unions are typically instrumental, grievance oriented. What has to be asked is whether there is or not a dynamic force inherent in this instrumentalism. Goldthorpe et al. show the adjustment between labor union and working-class orientation toward work: "The orientation of workers toward trade unionism reflects their orientation towards their employment generally; and where the latter is predominantly instrumental, it is not to be expected that unionism, any more than work itself, will be seen as a way of satisfying other than economic needs."[26] Others, like Mallet, make a distinction between the worker in his role as producer and as consumer.[27] While as a consumer the worker lost his isolation and participates in the affluent society, in the process of production "the basic characteristics that separate the working class from the other social classes have not changed." If workers in the most modern plants have increasing responsibility in the process of production, can express this responsibility through their union representatives, and come to perceive that they share common interests with technicians and other employees; then they could as well realize their potential power and eventually assume the complete control of production, replacing capitalist owners and managers and totally changing the established power structure.[28]

When looking at ideological orientations and political participation against the hypothesis of increasing conservatism and support of the status quo, critiques of the embourgeoisement hypothesis show that support and voting for parties offering leftist alternatives do not diminish—if anything they increase—in spite of rising standards of living and changes in working conditions of the working class.[29]

This is a formal and naive argument, unless the meaning and content of these leftist alternatives are analyzed, and historical changes are discovered in them. Few authors do this. Bottomore, for instance, claims that the language and tactics of parties change over time, reflecting shifts in the sociopolitical structure, but the basic and long-term goals of the working class remain the same: increasing control and greater social equality. Others claim that changes in language and tactics usually involve substantive changes in goals, at least insofar as there is an acceptance of the rules of the game. No doubt the political conflicts and confrontations between classes change when civil rights become universal in any given country.[30] However, there is a vacuum in studies of the relationship between changes in the content of political ideologies "offered" to the working class and the orientations and behavior of the mass of workers under shifting historical and structural contexts.

A REFORMULATION OF THE ISSUE OF EMBOURGEOISEMENT

Embourgeoisement is a hypothesis of historical change in a social class. At the same time, it raises the issue of the direction of this change: the working class is gradually coming closer to the bourgeoisie. In this context, the first question to be asked is, who is the bourgeois of the embourgeoisement? The comparative frame used to describe workers' actions in the hypothesis of embourgeoisement is certainly not Sombart's bourgeois, Weber's bourgeois spirit, or Marx's bourgeoisie. It seems as if the authors are rather thinking of Mills's white collar, or Whyte's organization man.[31] The use of the term embourgeoisement is so vague and blurry that authors who, for ideological and theoretical reasons would refuse to talk about a bourgeoisie have no misgivings when discussing the process of embourgeoisement.

The bourgeoisie or middle class implicitly taken as a standard for comparison with the modern working class is a heterogeneous category, including a variety of positions ranging from small entrepreneurs to managers of big enterprises, from highly specialized professional workers to office clerks. These occupational categories do not share either working conditions, levels of income, styles of life, or levels of consumption. In most writings about embourgeoisement, however, it would seem that routine nonmanual workers, the so-called "new middle class," are the ones in the back of the analysts' minds for the comparison, and not the bourgeoisie, the new managerial stratum, or even the petite bourgeoisie.[32]

It is hard to conceive of industrial workers and office clerks as two different social classes in advanced capitalist countries. Both are salaried workers, selling their labor power and thus subordinated, exploited and/or controlled by others.[33] The difference between the two strata is based on the prestige associated with the tasks, rather than on their position in the process of production. Therefore, the hypothesis of embourgeoisement, more than dealing with changes in the basic configuration of the class system in advanced capitalist societies, poses the convergence of two sections of the subordinate classes. These two sections are generally presented in sociological literature on stratification as qualitatively different, separated by the manual-nonmanual line (a distinction that is almost a classic "must" in studies of social mobility since Lipset and Bendix).[34] The usual distinction between white-collar and blue-collar workers, conceived as two different strata, is based on a rough and simplified prestige classification. Studies of prestige based on more refined and specific occupational categories show a high degree of overlap between prestige scores of specific manual and nonmanual occupations, suggesting that the separation is to a large extent artificial.[35]

Taking these considerations into account, the historical convergence of white-collar and blue-collar workers, if it exists, should be reinterpreted as a growing homogeneity within the working class in advanced capitalist societies. What does this convergence mean? Which are its relevant dimensions? In what direction does it move? From the standpoint of working conditions, it was stated above that there has been an increase in the proportion of blue-collar positions that require less physical effort and are cleaner. At the same time, important changes took place in the working conditions of white-collar workers. Office mechanization and automation imply greater similarity with blue-collar workers: the clerk has less control over what he is doing, his tasks are more routinized, he has less freedom to make decisions, less "substantive" rationality.

Changes in the working conditions of both industrial workers and clerks are due to technological and organizational shifts associated with increasing bureaucratization of economic activities. This implies greater intra-plant division of labor, an increase in the size of productive units, more formalization of rules and regulations, and growing work rationalization. Tasks and routines of each position are increasingly predetermined, leaving little room for on-the-job decision making. As bureaucratization grows, there is an increasing convergence in working conditions of manual and nonmanual workers, although it is not in the direction presumed by the hypothesis of embourgeoisement. It is not that workers become organization men, but rather clerks becoming programmed workers. This convergence does not mean homogeneity. Increasing division of labor, both among blue-collar and white-collar workers, implies a growing number and variety of positions, differing in terms of specialization, required abilities, technological context of work, and social relationships.

Convergence in terms of income level and style of consumption, discussed above, does not mean identity. Advanced capitalist societies are characterized by services organized on a profit-making basis and by the fact that most of the population, including manual workers, have a level of income above the minimum necessary for subsistence. Under these conditions, all social categories, including blue- and white-collar workers, share a series of life-style characteristics, and a series of demands for services. The way services are organized and offered implies a family-centered private life-style. It is not a bourgeois or middle-class life-style to which workers are getting closer. It is rather a life-style typical of affluent capitalist societies, and as such affects in greater or lesser degree all sectors of the population.[36] This fact, plus the increasing use of mass media to transmit a standard "ideal life-style" image, produce a certain homogeneity in the population, based on mass consumption.[37] Beyond this common core, affluent societies allow for a great deal of variation in life-style.

In the early stages of capitalist development in the central countries, a large proportion of the relatively small group of white-collar workers were the "executive arm" of the bourgeoisie: they were in charge of the direct control and immediate supervision of manual workers. This constant contact in everyday work activities, given its asymmetrical and hierarchical nature, could provide a basis for confrontation and antagonism between blue-collar and white-collar workers. The process of bureaucratization which took place during the past century meant an astonishing increase in the number and proportion of white-collar positions in the labor force. It also meant the routinization of the tasks of the bulk of white-collar workers. Nowadays, the majority of white-collar workers is not in direct contact with manual workers in supervisory positions; they work in offices manipulating symbols and papers, not workers. This change in the predominant tasks of the white-collar stratum means that one of the grounds for antagonism and confrontation—the direct asymmetrical link between the worker and his supervisor—is no longer the most common experience of white-collar/blue-collar contact. Thus, white-collar workers could increasingly accept their position as salaried workers, become more class conscious, perceiving that many of their interests are common to those of blue-collar workers. Eventually, this should lead to joint action, either in the labor movement, in political parties, or in both.[38]

During the first states of capitalist development, white-collar workers were offering a relatively scarce skill in the labor market—their education. They could take advantage of the favorable market situation for their skills. With growing educational facilities and opportunities, and the universalization and massification of education, conditions in the labor market changed for the white-collar worker: he is no longer offering a scarce ability, and his "semimonopolistic" position in the labor market is lost. Such change in objective position could bring about a change in the perception of his position. The white-collar worker no longer has a basis for seeing his position as a privileged one, monopolizing an important status symbol. It is much closer to the position of blue-collar workers who sell their labor power in the market. This stratum of white-collar workers could then gain a greater identification with the proletariat, and start engaging in the types of behavior prevalent among the working class. This is a hypothesis implying long-term change and refers to general trends. At any given moment, joint or separate political action by white-collar and blue-collar workers will depend on the historical juncture and structural conditions in each case.

The general problem of interpretation implicit in the embourgeoisement hypothesis is its lack of historical perspective. This shows up when considering living and working conditions and class-oriented actions, political ideologies, and the corresponding collective activities. As Bottomore points out, the thesis of the end of ideologies implicit in the description of the new working class rests "upon a tacit comparison between the present state of working-class consciousness and its state in some vaguely located and imperfectly known past age, which is seen as a time of heroic resolution and militancy."[39] This historical vagueness is compounded by the mistake of comparing the most prosperous and less distinctive sectors of the working class in the present with the less prosperous and more characteristic sectors of the working class in the past.[40]

These errors have important consequences for the analysis of the trends in the political and ideological dimensions of embourgeoisement. Certain orientations are characterized as new when they actually have a long tradition. Thus the aspiration of an increasing standard of living is viewed as novel, when in fact it has been an almost constant and universal goal of the working class since its inception with the industrial revolution.[41] They may show up under different ideological bents and within different structural contexts, but instrumental grievances such as better physical conditions of work, higher wages, a shorter working week, and so on are constant along the history of the labor movement, rather than the result of recent trends toward embourgeoisement.[42] Different observers, according to their varying theoretical and ideological orientations, interpreted them in different ways—as short or long-term trends, as constant or transitional features. Throughout the history of the labor movement, instrumentalism caught the attention of analysts. Engels was concerned with the instrumentalism of the English worker, including his search for "bourgeois respectability."[43] Lenin discussed at length the issue that if the working class were left to itself—with the leadership only organizing and articulating the preexisting interests of the mass of workers—the labor movement would become pure trade unionism, preoccupied only with the more immediate bread-and-butter issues.[44] And presently we talk about embourgeoisement and instrumentalism.[45]

Usually the attitudes and opinions of the mass of manual workers (generally measured through surveys) are compared with a stereotyped image of what the working class was in a vaguely specified and undefined past. The "past" is usually based on heroic images of highly politicized and ideologically challenging movements, such as anarchism. In their heroic moments, such movements involved only a small number of very active working-class members and were highly visible. The image of the present is based on individual verbal attitudes of the mass of workers, and not on any active social movement, whether of a minority or of the whole class. Data drawn from different units cannot be automatically considered as indicators of the same underlying phenomenon. Neither can a strike, or public speeches of labor union leaders be taken as indicators of attitudes and orientations of the working class; nor can results of attitudinal sample surveys of the mass of workers be taken as indications of the views of labor organizations, or used to predict probably collective actions the class might engage in.

Trends are analyzed as if the historical context and the larger social structure were constant along the whole period considered in the hypothesis. A century ago, the labor movement in most European countries was against the established political system. It was illegal and "revolutionary" to some extent simply because it was forbidden. As it gained legitimacy and was legalized, it lost some basis for being revolutionary. Legalization of workers' organizations, recognition of collective bargaining, and increase in labor union power, all these show that illegal and violent action decreases and is replaced by peaceful bargaining. Although the content of the struggle may be relatively unchanging, the change in form and in means has an important effect. In a society where workers are denied the basic civil rights (free association, citizenship, access to education, voting rights, etc.), active demands of these rights, as well as almost any tactical means used to achieve them will be officially labeled as "revolutionary." Although the ideological content was clearly not a challenge of the existing social structure, attaining these basic civil rights was to a large extent the result of workers' struggles with tactics that in their time were defined as revolutionary. When the institutional framework changes and includes the formal recognition of these rights, there will be a reinterpretation and reformulation of the goals of the working class, both at the political and at the union level.[46] What was revolutionary loses its revolutionary meaning; new issues emerge, new tactics are developed. Class conflict and challenging ideologies change, but they do not disappear.

We are not denying the existence of secular changes in the working class. After looking at the way these changes are presented and interpreted in the hypothesis of working-class embourgeoisement, what can be concluded is that we still do not have the historical evidence to support or refute the hypothesis. But more important, changes in the working class cannot be taken out of their historical context. They gain meaning only within the framework of a historical analysis of class relations and class conflict.

NOTES

1. Ralf Dahrendorf, "Recent Changes in the Class Structure of European Societes," in *A New Europe?*, ed. S.R. Graubard (Boston: Beacon Press, 1967).
2. Andre Gorz, *Estrategia obrera y neocapitalismo,* (Mexico City: Era, 1969); and Thomas E. Bottomore, *Class in Modern Society* (New York: Random House, 1966).
3. John H. Goldthorpe et al., *The Affluent Worker in the Class Structure* (Cambridge, England: Cambridge University Press, 1969).
4. Ferdynand Zweig, *The Worker in an Affluent Society* (New York: Free Press, 1962); and H. Popitz et al., *Das Gesellschaftsbild des Arbeiters* (Bubingen: J.C.B. Mohr, 1957).
5. Bottomore; and John H. Goldthorpe et al., *The Affluent Worker: Political Attitudes and Behavior* (Cambridge, England: Cambridge University Press, 1968).
6. Robert E.L. Faris, "The Middle Class from a Sociological Viewpoint," *Social Forces* 39 (October 1960); Kurt Mayer, "The Changing Shape of the American Class Structure," *Social Research* 30 (Winter 1963); and Jessie Bernard, "Class Organization in an Era of Abundance," *Transaction of the Third World Congress of Sociology* (London), vol. 3, 1956.
7. Dahrendorf.
8. Harold Wilensky, "Work, Careers, and Social Integration," *International Social Science Journal* 12 (1960); and Wilensky, "Mass Society and Mass Culture," *American Sociological Review* 29 (April 1964).
9. Wilbert R. Moore, "Changes in Occupational Structure," in *Social Structure and Mobility,* ed. N.J. Smelser and S.M. Lipset (Chicago: Aldine, 1966).
10. Arthur Stinchombe, "Social Structure and Organization," in *Handbook of Organization,* ed. J. March (Chicago: Rand McNally, 1965).
11. John H. Goldthorpe et al., *The Affluent Worker: Industrial Attitudes and Behavior* (Cambridge, England: Cambridge University Press, 1968).
12. Reinhard Bendix, *Work and Authority in Industry* (New York: Harper, 1963).
13. Elizabeth Jelin, "Estructura ocupacional, cohortes y ciclo vital," in *Actas de la Conferencia Regional Latinoamericana de Población,* vol. 2 (Mexico City: Colegio de México, 1970).
14. Simon Kuznets, "Economic Growth and Income Inequality," *American Economic Review* 45 (March 1955); Gabriel Kolko, *Wealth and Power in America* (New York: Praeger, 1962); R.M. Titmuss, *Income Distribution and Social Change* (London: George Allen, 1962); and Herman P. Miller, *Income Distribution in the United States* (Washington, D.C.: U.S. Department of Commerce, 1966), among others.
15. Alessandro Pizzorno, "The Individualistic Mobilization of Europe," in *A New Europe?,* ed. S.R. Graubard (Boston: Beacon Press, 1967).
16. Robert Blauner, *Alienation and Freedom: The Factory Worker and His Industry* (Chicago: University of Chicago Press, 1964).
17. Ibid.; and John K. Galbraith, *The New Industrial State* (London: Hamish Hamilton, 1967).
18. Dahrendorf; and Galbraith.
19. Pierre Naville, *L'Automation et le travail humain* (Paris: 1961) and Alain

Touraine et al., *Les Travailleurs et les changements techniques* (Paris: OCED, 1965).

20. Goldthorpe et al., *Industrial Attitudes.*

21. Ely Chinoy, *Automobile Workers and the American Dream* (Boston: Beacon Press, 1965); and Robert Blauner, "Worker Satisfaction and Industrial Trends in Modern Society," in *Class, Status and Power* (2nd ed.), ed. R. Bendix and S.M. Lipset (New York: Free Press, 1966).

22. Gorz. Unlike Goldthorpe et al., *Industrial Attitudes*, Gorz (p. 90) interprets attitude within the broader conceptual framework of alienation. The quote goes on: "Inversely, whatever the price freedom is sold for, the price will never be high enough to compensate for the net qualitative and human loss. Whatever the worker is able to get from his boss, it will never give him control and authority over his professional life, or the freedom to determine by himself his own condition."

23. David Lockwood, "The 'New Working Class,'" *European Journal of Sociology* 1 (1960).

24. Gorz, p. 131. Usually, other dimensions such as life-styles and types of social relations outside the work situation are also the subject of comparisons between blue-collar and white-collar workers. These are not discussed in this paper. See Goldthorpe et al., *Industrial Attitudes;* Goldthorpe et al. *The Affluent Worker;* Bennet M. Berger, *Working-Class Suburb* (Berkeley: University of California Press, 1960); and Richard F. Hamilton "Affluence and the Worker: The West German Case," *American Journal of Sociology* 71 (September 1965).

25. Galbraith; Solomon Barkin, "The Decline of the Labor Movement," in *The Corporate Takeover,* ed. A. Hacker (New York: Harper, 1964); Alain Touraine, "Management and the Working Class in Western Europe," in *A New Europe?,* ed. S.R. Graubard (Boston: Beacon Press, 1967); and Alain Touraine and Bernard Mottez, "Clase obrera y sociedad global," in *Tratado de sociología del trabajo*, ed. G. Friedmann and P. Naville (Mexico City: Fondo de Cultura Económica, 1963).

26. Goldthorpe et al., *Industrial Attitudes,* p. 114.

27. Serge Mallet, *La nouvelle classe ouvrière* (Paris: Editions du Seuil, 1963), p. 9.

28. Mallet; Gorz; and Touraine.

29. Goldthorpe et al., *Political Attitudes;* Bottomore; and Seymour M. Lipset, "The Changing Class Structure and Contemporary European Politics," in *A New Europe?,* ed. S.R. Graubard (Boston: Beacon Press, 1967).

30. T.H. Marshall, *Class, Citizenship and Social Development* (Garden City, New York: Doubleday, 1964).

31. C. Wright Mills, *White Collar* (New York: Oxford University Press, 1951); and William H. Whyte, Jr., *The Organization Man* (New York: Simon & Schuster, 1956).

32. Dahrendorf; Goldthorpe et al., *Industrial Attitudes*; Goldthorpe et al., *Political Attitudes;* and Goldthorpe et al., *Affluent Worker.*

33. Ralf Dahrendorf, *Class and Class Conflict in Industrial Society* (Stanford: Stanford University Press, 1959).

34. Seymour M. Lipset and Reinhard Bendix, *Social Mobility in Industrial Society* (Berkeley: University of California Press, 1959).

35. Robert W. Hodge et al., "Occupational Prestige in the United States: 1925-1963," in *Class, Status and Power,* ed. R. Bendix and S.M. Lipset (New York: Free Press, 1966).

36. Eric J. Hobsbawn, "Industry and Empire: From 1750 to the Present Day," in *Pelican Economic History of Britain,* vol. 3 (Baltimore: Penguin, 1969).

37. This does not mean that class subcultures disappear. Even when members of different strata share many features of their life-style, they diverge in others. Moving to a suburb, for instance, does not transform the worker into a typical middle-class suburbanite. Workers do not become members of voluntary associations, nor do they actively participate in religious activities. There need not be a change in interaction patterns between sexes, among friends, or within the family group. See Berger; and Herbert J. Gans, *The Urban Villagers: Group and Class in the Life of Italian-Americans* (New York: Free Press, 1962).

38. Mallet; Touraine.

39. Bottomore, p. 89.

40. Lockwood.

41. E.P. Thompson, *The Making of the English Working Class* (New York: Random House, 1963); and Jurgen Kuczynski, *The Rise of the Working Class* (New York: McGraw-Hill, 1967).

42. Edouard Dolleans, *Historia del Movimiento Oberero,* 3 vols. (Buenos Aires: EUDEBA, 1961).

43. Friedrich Engels, "The English Elections," in *On Britain, K. Marx and F. Engels* (Moscow: Foreign Language Editions, 1953).

44. Vladimir I. Lenin, "What is to Be Done?," *Complete Works* (Moscow: Foreign Language Press, 1947).

45. Gorz; Goldthorpe et al., *Industrial Attitudes;* Goldthorpe et al. *Affluent Workers.*

46. Marshall; and Reinhard Bendix, *Nation Building and Citizenship* (New York: Wiley, 1964).

Contributors

Henry Berger is Associate Professor of History, Washington University, St., Louis.

Robert Bibb is a member of the faculty of the Sociology Department of Vanderbilt University. His work has appeared in such journals as *Social Forces.*

Edna Bonacich is Associate Professor of Sociology at the University of California at Riverside.

William H. Form is Professor of Sociology and a member of the Institute for Labor and Industrial Relations, University of Illinois, Urbana.

Irving Louis Horowitz is the Hannah Arendt Professor of Sociology and Political Science at Rutgers University. He is the editor-in-chief of *Transaction/Society* and author of *Ideology and Utopia in the United States 1956-1976* and *Genocide: State Power and Mass Murder.*

Elilzabeth Jelin is a member of the faculty of Universidade Federal de Minas Gerais.

Gabriel Kolko is Professor of History at York University.

John H. M. Laslett is Associate Professor of American History at UCLA and has taught at the University of Chicago. He is coeditor (with Seymour Martin Lipset) of *Failure of a Dream? Essays in the History of American Socialism.*

John C. Leggett is Associate Professor of Sociology at Livington College, Rutgers University, and author of *Class, Race, and Labor* and *Race, Class, and Political Consciousness.*

S. M. Miller is Professor of Sociology at Boston University.

Martin Oppenheimer is Associate Professor of Sociology at Livington College, Rutgers University, and is the editor of *The American Military.*

Edna E. Raphael is Associate Professor of Sociology and Labor Studies at Pennsylvania State University.

Frank Riessman is Professor of Education, Queens College, New York and editor of *Social Policy* magazine.

Helen Icken Safa is Professor of Anthropology, Livingston College, and director of the graduate anthropology program of Rutgers University. She is the coeditor of *Social Problems in Corporate America.*

Name Index